A HISTORY OF BRITISH FOOTBALL

*

Percy M. Young

A History of British Football

Foreword by The Earl of Harewood

ARROW BOOKS

ARROW BOOKS LTD
3 Fitzroy Square, London W1

AN IMPRINT OF THE  HUTCHINSON GROUP

London Melbourne Sydney Auckland
Wellington Johannesburg Cape Town
and agencies throughout the world

First published by
Stanley Paul & Co Ltd 1968

Arrow edition 1973

*Made and printed in Great Britain
by The Anchor Press Ltd.,
Tiptree, Essex*

ISBN 0 09 907490 7

Contents

Illustrations

Between pages 96 and 97

Presentation of the World Cup, 1966
Celtic *v.* Internazionale Milan
'A Match at Football', 1871
'My First Football Match', 1879
Wolverhampton Wanderers, *c.* 1880
'A Maul in Goal', 1882
'The Association Game', *c.* 1885
Queen's Park F.C., 1873–4
Season tickets, 1883–95
The Inauguration of The Dell, Southampton, 1898
Crowd disorder and military intervention, 1888
The end of an era
Billy Meredith in the 1904 Cup Final
England *v.* Scotland, 1893
Newton Heath, newcomers to the English League, 1892
Woolwich Arsenal *v.* Newcastle United, 1893

Between pages 192 and 193

Southampton *v.* Reading crowd, 1913
'St. Merville's College' *v.* 'Wilchester Grammar School'
Everton *v.* Newcastle United, 1906
Musical Tribute to Tottenham Hotspur, 1908
Sheffield Wednesday F.C.
Bolton Wanderers *v.* Notts Forest, 1926
The dignity of management, 1939
Manchester United F.C., 1958
Red Star, Belgrade *v.* Manchester United, 1958

Foreword
by The Earl of Harewood

This book came at the right moment, first issued after the World Cup series in 1966 had introduced hosts of new followers to the game and ushered in a new period of potential popularity and prosperity. British football, which it chronicles, has touched new heights with the victory in the World Cup and club successes all over Europe, culminating in Celtic's astonishing achievement in 1966–7. Enormous numbers play the game every week-end in Britain, and we flatter ourselves that 'our' game is the world's most widely popular. Against this, in the realms of professional football gates are far smaller than they were in the immediate post-war period, only a comparatively few leading clubs take in a season more than they spend (the others raise money from outside the game, or leave it), statistics are constantly quoted to prove that demeanour on the field is deteriorating and that the behaviour of crowds inside and outside grounds is sometimes disastrous. So the game remains in a way controversial, and it is even possible to build up a case to indicate that a state of crisis exists.

But the real devotees will never see it that way. I was lucky in that I played football at school from the time I was nine (not unfortunately after I was thirteen) and the enthusiasm for it that was natural to a soccer school (whose founder was a famous centre-forward of the eighties and nineties, G. O. Smith: see page 187 has stayed with me more or less ever since. The first professional game I saw, more than thirty-five years ago, had Alex James, Cliff

Bastin, David Jack, Eddie Hapgood and Joe Hulme on one side and Willis Edwards and Wilf Copping and Jack Hart on the other. Since then, at least partly as a direct result, any Saturday during the season when I don't watch football seems to me a day that has got unaccountably out of step— like prolonging the week-end over Monday. I think this book is written for me and many thousands like me.

Introduction

There are two nightmares that afflict an author. The first is this: that one day he should be cast up on a desert island with a companion who had read none of his books. The second envisages a worse fate: the possibility of being left in the company of someone who *had* read one of his books. It was on an island—not quite a desert island—that I once touched the edge of reality in respect of the second hazard. A casual acquaintance revealed in passing that he had come across a history of a certain football club. He was more trenchant than a whole consortium of professional critics. What worried him about the book was that it was what it set out to be: not a history of one, two, or even five seasons, but of fifty, sixty, or seventy. So it happened that many once-familiar names were beyond his knowledge, and being so were to be disregarded. Yet it was those who had been forgotten (as alas! the great majority of the present eminences will be) who mattered. For in the broad sense it was the Alcocks, Kinnairds, Cleggs, Bloomers, Merediths, Barsons, Deans, and so on (as well as more distant predecessors), who made football. Without them England would not have won the World Cup. There would not have been a World Cup.

Association football is a national institution. As such it exists not only in its own right but in relation to every other sort of institution. The early promotion of the game, indeed, was owed to the involvement of representatives from almost every department of national life (hence, maybe, its basically democratic character). In some cases wider aspects of biography are indicated in order to emphasise the point. As one in this way draws together different strands of thought and action one is in effect constructing a history of the nation—from a particular angle.

A football match is ephemeral, but football itself is not. It has (as is shown) been with us since the beginning of time. And what was, is. That is to say, the movements of which the game is compounded symbolise many aspirations and intentions; so that in the end, the game now being of universal significance, it may be seen to have become the plain man's guide to philosophy. Whether this is overstating the case or not the reader must determine. For my part, however, I maintain that the subject is a serious one, to be approached in suitably serious mood. This thesis is supported by the fact that if one were to deal with the matter flippantly it would be regarded as infinitely more heinous than laughing in church.

Serious, however, is not dull, and one should retain a continual awareness of the liveliness, colour, humour, and unexpectedness of the game. Thus I have tried to bring together the scientific and the artistic aspects of the subject. Especially in respect of football it is all too easy to get bogged down with statistical minutiae. Realising that there are admirable handbooks which detail the arithmetic of the game, I have for the most part avoided reiterating items which, historically speaking, are of minimal significance. It is possible to go on for ever with record-breakers; but since the game does not exist for the purpose of breaking records what concerns us here is the main line development. For one, reasonably comprehensive, study in depth this is enough.

There are, I think, a number of facts that hitherto have not been generally accessible. Some, as for instances references to Italian influences of long ago, show that Europe was never quite out of sight from the British football arena,

Others—and these are of major importance—demonstrate the acceptance of football at an early stage as one constituent of liberal education, while the analysis of Matthew Concanen's famous poem of 1720 shows how far back impulses towards regulation and refinement were beginning to operate. Taken together, these and other factors indicate the tradition that was picked up and refurbished in the decisive middle years of the last century.

As in other fields of research I am not content that we should in England continue to believe in the assumption that *English* is what matters. Apart from important historical developments in Scotland, Ireland, and Wales, the English League would have been infinitely poorer had it not had access to the skills of the British footballing community as a whole. From where, in fact, comes the sparkle and vivacity that warms cold winter afternoons and evenings?

It is sometimes said (for example, in the popular press) that British football is slow to change its habits. What is not understood is that radical changes in the structure are coincidental on similar changes in the general social pattern. Football, as we know it in these islands, is not an accretion to life; it is part of the way of life. If we believe in one, then we believe in the other. The American millionaire who wishes to buy up British football needs to tune in to this wave-length before he loses a fortune.

For my part, what I pay in gate-money each week is a modest investment; but its interest yield is not to be surpassed.

P.M.Y.

Acknowledgements

The author wishes to thank the following for providing material, or answers to specific questions: The Football Association; Mr. Brian Belk (Uppingham School); Mr. Richard S. Burkett (The Charterhouse); Mr. James Lawson (Shrewsbury School); Mr. J. F. Leaf (Harrow School); Lutterworth Press; Mr. Frank Singleton (Librarian, *The Guardian*); Mr. L. J. Verney (Old Harrovian); Mr. V. H. Wayling and the Hitchin Town F.C.; and the many League and non-League clubs with whom I have had friendly associations over many years.

For permission to include copyright material in respect of illustrations the courtesy is acknowledged of: Borba, Belgrade; *The Chester Chronicle*; *The Guardian*; *Herts. Pictorial*; Hitchin Town F.C.; Lutterworth Press; The Press Association Ltd.; Thomson Newspapers Ltd.; Uppingham School; Wiltshire Newspapers Ltd.; and Mrs. F. H. Mugliston, widow of the late F. H. Mugliston.

1

Tribal Origins

In the absolute there is no such thing as a national idea, an idea being both above and aloof from such consideration. An idea, however, may be developed, and in the process of development there may be observed inclinations characteristic of a man, or of a group of men (and, in most cases, of women too); of a tribe, or of a nation. Or, if it comes to that, of a group of nations. By the side of the development of the idea the idea itself is necessarily maintained. Sometimes it is recognised and named as an ideal.

So it is with football: what is seen is compared with what might be, or what should be, seen. Of this there can be no doubt. The evidence is to hand weekly, if not daily.

It is convenient to come to this by way of Plato. For Plato laid out the basic theory of the 'idea' which is cursorily noted above, while as an educational pioneer he had something to do with the principle that the body and the mind work in some kind of harmony. This principle underlines the cult of games in general, and of football in particular, in British education, and has done so for a long time. In one way or another the development of football in Britain has been closely interwoven with that of education. This is one reason for the serious attention paid to the subject by the British people; so serious that in one brief moment of time it almost seemed that the winning of the World Cup by the English was sufficient recompense for the loss of an Empire.

The events of the summer of 1966 in fact took us back to the beginnings of football—at least to the tribal beginnings.

They also underlined the ubiquity of the idea of football, and the various discrepancies and idiosyncrasies of its development.

In the sense that every man is an artist—though some, either through heredity or opportunity, more so than others —so is every man a footballer. That is to say, the basic movements are inborn. So too is the intention which ultimately directs the movements. The fundamental intention is of aggression. Through the movements, which are controlled more or less purposefully, the aggression is at least partially sublimated. The more it is sublimated, the more the action becomes ritualistic and symbolic, though accepted as an apparent end in itself. At this point it approaches to the frontiers of art, for aesthetics are to be considered.

All of this was clarified by the final round of the 1966 series of World Cup matches, wherein the individual artist was acclaimed, particular patterns of national life acted out, the unknown (and sometimes the known) gods invoked, and tribal instinct for survival and supremacy exercised.

The insularity of the English across the centuries ensured that the vision of the game as a world game to many eyes was a new vision. Yet it is with a world game that we both begin and end. In between, however, there is a particular and persistent local zest, accompanied by various forms of developing skill, that can realistically be defined in sum as the British football tradition.

When the Han dynasty ruled in China—for some two centuries and until AD 25—a stylised form of Tsu Chu (or 'kick-ball') was ceremoniously practised on the Imperial birthday. Possibly due to Chinese influence the Japanese evolved a ball-game known as Kemari, which was well known by the sixth century of the Christian era. Ball-games were part of the great athletic-poetic-dramatic festivals of classical Greece. The nearest approach to an account of a game in some way related to football (but in which the hands were freely used) comes from the dramatist Antiphanes, who lived in the fourth century before Christ: 'Pass out. Throw a long one. Past him. Down. Up. A short one. Pass it back. Get back.' The excitement of more than two thousand years ago communicates itself through the staccato wording of a report by Antiphanes.

Since the Romans attempted to take over Greek culture, lock, stock and barrel, it is not altogether surprising that a similar activity also became a feature of Roman life. Known as Harpastum, it engaged two rival teams who, facing each other across a rectangle of land, endeavoured to take the ball—a small hard ball in this case—across the opposing base-line. In the process of attempting to do so a participant, unprotected by any detailed code of conduct, was liable to suffer damage. The Romans being an imperialist people successfully imposed their way of life on others; thus, as was testified by the fifth-century writer Sidonius Apollinaris, Harpastum was familiar all over Gaul.

That the Romans occupied most of Britain for a considerable period is not unknown. It may be assumed that those of the Britons and Celts who then made up the native population were, from time to time, involved in the Roman game. At the same time it may safely be assumed that the native population had evolved their own kind of ball-play, just as when English colonists desirous of exporting football to America found that the indigenous Indians had a football game of their own already firmly established.[1]

Of all games football is the most primitive in that the performer is rarely unaware of the fundamental significance of the phrase 'down to earth'. The earth even becomes a protagonist. Thus even now we may from time to time watch the anguished player, having prostrated himself in a vain effort either to score or to prevent a goal, beating the

1. F. P. Magoun, *History of Football, from the beginnings to 1871, Kölner Anglistische Arbeiten 31*, Bochum, 1938, p. 2, fn. 5.

ground as the author of his misfortune. Further back in time the dark gods of fertility were served through the ceremonies of ball-play. Thus the ball was driven towards the goal—the sanctified landmark of tree or stream. The ball, the emblem of the sun, was carried home as a guarantee of good fortune. Variations on such themes, beloved of anthropologists, may be discovered in all folklore. Some of them are hardly yet out of view, even in Britain.

A historian knows that to speak of any phenomenon as being the first of its kind is either impossible, or impolitic, or both. It is, however, not unfair to look to Derbyshire as a cradle of English football if only because the lower strata of the game's history are not entirely hidden. On Shrove Tuesday the annual football game is still played in Ashbourne. The Ashbourne game represents one group of myths and rituals, and enshrines the ancient invocations to the deities of earth, and air, and water. In Derby itself other causes have been ascribed. Remembering that Derby was once inhabited by a tribe known as the Coritani, the legend of a local victory by them has been worked into theories, or speculations, on the origins of football. 'It is said', wrote T. B. Trousdale, of the Derby game, 'to have been in commemoration of an occurrence as early as the year 217, when the Britons beat a team of Roman soldiers.'[2] Alternatively, Edward Bradley recorded 'The custom is said to commemorate some notable battle between the Saxon inhabitants and Danish invaders.'[3]

In later times all kinds of rituals (disguised as diversions) were assigned to Shrove Tuesday. Among them was football. Thus, in Derby, 'the pancake-bell was rung at midday as a signal that the apprentices were to be set at liberty, in order that they might repair to the Market-Place and join the populace assembled there to witness

2. *All about Derby*, ed. E. Bradbury and R. Keane, Derby, 1881, pp. 15–16.
3. ibid.

the throwing-off of the ball'. In due course:

'Then commenced that giant match, "All Saints' *versus* St. Peter's" . . . All Saints' goal was at Nun's Mill, the waterwheel of which had to be knocked three times. St. Peter's goal was a nursery-gate about a mile from the town . . .

'The ball was delivered over to the players, the contest commenced. There were no rules for them to trouble their heads about; the survival of the fittest was the only rule necessary to remember. Hard kicking, hard hitting and hard running were now the order of the day . . . On the following day, Ash-Wednesday, the game was repeated for the benefit of boys, whose youth had disqualified them from participating in the struggle of the previous after-noon.'[4]

Not far from Derby the Ashbourne game—still to be seen—took place on the same day:

'It had been the custom, time out of mind, for Compton and Ashbourne to play an annual match at football, the goals being the church gates at one end and, I think, Ash-bourne Hall gates at the other. The game was played in a very rough fashion, and many injuries were the result, besides the public being driven out of the main street and windows having to be shuttered up. Frequently the ball was pursued along the meadows, crossing and re-crossing the dividing stream; but no amount of ducking was suffi-cient to damp the ardour of the contestants. The magistrates at last decided to stop the game in the town, and permission was obtained to play it in Ashbourne Park. Going down from Osmaston, however, on the day of the match, my father found a furious conflict going on along the for-bidden street. Riding at once into their midst, with "Throw me up the ball, lads!" the ball was at once pitched to him, in a half surprise. "Follow me, boys!" and away he rode

4. Theo. Arthur, 'The Derby Game', in *Bygone Derbyshire*, ed. William Andrews, Derby, Hull, London, 1892, pp. 218–19.

to the border of the park, where he threw it over the wall. I do not think there was another man from whom they would have brooked this interference, or would have ventured upon it.'[5]

In both cases the totemistic nature of the goals is apparent. In both cases the apparent futility of the exercise and the general accumulation of moderate disorder provoked censure and oppressive action. Mayor Isaac Borrow tried to remove the annual football game from Derby in 1731. Fifteen years later Humphrey Booth, the Mayor of that time, published a denunciation in the local newspaper. The game, however, continued until, after a player had been drowned in the Derwent, another prohibition was sounded. The *Derby Mercury* made the suppression of football a crusade. In 1845 an attempt to substitute athletic sports was made. But football and footballers were irrepressible. And, as this anecdote shows, they had their well-wishers:

'In the year 1847 the Derby football game was threatened with extinction. The Mayor, Mr. William Eaton Mousley determined to suppress it as a public nuisance, conducive to riot and disorder. But the populace were not going to be deprived of a game which they looked upon as a birthright, inherited from their forefathers, without putting the authorities to considerable trouble. Horse-soldiers had to be called upon to assist the police. It was forbidden that the ball should be brought into the Market-Place, but it was forthcoming there all the same at the appointed hour, thanks to the offices of Mother Hope, who entered the Market-Place, with a basket of nuts on her arm, and the football concealed under her petticoats.'[6]

Thirteen years later a similar prohibition was issued in Ashbourne, Mr. Frank Wright then being Mayor. The players of Ashbourne (supported by many of the more

5. Francis Beresford Wright, on the history of the Beresford family, *The Notts and Derbyshire Notes and Queries*, III, 1895, p. 54.
6. Theo. Arthur, op. cit., p. 220.

virile citizens) refused to accept mayoral authority[7] and appealed to the Court of the Queen's Bench on November 14, 1860. Alas! the verdict of the Ashbourne magistrates was there upheld. Unabashed, those who reverenced their tradition found a way of maintaining it. The 'Death of the Right Honourable Game of Football' was announced:

'The funeral was public, though without ostentation, and the expenses (£200) [of the legal action] were subscribed by his sorrowing friends. We understand,' the notice continued, 'that the Honourable Gentleman is succeeded by an only son, a young man of Herculean strength, who inherits the valour of his father, and his coming of age will be celebrated by Playing at the Old Game next Shrovetide.'

Finally, 'The following Epitaph will be found on the Hon. Mr. Football's Tombstone:

> May Liberty meet with success,
> May Prudence protect her from evil;
> But may Tyrants and Tyranny tine[8] in the mist,
> And wander their way to the Devil.'[9]

Games of similar character, though with their own

7. The players were prosecuted by the police for having contravened the Highways Act. Their case was argued before the Queen's Bench by Sergeant O'Brien.
8. tine = kindle.
9. Theo. Arthur, 'The Ashbourne Game', *Notts & Derbyshire N. and Q.*, III, p. 220.
A lengthy ballad in honour of Ashbourne football was composed, and sung in Ashbourne, in 1821, by the comedian John Fawcett. The last verse runs:

> If they get to the Park, the Upwards men shout,
> And think all the Downwards men put to the rout,
> But a right about face they soon have to learn,
> And the Downwards men shout and huzza in their turn.
> Then into Shaw Croft, where the bold and the brave
> Get a ducking in trying the foot-ball to save;
> For 'tis well known they fear not a watery grave,
> In defence of the foot-ball at Ashbourne.

inflections, were held at Shrovetide in different regions. At Corfe Castle, Dorsetshire, the football game was combined with an initiation ceremony for newly elected Freemen of the borough. In Cornwall the Celtic word 'hurl' (perpetuated in the extant Irish game of hurling) was used to describe the Shrovetide ball-game. Uninformed travellers were sometimes taken by surprise when they arrived in towns where shops were shut, boarded up, and barricaded, as though against civil strife. A 'Mr. P.' passed on to William Hone a letter he had had from a 'Friend' in March, 1815:

'Having some business which called me to Kingston-upon-Thames on the day called Shrove Tuesday, I got upon the Hampton-court coach to go there. We had not gone above four miles, when the coachman exclaimed to one of the passengers, "It's Foot-ball day"; not understanding the term, I questioned him what he meant by it: his answer was, that I would see what he meant where I was going . . .'

Clearly, like arriving nowadays at Euston Station on Cup Final day, and asking what all the fuss is about. Having seen for himself, Hone's friend's friend finished his letter by saying:

'I was rather surprised that such a custom should have existed so near London, without my ever knowing of it.'[10]

The ancient custom of playing at football in the public streets was observed at Nuneaton (Warwickshire) on the afternoon of March 1. 'During the morning a number of labourers canvassed the town for subscriptions, and between one and two o'clock the ball was started, hundreds of roughs assembling and kicking it through the streets. The police attempted to stop the game, but were somewhat roughly handled.'[11]

10. William Hone, *The Every-day Book*, 3 vol., 1841 edition, London, I, p. 246.
11. E. H. Coleman, in *Notes and Queries*, VI, 3, 1881, p. 207.

Civil disturbances tended to be a concomitant of the foot-ball tradition of this order, and Dorking, in Surrey, acquired a bad name. The *Daily News* of February 11, 1880, gave a full account of a wild match played there on Shrove Tuesday that year, while twenty years later 'fifty of the townspeople . . . were summoned before the Dorking magistrates for obstructing the highway on the occasion of the annual football match held in the streets on Shrove Tuesday. The Bench fined each of the defendants 1/- and costs, saying the practice was "an obstruction of the high-way and a danger to life".'[12]

If, however, real vigour was to be sought, then the intrepid student of folk custom made his way to Working-ton to see what was described by one such student as 'an amalgamation of football, cross-country run, and Donny-brook Fair'.

There was, the account continued, 'an almost primeval disregard of life and limb. It usually resolves itself into a stern contest between the colliers and the sailors of the town. The former are known as the "Uppies": the latter are styled the "Downies". The aim of the colliers is directed to successfully carrying the ball over the gates of Curwen's Hall, at the high end of the town: the sailors' breezy efforts intimate a wild desire to "hale" the ball at the capstan on the harbour.

'So popular is this annual event that excursion trains run to Workington from all parts of the county, and as many as 50,000 persons witness the struggle for supremacy. The game commences on the "Cloffocks", a level piece of ground with a thick covering of mud deposited by the high tide. Here some four or five hundred men, stripped to the waist, may be seen floundering and spluttering in the slimy mixture.

'Some of the unrehearsed involuntary antics of the

12. A. Gibson & W. Pickford, *Association Football*, London (1907), 4 vol., I, p. 18.

players may not be particularly pleasing to themselves, but as a spectacular attraction leave nothing to be desired. During the whole game the onlookers see little of the ball, for it is usually the very focus of a dense mass of struggling, sweltering humanity. When the play occasionally veers into the adjacent side streets, the excitement is redoubled: fences are torn down; walls are scaled; and the game waxes fast and furious in the back-yards of unoffending and peaceable citizens. At times the shades of night are closing in before the goal is reached and the contestants retire to remove the traces of the fray, which in many cases is only attained after many days, with a liberal treatment of arnica and sticking-plaster.'[13]

The kind of primitive game thus described—and many more instances can be dredged up from history—gives us the aggressive idea that underlies football in more or less simple terms. The contestants, unaware of anything other than a compulsion to hold on to an object and to mark their warrant to maintain it trophy-wise by symbolically capturing the defences of those who would obstruct their intention, fight for supremacy. Unhindered by rules, or codes of conduct, emboldened by the high stimulant of mass hysteria, and increasingly strengthened by traditions of indisputable title, they emulate nature in the raw.

The ancient ball-game was oftentimes a brutish business. It is small wonder that continual attempts were made to prevent it. And yet it proved ineradicable. The question is why?

The answer to this question is as complex as it is important, for it relates also to many facets of football-in-society as we generally know it today. Man by nature is gregarious, preferring to act in unison with others; indeed he is often

13. 'Quaint Survivals of ancient Customs', *The Windsor Magazine*, December, 1903, p. 102.

See also, Daniel Scott, *Bygone Cumberland and Westmoreland*, London, 1899, p. 200; William Whellam, *History of Topography of Cumberland and Westmoreland*, Pontefract, 1860, p. 479.

under compulsion to do so. The group exists for security and survival, and primarily acts to defend its possessions, its rights, and its privileges. Conscious and unconscious motivation produces a twofold consequence of the desire for security: physical exertion on the one hand and the underwriting of this by appeal to or placation of the unknown on the other. We all hope for 'good luck' and shed reason in pursuit of it.

The ball—from the entrails of an animal that once held their own supernatural mystery—is in itself symbolic. It means more than it is, an object of fecundity related to all that is fecund. To possess it, to control it, bestows magical powers on the successful performer. He, however, being of a group, brings prestige to the company to which he belongs. To possess the ball, to become its manipulator, entails strife. Now the ball-game is a fight, but in the absolute sense not a real fight. It is a mock-battle that is being enacted when the Ashbourne Shrovetide game takes place. The mock-battle, however, knows no precise zonal limitation: it can easily be mistaken for the real thing. When it has been then authority has stepped in.

But the fighting urge in itself is indelible. The clever exploit it through verbal contest. Those of different physical or intellectual formation exhibit it more patently. For them a game—a substitute for words and its motions a meaningful group of concepts—is a matter of conclusive seriousness. For the 'Uppies' and 'Downies' of Workington victory was important. It was not, of course, important to anyone else.

How far, in fact, have we grown away from the primitive? Perhaps, taking into account the actions of some players and some communities of spectators, not very far. It is still a sublimation, a mock-fight, a reflection of irresistible urges, of prejudices, and of aspirations that can find no fulfilment elsewhere. Our point of view in some respects, however, has altered. For some people, at least, view a match with the eye of the critic, the connoisseur, or the artist. The motions of a game are changed by writers and reporters into words of more or less sophistication, so that what has already been once removed is now twice removed from reality. But the reality is still there.

This is why the Mayors of Derby, the Justices of Ashbourne, and countless generations of legislators have failed to prevent football: what it stands for is, in a sense, what we are. In that the British have preserved the game against all opposition they show a radical conservation, not of faith but of feeling. In the end feeling turns back into a new faith.

The folk-football of ancient times has interest for the historian and the psychologist. It has wider interest, however, for what it represents is what, as ardent followers of the game, we are. In more than a thousand years the nature of football has not changed: its forms have. It is these forms that we study in the following chapters, to discover that they are congruent with other forms: those that we term, broadly speaking, as those of civilisation. British football is a mirror in which is reflected the British people; not the best people, nor the worst people, but the whole lot. That is why it infuriates while it pleases.

This brief observation on folk-football is preludial. But, as is the case with a Wagnerian prelude, the themes run throughout the whole course of the exposition of the story. Country football and street football will recur. But subsequent notices of them in this book will have a more specific purpose.

2

Lively Exercise in the Middle Ages

In the previous chapter the unifying characteristic is that which is the mark of all true folk-culture: anonymity. This makes it of no more than relative importance whether the idea of communal football is caught in the shadows of pre-history or in the outskirts of the records of the last century. Folk-football was an abiding function, of common expression, in rural life; and even when it was carried into the towns—as the St. George plays and the rhymes and rituals of All Souls' Day were taken by groups of mummers from the countryside into urban settings well within living memory—it still represented the rough philosophies of those who sustained themselves on and from the soil. The sense of the ancient folk-football may still be seen to survive in the spontaneity of children's games (just as folk-song only remains with us in the nursery rhyme): though even here sophistication and refinement set in perhaps all too soon.

The conviction has already been recorded that old meanings still lie behind the modern football game, and further reference will be made to this from time to time. Now what is 'modern football'?

Modernity to the unacademic follower of the game is represented by names. If in 1973 one speaks of Lee, or Todd, or Moore, or Dougan—or of Clough, Greenwood, or Docherty—one is presumed to be abreast of the times. (In 1974 or 1975, of course, the case might prove to be other-

wise.) The fascination exercised by the individual performer is the compelling feature of contemporaneity. Some-
how, then, we begin to seek a different concept of the
ancient game by noting either the influence of one person
on others, or the imposition of patterns that afford opportunity for the exercise of individual skill, judgement, or
initiative. In effect, it seems we have a renascence of a
Renaissance.

No doubt individuals emerged as such in folk-football.
If they did we know nothing about it. There was (and this
is true of other aspects of life) no good reason why individuality should be recognised when the fundamental intention was to affirm communal solidity. Individuality is, of
course, subject to considerations of relativity. It may exist
for a day, for a lifetime, or, occasionally, throughout posterity. The individuality of the football player is normally
confined. There are few whose personality in this sphere
persists for more than a brief period. Further, there are
even fewer of whom notice is taken beyond their own frontiers. Those who pass into the company of the immortals
do so because they have been captured by the chronicler.

The function of the commentator is, therefore, of importance. Not least of all because, beyond our own uncertain
memory, we are obliged to reconstruct our image of the
game from written records. As soon as these began to
collect football assumed a special position in relation to the
general art of living. For our purpose this appeared to
happen when concepts of nationhood first began to take
shape.

The Romans departed from Britain, and, presumably,
took the practice of Harpastum with them, its echoes linger-
ing, but ever growing more faint, in the indigenous, ritual,
handball-football. When the Normans reached Britain they
arrived not only as conquerors but also as heirs to a ball-
game tradition. The same kind of cross-country, through-
bush-through-briar, 'football' described in the first chapter

had long been practised both in Brittany and Normandy under the name of La Soule in the one region and Choule in the other. A cautious verdict in favour of a Celtic origin of football, based on the independent practice of football in regions of Europe which were or had been Celtic settlements, is delivered by Morris Marples.[1] Until further evidence is available, however, one would accept this verdict (unless Celtic in origin) with some reservation. However this may be, it is clear that little more than a hundred years after the Battle of Hastings 'football' was an established factor in the life of the urban population.

We say 'football', but still with a little less than certainty. In all literary references so far there had been mention of the *follis*[2] or of the *pila*.[3] But in no case was there ever a precise account of how the ball was used. The significant reference of the twelfth century is similarly imprecise in this particular, but a good deal more revealing in general. William Fitzstephen, a monk and a friend of Thomas à Becket, of whose martyrdom he was a witness, wrote a lively account of London life in 1175. Some part of this dealt with the amusements of the time. On Shrove Tuesday there was a variety of entertainment, including cock-fighting and the well-known *ludus pilae*. In the afternoon: 'all the youth of the city go to a flat patch of ground just outside the city for the famous game of ball. The students of every faculty have their own ball, and those who are engaged in the various trades of the city also have their own ball. The older men—the fathers and the men of substance—come on horseback to watch the competitions of the younger men. In their own way the older men partici-

1. *A History of Football*, Secker & Warburg, 1954, p. 10.
2. Latin word meaning leather bag or purse, and, later, an inflated (leather) ball, which was sometimes ballasted with feathers. The Roman writer Martial (first century A.D.) advised both young and old to play at ball: *Folle decet pueros ludere, folle senes*.
3. The Welsh chronicler Nennius (eighth century) described boys quarrelling during a game of ball, which he termed *ludus pilae*.

pate in the sporting activities of their juniors. They appear to get excited at witnessing such vigorous exercise and by taking part in the pleasures of unrestrained youth.'[4]

Fitzstephen thus defines what was a regular occasion. There were specific groups of performers—'teams'—of students on the one hand and apprentices on the other; a set venue, probably by Smithfield, a recognised centre for entertainment; a company of spectators, whose vicarious involvement was, it would seem, affected by the action on the field of play. It is also apparent that, under the patronage of the 'men of property', the *ludus pilae* of the reign of Henry II enjoyed a respectability that was thereafter frequently in doubt.

The fact that boys were keen on ball-play in early times is variously attested. The first specific observation on football as such comes by way of a famous ballad, 'Sir Hugh, or the Jew's Daughter'. No doubt the number of players involved in the game was symbolic rather than actual, and it is not quite reasonable to deduce that twelve aside was the thirteenth- or fourteenth-century norm. But there is no doubt at all that the star player was on the way. In this instance, of course, a backward-looking personality cult was induced by the circumstance of ultimate beatification —a rare honour for a football player.

> 'Four and twenty bonny boys
> Were playing at the ba',
> And by it came him sweet Sir Hugh,
> And he play'd o'er them a'.

4. *Descriptio Nobilissimae Civitatis Londinae:* '*Post prandium vadit in suburbanam planitiem omnis juventus ad ludum Pilae celebrem. Singulorum studiorum scholares suam habent Pilam; singulorum officiorum urbis exercitores suam feres singulis. Maiores natu, patres, et divites urbis in equis, spectatum veniunt certamina juniorum, et modo suo iuvenantes cum iuvenibus: et excitari videtur in eis motus caloris naturalis, contemplatione tanti motus et participatione gaudiorum adolescentiae libidinis.*'

He kicked the ba' with his right foot,
And catch'd it wi' his knee,
And throuch-and-thro' the Jew's window
He gard the bonny ba' flee.'[5]

The small Sir Hugh (of Lincoln), evidently a ball-playing genius of a type still known, asked for his ball. The Jew's daughter told him to come up for it. He did. He never came back.

It is sad thus to note the demise of a boy who clearly had some notion of the potential artistry inherent in the game, for it was to be many years—centuries indeed—before its general crudities were moderated. There is a long record of violence and misadventure to consider; some of it, however, not fairly attributable to the game itself. On Trinity Sunday, 1280, at Ulgham, Northumberland, one Henry, son of William de Ellington, was playing at football with a large number of his friends. In the course of play he ran against David le Keu, who was wearing a knife. The unfortunate Henry impaled himself on the knife and subsequently died.[6] In 1322 a Gilbertine Canon of Shouldham, Norfolk, William de Spalding, accidentally killed a friend in the course of a football game. He too was wearing an unsheathed knife. Having heard the evidence, Pope John XXII absolved William.[7]

There were more sinister happenings. On March 25, 1303, an Oxford student, Adam of Salisbury, was performing his football skills in the High Street. He was attacked by a gang of Irish students, and mortally wounded.[8] Eighteen years later a nasty episode took place in the heart

5. *Old Ballads*, selected by A. T. Quiller-Couch, Clarendon Press (n.d.), p. 49.
6. *Calendar of Inquisitions*, Misc. (Chancery), London, 1916, I, p. 599, item 224.
7. W. H. Bliss, ed., *Calendar of Entries in the Papal Registers relating to England & Ireland*, London, 1895, II, p. 214.
8. H. E. Salter, *Records of Medieval Oxford*, Oxford, 1912, p. 11.

of Cheshire. John de Boddeworth, a servant at the great Cistercian Abbey of Vale Royal, was murdered near the sister house of Darnhall by two brothers named Oldyngton. The murderers (aware, it may be, of the horrific Derby tradition which allowed the victorious Anglo-Saxons to substitute a Danish head for a ball) took his head and used it as a football: *'ad modum pilae cum pedibus suis conculcaverunt'.*[9]

Life was hazardous enough without football adding to its dangers. Therefore authority stepped in and on April 13, 1314, the citizens of London heard a proclamation in the King's name: 'For as much as there is great noise in the city caused by bustling over large balls . . . from which many evils might arise which God forbid: we command and forbid on behalf of the king [Edward II], on pain of imprisonment, such game to be used in the city in future.'[10] As events were to show it was easier to issue such edicts than to bring to an end a diversion which had won an inalienable place in the traditions of the people. Nevertheless further attempts to prevent the game were made with some regularity.

Attacks on football came from three directions, from the King, from the Church, from the municipality. Justification for thus interfering with the pleasures of the people was based on two articles. The first, as has been seen, was that violence was to be deprecated. The second—more sinister —was that football wasted time. Both criticisms run down the course of history as themes on which the censorious often take pleasure in inventing variations. During the long French wars of the fourteenth century the English commanders found themselves running short of expert bowmen. Edward III accordingly wrote to the Sheriffs of London, in

9. George Ormerod, *The History of the County Palatine and City of Chester* (2nd, enlarged edition), Chester, 1882, II, p. 162.
10. Quoted in M. Shearman, *Athletics and Football* (The Badminton Library), London, 1887, p. 248.

1349, observing that 'the skill in shooting with arrows was almost totally laid aside for the purpose of useless and unlawful games', of which football was named as one, and that the Sheriffs should see to it that 'such idle practices' were suppressed.[11] In 1389 Richard II turned aside from his personal difficulties to restate the prohibition in uncompromising terms, expressly forbidding 'all playing at tennise, football, and other games called corts, dice, casting of the stone, kails, and other such importune games' throughout the realm.[12] In 1401 the Statute was re-enacted by Henry IV.

It was now the turn of Scotland. In 1423 James I of Scotland went back to his kingdom (a suitable ransom—or perhaps 'transfer fee'—having been paid) after spending nineteen years in the custody of the English. It is apparent that in captivity he adopted certain wrong ideas, for immediately after his return home he presented the Scots with twenty-seven Acts of Parliament, among which was the following:

'It is statute, and the King forbiddis that ne man play at the futeball under the paine of fiftie schillings, to be raised to the Lord of the land als oft as he be tainted, or to the scheriffe of the land, or his Ministers, gif the Lordes will not punish sik trespassours.'[13]

Up to a point the Church in England helped to preserve certain libertarian notions merely by affording a convenient meeting-place. The churchyard was often used as a playground (so it was in my childhood, but that is another story), and football, like minstrelsy and other secular convivialities, was generously supported by some of the clergy

11. Rot. Claus. 39, Ed. III, memb. 23. Rymer, *Foedera,* I, 1869.
12. Rot. Claus. 12, Rich. II, c. 6, ibid., II, 1873.
13. Act of Parliament, James I of Scotland, 1424, c. 17. James II, James III, and James IV, repeated the Statute in 1457, 1471 and 1491, James VI took a prejudice against football back to England (see p. 58).

themselves. The case of William de Spalding has already been cited. During the fourteenth century the Feast of St. Catherine the Martyr was celebrated football-wise, '*Indentibus ad pilam pedalem*,' in the grounds of Bicester Priory, in Oxfordshire.[14] In view of the fact that the Prior was willing to sanction gifts to the football players to the sum of fourpence it may be allowable to accept St. Catherine's Day (November 25), 1425, as that on which professional football was first recognised and recorded.

From time to time Puritanism in its primal form reared its head. John Mirc, Prior of Lilleshall, Shropshire, first brought that now celebrated football locality into prominence at the beginning of the fourteenth century, by instructing parish priests not to 'indulge in casting axle-trees and stones there; [and to] banish from the churchyard ball and bar and similar games'. Mirc, as a Prior, fortunately had no control over parochial clergy, so it may be supposed that his injunctions were noted rather than acted on. In 1364, however, the Synod of Ely, with full authority so to do, firmly pronounced against the clergy playing football.

And yet the game persisted. One may like to believe that an amiable relationship between it and everyday life was developed by the early masters of our national literature, who discovered in football a useful supply of effective similes. That they did so tells its own story. A simile comes best from what is familiar rather than from what is unfamiliar.

In the third part of *The Knightes Tale* (a tale supposedly told to a pretty representative section of the English people) Chaucer gives a splendid eyewitness account—so it reads—of a knightly joist: between Arcite (red banner) and Palamon (white banner). At the height of the combat one, un-

14. White Kennett, *Parochial Antiquities*, Oxford, 1695, p. 578; 2nd. ed., Oxford, 1818, p. 259.

named, knight was unhorsed. Then, said Chaucer: 'He rolleth under foot as dooth a bal.'[15]

The association of football with chivalry (as it was called) is here fortuitous, but there was a nice legend in Scotland which hopefully asserted a more direct connection. In the *Statistical Account of Scotland* Sir Frederick Eden (1766–1809) supposed 'that the game had its origin in the days of chivalry, when it is alleged that an Italian who came into Scotland challenged all the parishes in the neighbourhood of Scone under a certain penalty should they decline his challenge. This was generally done; but Scone accepting, beat the foreigner and in consequence the game was instituted . . .'[16] This was an attempt, made in an age when reason was esteemed, to attribute causes where none were apparent. One rejects legends with reluctance, and, as will be shown, an Italian association at least was not entirely improbable.

If Eden reflects a facet of chivalry, which lies somewhere within the idea of football, Chaucer's near-contemporary John Wycliffe uses the game referentially in order to inveigh against the abuses of the age. Here the great reformer, the champion of the liberties of the underdog, blasts the pretensions of authoritarianism:

'Now Cristene men be chullid, now with popis, and now with bishopis, now with Cardinalis of popis, now with prelatis under bishopis; and now be clouten per shone with censuris, as who shulde chulle a foot-balle.'[17]

---

15. *The Knightes Tale*, line 1756. Dryden translated this line somewhat freely, as

'One rolls along a football to his foes.'
Cf. 'Hedes reled about over-al
As men playe at the fote-bal.'

from description of a Greek naval battle in the *Laud Troy Book* (c. 1400).

16. See *Notes and Queries*, VI, 11, 1885, p. 287.

17. John Wycliffe, *Select English Works*, ed. Thomas Arnold, London, 1871, p. 280. The passage may be represented by: 'Nowadays Christian men are kicked about by pope, bishop, cardinal, and other

Chaucer and Wycliffe were acquainted with football. As promoters of the general idea of personal liberty it is to be supposed that they viewed the game sympathetically. If so then they were in dissent against official opinion. After the King and the Church the governments of the towns began to legislate in disfavour of football. That they were under some pressure from above is shown by the fact that in 1410 Henry IV—again with the requirements of the French wars in mind—imposed a fine of twenty shillings on mayors of towns where unpermitted games were discovered to be taking place. In 1450 dice, bowls, and football were placed under the penalty of a shilling fine on anyone taking part in them in Halifax. In Leicester—more liable to visitation by officials from London—instructions forbidding a variety of games were made known in 1467 and again in 1488. On June 5 of that year it was advised: 'that no man of the town or the country play within the franchise of this town . . . at unlawful games . . . dice . . . tennis . . . football . . . on pain of imprisonment. And the owner of the house, gardens, or places where these games are practised, as often this is discovered and practised, shall pay the chamberlain 4 pence, and every player 6 pence to those same chamberlains for the use of the community.'[18]

That the legislation started against football in the Middle Ages is still to some extent effective is shown by a recent essay on the Criminal Justice Bill of 1966: '. . . the old-time fines for the more familiar offences make some inflationary jumps, varying from a 2,500 per cent increase for obstructing a highway and a 1,000 per cent one for street football . . .'[19]

high clergy. These men clout their censures with shoes, just as one treats a football.' The word 'chulle' (meaning 'to kick') is derived from the French *soule* (see p. 31).

18. Mary Bateson, ed. *Records of the Borough of Leicester*, London, 1901, II, p. 290.

19. C. H. Rolph, in the *New Statesman*, December 9, 1966, p. 178. Prosecutions are now undertaken according to Section 140 (Subsection

The condemnation of football is a strong theme to develop, even if one is frequently so prejudiced as to wish to condemn the condemners. But sometimes one chances on a more subtle attempt at prohibition. It being granted that the fundamental idea of strife is so irresistible as to be ineradicable there are those in authority willing to try to persuade the community to a higher degree (as it might seem) of sublimation. There is, for example, the instance of the cancellation of football in Chester, where the ancient game had taken on a new significance somewhere during the Middle Ages to serve, almost in a modern sense, as an accessory to trade. So Archdeacon Robert Rogers, who died in 1595, wrote in his account 'Of the laudable Exercises yearly used within the cittie of Chester':

'Mem: That whereas the companye and corporation of shoemakers within the cittie of Chester, did yearely, time out of memory of man, upon Tewsday, or otherwise *Goteddesse* day afternoon, at the cross upon the Rood Dee, before the mayor of the said cittie, offer unto the company of drapers of the said cittie, a ball of leather, called a footeball, of the value of 3s. and 4d. or thereabout: and by reason of greate strife which did arise among the younge persons of the same cittie (while diverse parties were taken with force and stronge handes to bringe the said ball to one of these three houses, that is to say, to the mayor's house, or any one of the two sheriffs' houses of the time being), muche harme was done, some in the great thronge falling into a trance, some having their bodies bruised and crushed; some their arms, heades, or legges broken, and some otherwise maimed, or in perill of life; to avoid the said inconveniences, and also to torne and converte the saide homage to a better use; it was thought good by the

3) Highways Act (1959) where a maximum penalty of £2 is laid down. But a case before the magistrates of Barnsley, Yorkshire, on August 1, 1967, where a boy when proceeded against pleaded that he had only headed the ball opened a battle of legal semantics. What is football? (See *Daily Mail* and *The Times,* August 2 1967.)

mayor of the said cittie, and the rest of the common-
council, to exchange of the saide foote-ball as followeth:
that in place thereof there be offered by the shoemakers to
the drapers six gleaves [darts] of silver, the which gleaves
they appoynted to be rewards unto such men as would
come, and the same day and place, passe and overcome
on foote all others . . .'

This took place during the Mayoralty of Henry Gee, in
the year 1539.[20]

The history of football is full of anomalies. There is continued opportunity for exercising the talent for reading
between the lines. The medieval footballer was a vigorous
fellow. He was liable to excesses of enthusiasm. These,
especially when let loose in the narrow, ordurous, streets
of the towns, were at least tiresome. There were those too
whose zealous pursuit of games contrasted with their
indifference to other obligations. The idle apprentice earned
a bad name not only for himself but also for his com-
panions. On the other hand there is ample evidence—in
the shape of literary references representative of a broad,
country-wide, acquaintance with the game—that where
order was not at peril then football was not disapproved.
The Brewers' Company of the City of London at all events
were not reluctant to hire out their Hall for a football
dinner. In the accounts of the Company relative to the years
1421–3 an item records: 'by the football players twice . . .
20 pence'.[21] From this it is to be concluded that these footballers—presumably maintaining the conventions defined
by Fitzstephen—were an organised body. This being the
case it may also be supposed that their game was conducted
within some framework of acceptable rules, and that, since

20. Joseph Hemingway, *History of the City of Chester*, 2 vols.,
Chester, 1831, pp. 207–8. Rogers also tells how the Saddlers' ball—of
silk and as large as a bowl—was changed for a silver bell to be competed for by horses. Thus began the Chester Races.
    21. Magoun, op. cit., pp. 11–12.

they comprised a corporate body, they had some pride in their activity.

Football players, then as now, were, as has been seen, subject to injury. While it is not entirely probable that the modern footballer will impale himself on an opponent's knife it is quite probable that at some time or other he will break a leg. Two Sussex footballers of the early fifteenth century found such an accident a convenience in later time for giving accurate testimony to dates.[22] At the end of the century the record of another accident throws additional light not only on the game of football as then practised but also on a prevalent attitude to life—both this and the next.

Henry VI was murdered in the Tower of London in 1471. Before long he was accorded saintly rank, to which he appeared entitled by the miracles of which he was capable. One such miracle preserved the life, and perhaps, the football career, of a player named William Bartram, of Caunton, near Newark. He 'was kicked during a game, and suffered long and scarce endurable pain, but suddenly recovered the blessing of health when he had seen the glorious King Henry in a dream.' The chronicler continues as follows:

'The game at which they had met for common recreation is called by some the foot-ball-game. It is one in which young men, in country sport, propel a huge ball not by throwing it into the air but by striking and rolling it along the ground, and that not with their hands but with their feet. A game, I say, abominable enough, and, in my judgement at least, more common, undignified, and worthless than any other kind of game, rarely ending but with some loss, accident, or disadvantage to the players themselves.

'What then? The boundaries had been marked and the game had started, and, when they were striving manfully kicking in opposite directions, and our hero had thrown himself into the midst of the fray, one of his fellows, whose

22. *Sussex Arch. Collect. XII* (1860), p. 43; *XV* (1863), p. 213.

name I do not know, came up against him from in front
and kicked him by misadventure, missing his aim at the
ball.'[23]

In that account there is an indication that the game in
question, unlike the folk-game, was an organised exercise.
There were two opposing sides. The ground was specifically marked out. That there were goals is implicit. The
writer cancels the censorious note which he felt obliged to
introduce into this context for ideological or theological
reasons by the vividness of his description. He was watching the game closely. So closely that he was able to absolve
the player whose name he did not know from the suspicion
of having committed a foul.

Concerning football in the later Middle Ages, the operative word is enthusiasm. The game was ineradicable
because the people would not see it suppressed. In the
sense that democracy is intended to fulfil the will of the
people the survival of football has proved a triumph for
democracy. It is one of the few such victories which is attributable to a true consensus of opinion. In the fifteenth and
early sixteenth centuries finer points of constitutional propriety, or systems of government, or details of philosophy,
were not discussed at tavern level. What was there
approved, however, represented some kind of rough judgement. Thus in the Morality Play entitled *Mankind*, of the
reign of Edward IV, the character playing the part of New
Guise called out:

'What ho, hostler! Hostler! Lend us a football.'

23. R. A. Knox and S. Leslie ed., *The Miracles of Henry VI*, Cambridge, 1923, pp. 131–2.

3

Renaissance Sophistication

Nothing, of course, happens suddenly. Modern football is the culmination of a long tradition, so long that a British affection (now, as formerly, sometimes sorely tried) for the game is quickly assumed to be inborn. That it appears so is due to attitudes concerning it which were shaped centuries ago. During the sixteenth century the shape of these attitudes began to show more clearly.

That century belonged to the Tudors. It was marked by a surgence of national pride, which stemmed from the increasingly refined efficiency of the language (the cornerstone of all nationalism) as a vehicle for conveying thoughts and emotions, from achievement in consolidating independence against threats of foreign domination, and from economic and artistic accomplishment. It was an age of paradox. The nation was united, but also, through religion, divided. Life was hard and often squalid. Yet the literature and the music of the Tudor epoch have never been surpassed. In general there was a distaste and even contempt for the foreigner. But Italians, Germans, Flemings, Dutchmen, and others immigrated, to influence especially architecture, literature, music, and education. While the English upper and middle classes, and actors and composers, eagerly sought opportunity to bring themselves abreast of modern cultural developments by paying long visits to the Continent.

Football as an institution will, at the end of the story, be seen to have acted as a mirror of society; not the only one,

but that which has in fact been held up most often to the
gaze of many. During the Tudor period there were, as previously, objections against the practice of football playing;
but there was also a more resolute championship of the
game. The objectors, often repeating phrases that had lost
their significance, were reactionary. The champions, basing
their views on newer theories that became fashionable
during the Renaissance, were in the van of progress. In both
cases, however, the argument centred not on a game but on
ways and means of building a civilised society, and, particularly, of nurturing a sound body of men to lead that
society. In these terms the problems then faced sound
contemporary.

One aspect that is immediately attractive is the sixteenth-
century appreciation of the spectacle and the charm of
football.

Country life was idealised through the poetic conventions that were born of the union between English verse
traditions and Italian techniques. Alexander Barclay, a
Scottish Benedictine who settled in Ely, there composed in
1514 a beautiful set of *Eclogues*, in the fifth of which the
familiar figure of the farm labourer is thus elevated to bliss
by way of what by now had become the distinctive winter
game:

> 'The sturdie plowman, lustie, strong, and bolde
> Overcometh the winter with driving the foote ball,
> Forgetting labour and many a grevous fall.'

A gesture of support for football from the young women of
Elizabethan times is indicated by an Eclogue of 1587 by
Robert Greene whose Carnela thus addresses Doron:

> 'Ah leave my toe, and kisse my lippes, my love,
> My lippes and thine, for I have given them thee:
> Within thy cap 'tis thou shalt weare my glove,
> At football sport, thou shalt my champion be.'

From which it may be concluded that Carnela was present to cheer her lover on, and that Doron's cap was a necessary part of his football gear. In fact the use of distinctive colours in sporting (?) encounters was suggested by Chaucer. The same colours, red and white, distinguished those football players who performed in France during the early part of the sixteenth century under the patronage of King Henry II, while in Florence the ritualised *Calcio*, also a variant on the idea of football,[1] required one group of players in red, the other in green livery. We may then see Doron, the bucolic footballer of Greene's fancy, proudly wearing his cap,[2] and reflect that because he did, then so does the international player of today carry a symbolic cap.

Nicholas Breton, an engaging limner of the English pastoral scene, carries us into the reign of James I. In his *The Honour of Valour* written in 1605 he outlines some facets of manly character:

> 'Hee that can whistle at a Plowe and Cart,
> And catch a Weesle in a cony hole;
> Hee that can eate up a whole aple tarte,
> And overleape a blinde mare and her fole,
> Or strike a football strongly through a goale;
> These may be too, a kinde of men, and so,
> But no such men as honour knowe.'

Each man catches his own impression. Breton, as spectator, clearly kept his eye on the goal. In fact he was not the first writer to mention this necessary apparatus. That honour would appear to belong to Richard Stanyhurst, a versatile, often contentious, scholar, who in 1577 was disputing with one (Alan?) Cope on the subject of there being no snakes in Ireland. 'I purpose', he wrote, 'under Mr. Cope his correction to coape and buckle with hym herein, and before

1. See also p. 68.
2. Cf. p. 80.

he beare the ball to the goale, to trippe him, if I may, in the way.'³ Breton and Stanyhurst had been students at Oxford (of which University Greene, after graduating at Cambridge, was also a member). Both may well have learned the game there, even though one college—St. John's—had prescribed the game of *pila pedalis* in a Statute of 1555. Stanyhurst was clearly more aware of the techniques of football than of its aesthetics.

Still on the subject of football as part of the landscape reference must be made to the game as played on ice.

'This yere 1564 was a sharpe froste, which began on Seynt Thomas daye before Christmas, on ye 21 daye of December, beying, Thursday, and contynewyd tyll ye 3 day of Janewarie. This frost was so sharp that on newyeres even men went ovar ye Thams as saffe as on the dry land, and ye same newyers even, beyinge Sundaye, people playd at ye footballe on ye Thams by great numbars.'⁴

A similar scene—which would have appealed to the Dutch painter van der Neer—was enacted in Chester in 1589 on the frozen Dee.

The spectacular attributes of football emerge when two conditions are fulfilled: when the action being both purposeful and skilful is moved several degrees away from actuality, and when it is seen to be related to setting. Folk-football, to continue all down the line, is in one sense real. It is also crude in execution, and unconfined. The Florentines who in Renaissance times made the game of *Calcio*

3. 'Description of Ireland', in Holinshed's *Chronicles*, 1577, Ch. 2. Regarding tripping, cf. Shakespeare:
Steward: I'll not be strucken, my Lord.
Kent: Nor tripped neither, you base football player (*tripping up his heels*).
Lear: I thank thee, fellow.

King Lear, I. 4. 95.
Shakespeare otherwise alludes to football in *A Comedy of Errors*, II. 1. 83.

4. *Almanac*, 1564.

famous did so because it expressed a philosophy. The philosophy simply was *mens sana in corpore sano* and it embraced fitness and grace. The *Calcio* players were by rank aristocrats. They performed the game, in which the principles of an older manner of chivalry were enshrined, in the *Piazza di Santa Croce*. The season ran from the Feast of the Epiphany up to Lent.

The brighter young Elizabethans aspired to reaching, if not surpassing, the intellectual and cultural standards attained by the Italians. In many respects they proved themselves at least apt pupils. It was not, in fact, until the second half of the seventeenth century that literature in English relating to Florentine football appeared,[5] but there can be no doubt that it was at the back of the mind of many Englishmen throughout the sixteenth century. Not least of all because of the patronage of the game by the upper classes.

On March 5, 1600, that inveterate letter-writer John Chamberlain wrote to Dudley Carleton, later Viscount Dorchester, inviting him to 'come and see our matches at football, for that and bowling wil be our best intertainment'.

This is in line with the implied interest of the poets in the game, and with a general influence in the sphere of higher education. One of the purposes of education was to breed a ruling class. A pioneer in the provision of manuals intended to achieve this end was Sir Thomas Elyot (1490?–1546). Elyot, a disciple of Erasmus and the Italian humanists, and a friend of Sir Thomas More, was scholar, jurist, and diplomat. His works included *The Booke called the Government* (1531), to which he is said to have owed his appointment as Ambassador to the Emperor Charles V, *The Doctrine of Princes* (1534), a translation from the Greek of Isocrates, and *The Image of Government* (1540), also translated from the Greek.

In *The Governour* Elyot expressed a formal opinion

5. See p. 69

condemning football. The terms of his condemnation were those used on many previous occasions.

'Some men woulde say', he wrote, 'that in the medio-critie, which I have so much praysed in shootynge, why should not bouling, claishe pynnes, and koytynge, he as moche commended? Veryly as for the two laste, be to be utterly abiected of all noble men, in lyke wyse foote balle, wherein is nothynge but beastely fury, and extreme violence, whereof procedeth hurte, and consequently rancour and malice do remayn with them that be wounded, wherefore it is to be put in perpetuall sylence.'[6]

Three years after he had written this Elyot, who was now unwillingly trying to persuade the Emperor to approve Henry VIII's divorce intentions, recanted to this extent: that he applauded a 'compounde of violent exercyse, and swyfte, when they are joyned together at one tyme, as daunsing of galyardes, throwing of the balle and renning after it; footeball playe may be in the numbre thereof . . .'[7]

The Elizabethans tended to be obsessed with the subject of health. This, taking into account a generally brief expectation of life and an infinity of aggressive contagions, was reasonable enough. The development of new skills and of a scientific way of examining problems encouraged hope that by due care and consideration life might be lengthened. The idea that health came under the heading of education was also promoted by the great composer William Byrd, who advocated the practice of singing as conducive to good health.

One of the most notable of Elizabethan educationists was Richard Mulcaster, Headmaster of Merchant Taylors' School from 1561 to 1586, and High Master of St. Paul's School from 1596 to 1608. Mulcaster, a characteristic figure of the Renaissance, promoted the idea that education was effective in so far as it developed the whole man. He

6. 1537 ed., f. 93.
7. *The Castell of Helth* (1541 ed.), f. 50.

believed, therefore, in a broad scheme of training which should include music, drama, and athletics; as well, of course, as the basic studies in the classics. The debt which football owes to Mulcaster is indicated by the following, visionary, passage: '. . . the Footeball play, which could not possibly have growne to this greatnes, that it is now at, nor have been so much used, as it is in all places, if it had not had great helpers, both to health and strength. And to me the abuse of it is a sufficient argument that it hath a right use: which . . . will both helpe, strength, and comfort nature, though as it is now commonly used, with thronging of a rude multitude, with bursting of shinnes, and breaking of legges, it be neither civil, neither worthy the name of any traine to health. Wherein any man may evidently see the use of the tra[i]ning maister. For, if one [a trainer] stand by, which can judge of the play, and is judge over the parties, and hath authoritie, to commaunde in the place, all those inconveniences have bene, I know, and wil be I am sure very lightly redressed, nay, they wil never entermeddle in the matter, neither shall there be complaint, where there is no cause.

'Some smaller numbers with such overlooking, sorted into sides and standings [positions on the field of play], not meeting with their bodies so boisterously to trie their strength: nor shouldring or shuffing one an other so barbarously, and using to walke after, may use football for as much good to the body, by the chiefe use of the legges, as the arme ball, for the same, by the use of the armes.

'And being so used, the Football strengtheneth and brawneth the whole body, and by provoking superfluities downeward, it dischargeth the head, and upper partes, it is good for the bowells, and to drive downe the stone and gravell from both the bladder and kidnies. It helpeth weake hammes, by much moving, beginning at a meane, and simple shankes by thickening of the fleshe no lesse than riding doth. Yet rash running and to much force oftentime breaketh some ineward conduit, and bringith ruptures.'[8]

In his refinements Mulcaster had Italian practices in mind. But, a man of the world and of wide experience, he was basing his observations on what was near at hand. Reason told him that football would be a better game if there was agreement as to the number of players permitted to take part, if teams were properly selected, if players fulfilled defined functions, if they were supervised by an instructor ('training maister') who would also act as referee. Mulcaster was for skill rather than vigour. Shoulder-charging and shoving he considered unseemly and unnecessary. The advocacy of such gentility, apparently inherent in the Florentine game, was premature. Appreciation of 'continental' styles did not begin to show itself in England until nearly four hundred years after Mulcaster had written his essay. Nevertheless what Mulcaster did achieve was to regularise the notion that football might justifiably be accepted within the conditions of a superior education. From that point the influence of certain schools and of the universities was strong and continued so until our own day.

The situation regarding football at Cambridge at the time when Mulcaster (a graduate of Oxford) was writing is graphically described in a report from the Vice-Chancellor to Lord Burleigh sent on May 7, 1581. It should be remembered that students were then admitted to the universities from the age of fourteen. Here we see the University football team in trouble in respect of an away match:

'Thomas Parishe being head constable dwelling at Chesterton, when ther was a match made betwixt certain schollers of Cambridge and divers of Chesterton to play at the foteball, about two yeres past, the sayd schollers resorting thither peaceable withowte any weapons, the sayd townsmen of Chesterton had layd divers staves secretly in the church-porch of Chesterton, and in playing did pike

8. *Positions*, 1561, Chapter 27, 'Of the Ball'.

quarrells against the Schollers, and did bringe owte their staves wherewith they did so beat the schollers, that divers had their heads broken, divers being otherwise greatly beaten, wear driven to runne through the river, divers did crye to Parish the constable to keep the Queene's peace, who then being a player at the foote ball with the rest, did turne to the Schollers, willing them to keep the Queene's peace, and turning himself to the townsmen of Chesterton willed them to beat the schollers downe.' Another witness reported how 'When they were hotte in playe sodenlye one cryed Staves! and incontinently some came forth with the staves and so fell upon the schollers that they caused them to swymme over the water. And Longe John, servant to Mr. Brakyn, did folowe one Wylton, Scholler of Clare, with a Javelyn; and if this deponent had not rescued him he believeth he would have run the said Wylton throughe.'[9]

Thus clearly was the need for an independent 'training maister', vested with judicial authority, shown. It is doubtful whether organised matches between Cambridge University and any of the surrounding villages took place again until the autumn of 1966 when the University, seeking new inspiration, turned to the preliminary rounds of the F.A. Amateur Cup in search of fresh fields to conquer. In fact the students were under restraint from looking for 'foreign' opposition in Tudor days. In 1580, and again in 1581, they were told by the Vice-Chancellor to play 'only within the precincts of their several colleges, not permitting any strangers or scholars of other colleges or houses to play with them or in their company, and in no place else. And if any person being not adultus shall break or violate any part of this decree and order, he shall for every default be openly corrected with the rod in the common school by some of the University officers.'[10]

9. J. Venn, *Early Collegiate Life*, Cambridge, 1913, pp. 122–3.
10. ibid., pp. 121–2.

During the Tudor period the usual crop of legal references to football are to be found. In some of them there is a greater amount of descriptive material than previously. Evidence of a strong Irish tradition is provided by an unusual edict issued in 1527 concerning the city of Galway. Once again a lack of interest and skill in archery was adduced as a reason for banning certain games; but in this case football was explicitly excluded from suppression: '. . . and also of no tyme to use ne occupye the horlinge of the litill balle with hockie stickes or staves [the developed game of "hurling" as at present known], nor use no hande ball to playe without the walles, but only the great foote balle, on payne of the paynis above lymittid'.[11]

Football figured in a case of *lèse majesté* when, on February 27, 1535, one George Taylor was jailed at Brickhill, Buckinghamshire, on account of his having been alleged to have said: 'I set not by the King's crown, and, if I had it here, I would play at football with it.'[12] George Taylor was no true republican. He excused himself before the Justices; first, by denying that he had said what he was supposed to have said, second, by pleading that if he had said it he was drunk at the time and, therefore, in a state of unawareness and not to be held responsible. Nevertheless, he went to prison.

Shrove Tuesday football continued to exercise the authorities. In the last year or so of the reign of Elizabeth I, an unusual occurrence was detailed in Shrewsbury when John Gyttings, the younger, petitioned the Queen for his discharge from prison, where he had been committed 'for playing at the foot balle upon Shroftusdaie, and for throwinge the balle from him when the serigent Hardinge

---

11. Tenth Report, *Roy. Comm. Hist. Mss.*, London, 1885, App. V, p. 402.
12. J. Gairdner, ed., *Letters and Papers, Foreign and Domestic, of the Reign of Henry VIII*, London, 1885, VIII, p. 114.

demanded the same'.[13] One has not far to go to discover some modern Gyttings junior of the Football League throwing the ball away when asked for it by the contemporary counterpart to Serigent Hardinge—the referee. It may be observed that in some particulars human nature is relatively immutable: one says relatively in this instance only because prison is not now the penalty for ungentlemanly behaviour at football.

In Tudor times ungentlemanly behaviour was by some readily collated with ungodly behaviour and the proper antidote was seen in a rigorous diet of fundamentalist theology. The Puritan voice was powerful in the land; it continued so for a long time to come. The loudest cry of commination in the sixteenth century came from Philip Stubbs, a graduate both of Cambridge and Oxford, who found it profitable to publish Puritan pamphlets. His most notorious work was entitled *The Anatomie of Abuses*, 1583. He proclaimed that the end of the world was at hand. That this was the case was in large measure due to 'football playing and other develishe pastimes' on the Sabbath Day. Sunday and holy days, of course, had been consecrated to recreation from time immemorial; the custom—it being understood that church attendance was also made—was approved by the pre-Reformation Church. In his diatribe Stubbs allows us a view of an unreformed game.

'Lord', he prayed, in the person of Philoponus, 'remove these exercises from the Sabaoth.[14] Any exercise which withdraweth us from godlines, either upon the Sabaoth or any other day els, is wicked and to be forbidden. Now, who is so grosly blinde that seeth not that these aforesaid exer-

13. Fifteenth Report, *Roy. Comm. Hist. Mss.*, London, App. X., 1899, p. 62.
14. The Bishop of Rochester had indicated in his Visitation Articles (1572–4) that football should not take place on Sundays. In 1592 the Archdeacon of Essex fined a football player for organising a game during the time of Evensong on Easter Monday.

cises not only withdraw us from godlines and vertue, but also haile and allure us to wickednes and sin for as concerning football playing, I protest unto you that it may rather be called *a frendly kinde of fyghte* than a play or recreation—a bloody and murthering practise than a felowly sport or pastime. For dooth not everyone lye in waight for his adversarie, seeking to overthrowe him and picke [pitch] him on his nose, though it be uppon hard stones? In ditch or dale, in valley or hil, or what place soever it be hee careth not so he have him down. And he that can serve the most of this fashion, he is counted the only felow, and who but he?

'So that by this meanes, sometimes their necks are broken, sometimes their backs, sometime their legs, sometime their armse, sometime one part thurst out of joynt, sometime another; sometime the noses gush out with blood, sometime their eyes start out; and sometimes hurt in one place, sometimes in an other. But whosoever scapeth away the best goeth not scotfree, but is either sore wounded, craised [crushed], and bruseed [*sic*], so as he dyeth of it or else scapeth very hardly. And no mervaile! for they have the sleights to meet one betwixt two, to dash him against the hart with their elbowes, to hit him under the short ribbes with their griped fists, and with their knees to catch him upon the hip and pick him on his neck, with a hundered such murthering devices: and hereof groweth envie, malice, rancour, cholar, hatred, displeasure, enmitie, and what not els, and sometimes murther, fighting, brawling, contortion, quarrel kicking, homicide, and great effusion of blood, as experience dayly teacheth. Is this murthering play, now, an exercise for the Sabaoth day?'[15]

15. Stubbs could back his censure with a formidable body of evidence. On March 20, 1576, a number of tradesmen, of Ruislip, 'with unknown malefactors by the number of one hundred assembled themselves unlawfully and played a certain unlawful game called football, by means of which unlawful game there was amongst them a great affray likely to result in homicides and serious accident'. J. C. Jeaffreson, ed.,

The influence of Puritanism was strong in every part of life. The age-old tradition of Mystery and Miracle Plays came to an end during Elizabeth's reign; the Shrove Tuesday and Hocktide festivities were suspended in many places; church ornaments and musical instruments were wrecked. Yet football survived. It begins to show where this activity ranked in the British scale of values.

Middlesex County Records, London, 1886–7, I, p. 97. Five years later there was the unhappy case of Roger Ludforde, of South Mimms, which came before the Coroner's Court: '. . . Roger Ludforde ran towards the ball with the intention to kick it, whereupon Nicholas Martyn with the fore-part of his right arm and Richard Torvey with the fore-part of his left arm struck Roger Ludforde on the fore-part of the body under the breast, giving him a mortal blow and concussion of which he died within a quarter of an hour, and that Nicholas and Richard in this manner feloniously slew the said Roger.'

4

Roundheads v. Cavaliers

The secret of survival is adaptation. In the previous chapter it has been seen how the ancient game of football was changing in some particulars. It was changing because its function was submitted to analysis in the light of a new social philosophy. The end of medieval theological dogmas in their absolute form, and the civilising virtues that stemmed from Italian humanism, gave additional substance to the belief that this life was, perhaps, equally important as, if no more so than, the one to come. Slowly it began to dawn that the preservation of life, at least through measures to maintain health, was not an unimportant consideration.

The extent to which a gracious life was possible, for the few at least, should not be exaggerated. Nor should it be underestimated. The British of the Tudor epoch were a tough race, but they had high aspirations. The football game was a meeting point, for the artisan and the artist, for the peasant and the scholar, for the modest and the mighty. It characterised country life and town life, but it was revealing new subtleties of expression by which its rougher edges could be smoothed and which would give it its place among the pageantries.

The consequences of Puritanism, of Civil War, and rising capitalism, did considerable damage to the amenities of life. Utility became an end in itself and what was not utilitarian was under grave suspicion. Pageantry was diminished. Gradually football, substituted for other diver-

sions, assumed the character of a pageant, of a theatrical
display. That is where it stands today. The British have
much football, but little opera: the Italians have both.

A dramatic performance requires a theatre, a football
match an arena. Already in Elizabethan times a place
for football—a 'Fote-balle close'—had been allocated in
Hitchin, Hertfordshire.[1] In reserving suitable ground for
football matches the universities played their part. By 1620
such prohibitions as had existed now being abrogated or
merely ignored, certain Cambridge colleges were in the
habit of playing matches against one another. Those that
took football most seriously appeared to be St. John's and
Trinity Colleges,[2] though since Oliver Cromwell was a
doughty performer in his undergraduate days at Sidney
Sussex it would also appear that that house was also
reasonably placed in the football competition of the period.
At a later period in the seventeenth century Magdalene
College, Cambridge, also had its football fraternity. In
1679 it was there enjoined 'That no schollers give or
receive at any time, any treat or collation upon account of
ye football play, on or about Michaelmas Day, further
than Colledge beere or ale in ye open hall, to quench their
thirsts. And particularly, that that most vile custome of
drinking and spending money—Sophisters and Freshmen
together—upon ye account of making or not making a
speech at that football time, be utterly left off and
extinguished.'[3]

Sir Thomas Overbury (poisoned in the Tower of London
in 1612 by agents of Lady Essex) was a student at Queen's
College, Oxford, at the end of the sixteenth century, at
which time football was played at Bullington Green. He
testified to the fact that in his day football achievement was
regarded by some as a matter of college pride. To the

1. R. L. Hine, *The History of Hitchin*, London, 1927–49, II. p. 24.
2. Marples, op. cit., p. 74.
3. Fifth Report, *Hist. Mss. Comm.*, 1876, p. 483.

scholar, he wrote, 'the antiquity of his University is his need, and the excellency of his Colledge (though but for a match at football) an article of his faith'.[4]

Sir Henry Wotton, diplomat and scholar, too was a graduate of Queen's College, Oxford, as also of New College. He had been at school at Winchester, where football seems to have been practised. Wotton, following the example of Nicholas Breton, watched the game from the side-lines, where he concentrated on the romantic interest that it promoted in the countryside.

> 'Jone takes her neat-rub'd paile, and now
> She trips to milk the Sand-red Cow;
> Where, for some sturdy foot-balle Swaine,
> Jone strokes a sillibub, or twaine.'[5]

Behind the cult of the game at the universities lay encouragement in the grammar schools. There is documentary evidence relating to the practice of football both at Aberdeen and Winchester.[6]

When James VI of Scotland succeeded to the English throne as James I he was faced with the problem of devising a curriculum of education suitable for his heir, Prince Henry. Henry was intelligent, artistic, and an amiable companion. But he had instructions not to play football.

'From this court', wrote his father in his *Basilikon Doron*, of 1603, 'I debarre all rough and violent exercises, as the foot-ball, meeter for mameing than making able the users thereof, but the exercises that I would have you to use, although but moderately, not making a craft of them, are running, leaping, wrestling, fencing, dancing and play-

4. *The Misc. Works . . . of Sir Thomas Overbury*, ed. E. F. Rimbault, London, 1856, p. 87.
5. *On a Bank as I sate a Fishing—A Description of Spring*.
6. In a book called *Vocabule*, by the Master of Aberdeen, David Wedderburn; and in a Latin poem, *De Collegio Wintonensi*, by Robert Mathew. Both quoted in Marples, op. cit., pp. 70–1.

ing at the catch or tennisse, archerie, palle-malle, and such like other fair and pleasant field-games.'

Alas! Prince Henry escaped death (or maiming) at football, but was carried off by typhoid fever in 1612—a sad loss, it would seem, to the English people.

The King may have had strong views on the undesirability of the heir to the throne playing football. Towards the people in general, however, he was more indulgent. On June 11, 1613, King James and his Consort, Queen Anne, were entertained in Wiltshire in the course of a 'royal progress'. In charge of the entertainments customary for such occasions was the Rev. George Ferebe (Feribye, Ferrabee, or Ferraby!), Vicar of Bishop's Canning. Ferebe, a native of Gloucestershire, had been a chorister and later a student at Magdalen College, Oxford—where also Prince Henry had matriculated. His musical interest was maintained to the extent of his composing a madrigal—and from his parishioners conscripting a small group able to sing it as well as a wind consort to cover up such errors as the singers might make—which was presented to the royal party. Following the music there was a football match, the Bishop's Canning team being notable in those parts.[7] Royal approval of Ferebe's initiative came in the form of an appointment to a King's Chaplaincy.

The place of the 'sporting parson' in British (especially English) life is one of some importance. The manner in which the concept of the 'whole man' came into English educational philosophy has already been shown. Its influence remained with the clergy of the Established Church down to the last days of its effective power as a social influence. The celebrated Rev. K. R. G. Hunt, of Wolverhampton fame, the learned theologian Dr. J. O. F. Murray, once Master of Selwyn College, Cambridge, and Bishop Norman Tubbs, sometime Bishop of Rangoon and Dean of

7. John Aubrey, F.R.S., *Natural History of Wiltshire*, ed. J. Britton, London, 1847, p. 109. John Nichols, *Progresses of James I*, ii, p. 668.

Chester, all of whom were Corinthians, were, perhaps, the last to belong to the great tradition effectively inaugurated in England by George Ferebe.[8]

Scotland, of course, had its own collateral tradition, and, ecclesiastically speaking, it is doubtful whether comradeship on the football field ever exerted such influence on a career as in the case of James Law, who was elevated to the archiepiscopal see of Glasgow in 1615 through the advocacy of John Spottiswood, who had been lately promoted therefrom to the Primatial throne of St. Andrews. Away back in 1585, Law then being Minister at Kirkliston, both men then being in their early twenties, had been called to account by the Synod of Lothian for playing football on the Lord's Day.[9]

On the other hand it was left to the Scots to provide a distasteful example of double-dealing. As the tenets of John Calvin took firmer hold any idea of the Sabbath as a day of recreation became increasingly untenable. Nevertheless, there was a sufficient supply of Scots to uphold the manlier traditions of their race by defying the Kirk by playing football on that day. The Rev. Michael Potter (not otherwise known to posterity) determined to strike an effective blow for the suppression of liberty. As newly ordained Minister of Kippen, Stirlingshire, in 1700, he discovered to his horror that 'It had been the practice with some of the parishioners for years to play football on Sunday afternoons . . . Mr. Potter disapproved of this and he therefore one Sunday afternoon embraced the opportunity of going down when the people were engaged in the sport, and begged to be permitted to take part in the game. The players

8. Dr. Cuthbert Bardsley, Bishop of Coventry, was President of Coventry City F.C. when they were promoted to Division I, in 1967. For a description of episcopal deportment at a football match, see *The Times*, May 20, 1967. In 1973 their Bishop was chief cheer-leader for Norwich City F.C.

9. Hew Scott, ed., *Fasti Ecclesiae Scoticanae*, Edinburgh, 1915, I, p. 212.

were somewhat astonished, but made no reply, neither complied nor refused. Mr. Potter said it was proper that all their employment should begin with prayers, and he therefore pulled off his hat and began to pray. By the time he had concluded, the most of the players had skulked away, and the practice was in future discontinued.'[10]

A more gracious picture, however, may be taken from Cumberland at about the same time. The Rector of Ousby from 1672 until his death in 1719, Thomas Robinson, who was a natural historian of some distinction, had a nice appreciation of the merits of football. Thus, after Sunday afternoon prayers, he would regularly 'accompany the leading men of his parish to the adjoining ale-house, where each man spent a penny and only a penny: that done, he set the younger sort to play at foot-ball (of which he was a great promoter) and other rustical diversions'.[11] Blessed be the name of Thomas Robinson!

As well as the Church another of the professions took a lively interest in football—that of the Law. In Thomas Dekker's *The Whore of Babylon* (1607) Plain Dealing ran into a group of young lawyers:

'I wondered what they were,' he said; 'I asked one of them if they were going to foot-ball. "Yes", said he, "doe you not see those country fellowes? We are against them." "And who do you think shall winne?" said I. "Oh," said he, "the gowns, the gowns." '

In Peter Hausted's *The Rival Friends* (1632) Anteus observes to Nodle Emptie, of the Innes of Court:

'Why he is sent for far and near by the valiant of the Parishes, to play matches at football: I tell you here is the only Hammershin this Shire can boast of; not a serving man can keep a legge or an arme whole for him, he ha's

10. W. Chrystal, *The Kingdom of Kippen*, Stirling, 1903, pp. 121, 123.
11. W. Hutchinson, *The History of the County of Cumberland*, Carlisle, 1794, I, pp. 224–5. The Cumberland tradition of football is reflected in Hugh Walpole's account of an imaginary match of the eighteenth century in *Rogue Herries*, London, 1930, pp. 621–6.

pension from all the surgeons within the compasse of fortie miles, for breaking of bones.'

Hammershin, B.A. (for he was a university graduate), a character not quite unknown at the present day and aptly named by Rev. Peter Hausted, might be thought from this to have been no more than nominally an amateur performer.

In the classical days of English culture (broadly speaking, the seventeenth and eighteenth centuries) the fashioning of what is termed a democratic way of life was at least partly due to a community of interest and a mutual respect engendered thereby between contrasted groups of society. The distance between the so-called aristocrat and the peasant or artisan was much less than in Europe because there were activities in which collaboration or competition on equal terms was possible. The strength of the musical and dramatic records of that period depended on this fact to a large extent. Neither the music club nor the theatre was exclusive. Football, now coming to be seen as a unique fusion of folk-custom and Renaissance philosophy and practice, was another catalyst of social *mores*.

A number of writers have tended to put the wrong emphasis on the boisterous element in and about football. Those of Puritanical inclinations, whether old or new, have condemned disorder, but have not analysed the discontent that fathered the disorder. Often it was a discontent stemming from general frustration. In the seventeenth century the campaign for stopping football grew stronger, as the game itself increased in popularity. In 1608 the Court Leet of Manchester was greatly concerned and on October 12 ordained:

'Whereas their hath been heretofore greate disorder in our towne of Manchester, and the Inhabitants thereof greatlye wronged and charged with makinge and amendinge of their glasse windowes broken yearlye and spoyled by a companye of lewde and disordered persons usinge that unlawful exercise of playinge with the footbale in ye streets of the said towne, breaking many mens windowes and glasse at their plesure, and other great inormyties. Therefore Wee of this Jurye doe order that no maner of persons herafter shall playe or use the ffotebale in any streete within the said towne of Manchester sub pena to everye one that shall so use the same for everye tyme xiid.'[12]

This injunction was repeated in the following year and (not perhaps unexpectedly during the era of the Commonwealth) again in 1655 and 1656. Other towns had the same problem and among those where specific prohibitions were issued were Maidstone, Hexham, and Richmond, Yorkshire. Fatalities still occurred from time to time to provide additional ammunition for the suppressionists. A football game in Devonshire in 1627 ended in tragedy. In 1692 an unfortunate young man in Aldeburgh, Suffolk, was killed. (A luckless member of the family Grimes?) This continuing tale of intention and unintentional dislocation of civil life is otherwise annotated by William Davenant. In his *First Day's Entertainment at Rutland House* (1656), where a Parisian and a Londoner abuse each other's city, the former remarks: 'I would now make a safe retreat, but that methinks I am stopt by one of your heroic games, call'd football, which I conceive—under your favour—not very conveniently civil in the streets, especially in such irregular and narrow roads as Crooked Lane.' Since by this work Davenant hoped to establish a native music-drama this citation just qualifies as the first operatic reference to football.

On the other hand there was an increasing number of persons of quality with a direct interest in the game. Archibald Campbell (1576?–1638), seventh Earl of Argyll, later to be the scourge of the Macgregor clan, was remem-

12. J. P. Earwaker, ed., *The Court Leet Records of the Manor of Manchester*, Manchester, 1855, II, pp. 239–40.

bered for his 'playing at the foot ball with Achinbreak and other scholaris',[13] long after his apostasy (he became a Roman Catholic), his wanton extravagances, and his dangerous dalliance with treason, were forgotten.

George Chapman, a splendid and satirical observer of the habits of the courtier or the would-be courtier, relates folk-football to higher society when he allows his epony-mous hero in *Sir Gyles Goosecap* (c. 1601–3) to expound why he 'would fain marry'.

'Why, madam,' said Sir Gyles, 'we have a great match at football towards, married men against bachelors, and the married men be all my friends, so I would fain marry to take the married men's parts, in truth.'

To which Hippolyte observed: 'The best reason for marriage that I ever heard, Sir Gyles.'[14]

The fact that a footballer was a footballer and on the field was protected by no privilege of class was demon-strated in the unlucky case of Emanuel Scrope, Earl of Sunderland. On December 3, 1630, James Howell, a versa-tile Welsh scholar, diplomat, and writer, recounted in a letter

'. . . how many years ago my Lord Willoughby [of Eresby] and he [Sunderland] with so many of their servants (de gayeté de cœur), play'd a match at football against such a number [i.e. an equal number] of countrymen, where my Lord of Sunderland, being busy about the ball, got a bruise in the breast; which put him in a swoon for the present, but did not trouble him till three months after . . .'[15]

13. J. R. N. McPhail, ed., *Highland Papers*, Scot. Hist. Soc., 2nd Ser., V, Edinburgh, 1914, I. p. 184.

14. Some Shrove Tuesday games between Married Men and Bachel-ors were recorded in the eighteenth century: particularly in Scotland and Cornwall, as also in Normandy. The symbolic significance of this arrangement—even more so in the case of the Married Women *v.* Spinsters of Inveresk—is patent.

15. Joseph Jacobs, ed., *Epistolae Ho-elianae: the Familiar Letters of*

By this time the general condition of England was deplorable, Charles I having commenced his disastrous period of rule without Parliament. A young man named Oliver Cromwell—a former student of Sidney Sussex College, Cambridge, and, it is supposed, at one time a member of Lincoln's Inn—was considering emigration to America. But on this intention he had second thoughts. His subsequent career as soldier, politician, and 'Lord Protector' is familiar in outline. Like all extraordinary men Cromwell liked to think of himself otherwise. The more congenial aspects of his character—his love of music and sport—have, however, been obscured by the partial assessments of champions on the one hand and detractors on the other. In 1654 Cromwell attended a 'hurling' match in Hyde Park, at which he was attended by members of the Privy Council. The match was played, it was recorded, by 150 Cornishmen, one side designated by distinctive red, the other by white, caps.[16] Like the majority of English statesmen Cromwell's early life was not distinguished by academic success. He was 'more famous for his Exercises in the Fields than in the schools . . . being one of the chief Matchmakers and Players at Football, Cudgel, or any other boystrous sport or game'.[17] Moreover, he was wont in after years to recount his athletic experiences, remembering especially 'when he had been more special of meeting [John] Wheelwright at football, than of meeting an army in the field; for he was infallibly sure of being tript up by him.'[18] John Wheelwright (1594–1679), a native of Lin-

---

James Howell, London, 1892, I, pp. 282–3. These letters, generally written to imaginary recipients, belong to the epistolary convention which later blossomed into the novel.

16. The match was described by *The Moderate Intelligencer*, May 4, 1654. For previous use of red and white for sporting occasions, see p. 45.

17. *Flagellum: or the Life and Death, Birth and Burial of Oliver Cromwell, the late Usurper*, 1663.

18. Letter to George Vaughan quoted in J. Belknap, *The History of New Hampshire*, Boston, 1792, III, p. 339.

C

colnshire, was a Sizar at Cambridge. After ordination he became Vicar of Bilbsby, but in 1633 he was suspended from his living for nonconformity. Three years later, having arrived in Boston, Mass., he began a new career in a new land.

George Monck, a professional soldier of eminence, was among Cromwell's valued advisers. After Cromwell's death Monck, commander of the land forces, joint commander of the Navy, and head of a council of state, exercised great power, and it was he—reading the thoughts of his countrymen—who proposed and took effective steps towards the Restoration of the Monarchy. On the return of Charles II, Monck was created Duke of Albemarle.

It was expected that Charles II would renew a right cheerful spirit in the nation. This, in broad terms, was why he was asked back. After 1660 the blither spirits hauled out their maypoles and other instruments of gaiety, and former revelries that for twenty years had been restrained by discretion or forbidden by law came into the open again. As has been suggested things were not quite as bad as they are commonly conceived to have been during the Commonwealth, but the English at all times at heart are reluctant to admit of the virtues of austerity. There was, to put it mildly, an appreciable increase of licence in Restoration England. Football on the top level, however, fell into a ruminative phase. The rough stuff went merrily on, in town and country, but a certain sense of gallantry supervened. Thus it is reported that '. . . Charles II attended a match which was played between his own servants and those of the Duke of Albemarle'.[19] Whether or not this was the case (Shearman gives no authentication) the legend is sufficient to suggest that the game at that time had its powerful protectors. The reason—or a main reason—is proposed by two dramatists whose interest in the subject of class distinc-

19. M. Shearman, op. cit., p. 263.

tion tends in some instances to enhance the validity of this comment.

In *The bird in a cage* (1633) James Shirley thus shows Morello, a courtier, giving encouragement to Peronotto, Captain of the Guard of the Duke of Mantua:

'Your Lordship may make one at foot-ball,
'tis all the sport now-a-days. (*Sings*)
What other is the world than a ball,
Which we run after with whoop and into hollow?
He that doth catch it is sure of a fall,[20]
His heels tripp'd up by him that doth follow.'

In *The Antipodes* Richard Broome has his footballer nobleman Letoy speak thus to Blaze, a heraldic painter:

'They runne at ring, and tilt against one another,
I and my men can play at a match at football.
Wrestle a handsome fall, and pitch the barre,
And crack the cudgells, and a pate sometimes,
'twould doe you good to see 't.'

The Italian, chivalric, football, lay behind this. Shirley had been a pupil at Merchant Taylors' School, of which Mulcaster had been head-master; Broome an assistant to the Italophile Ben Jonson. Both moved in the world of fashion and came across countless enthusiasts for holidays in Italy. (The Italian States were really beginning to open up their tourist trade in the seventeenth century.) In different ways Thomas Coryate, the traveller, Henry Peacham, author of a celebrated guide to etiquette—*The Compleat Gentleman*,[21] John Dowland, the composer, Nicholas

20. One might not be far wrong if one supposed Bunyan's 'He that is down needs fear no fall' to have been an image drawn from the football game.
21. 1622.

Lanier, the keeper of the pictures of Charles I and also a composer, John Milton, and John Evelyn, wrote and spoke of the glories of Italy. The musical could hardly be unaware that Giovanni Bardi, the patron-founder of Florentine opera, was the author of a classic work on football: *Discorso sopra il gioco del calcio fiorentino*, Florence, 1580.

The game of *Calcio* reached the height of its glory just when Englishmen were sojourning in Italy for long periods as a matter both of duty and of pleasure.[22] It was thus described in the *Vocabolario della Crusca*, published in Venice, in 1612: '*É* calcio *anche nome di un gioco, proprio, e antico della città di Firenze, a guisa di battaglia ordinata, con una palla a vento, rossonigliantesi alla speromachia passato de' Greci a' Latini, e da' Latini a noi!*'[23]

Calcio, although not without its vigour, was a colourful, skilful, regulated spectacle. It not only had its origin in the patterns of medieval chivalry; it had also a tactical basis. The Florentines, with 27 players on each side, operated what in modern terms would be described as the 15—5—4—3 formation—15 *innanzi o corridori*, 5 *sconciatori*, 4 *datori innanzi*, and 3 *datori e dietro*.

The first account of *Calcio* to be made available to the English at home was in a translation of T. Boccalini's *I Ragguagli di Parnasso*[24] by Henry Carey, Earl of Monmouth, published in London in 1656. This account gives moral support to the pastime, indicating its value in society, and also some indication of the possibilities afforded to the individual to show his strength and his skill:

22. '*Il gioco del calcio toccò il periodo del massimo splendore in Firenza, all' epoca dei Medici*', *Enciclopedia Italiana*, 1930–9.
23. A game after the manner of a battle!
24. . . . or *Advertisements from Parnassus*: see (Ch.) xciii, pp. 88–90. 'The Florentines in their pastime called the Calcio, admit of a spruce Forreign Courtier, who wins the Prize.'

'The Noble Florentines plaid the last Tuesday at the Calcio in the Phebean field, which all the Litterati of *Pernassus* came to see; and though some, to whom it was a new sight to see many of these Florentine Gentlemen fall down to right cuffs, said, that that manner of proceeding in that which was but play and sport, was too harsh, and not severe enough in a real combat, yet the Vertuosi took delight to see it, for many praised the Gamesters swift running, their nimble leaping, and their strength; others were very well pleased with the invention of the game, which was very good to breed up youth to run, leap and wrastle, and many believe this to be the cause why it was instituted in that formerly so famous Commonwealth . . . the Commonwealth of Florence had done very well and wisely in introducing the Calcio amongst the Citizens, to the end that having the satisfaction of giving four or five good round buffets in the face to those to whom they bear ill will, by way of sport, they might the better appease their anger . . .'

Better, said the writer, than by the use of daggers. There was at this particular game a spectator—a 'Spruce Forreign Courtier'. It is not stated from where he came, and if one were to hazard a guess it would be from the direction of France or Britain. The Courtier asked:

'. . . that if they would permit him to play with them, he would teach these Florentine Gentlemen the true art how to take the ball, how to run with it, how to repulse the wrastlers dextrously, who would take it away, and other excellent master like tricks. . . .

'and presently the Ball was thrown up into the ayr by men appointed thereunto: which came no sooner to the ground, but that the nimble Courtier ran towards it, and having taken it up, clap it under his left arm; those of the contrary party ran to take it away from him: but he with great strength justled one, and thurst away another; and whereas the Florentines, who were masters of the sport, thought to have thrown him down, they were thrown down them selves; for the sturdy courtier did so freely lay about him on all sides with his arms, shoulders, head, and every part of him, as he made all keep aloof, so as the greatest part of the Florentines of the adverse part, were thrown to the ground; and some of them received such blows on their breasts, as they could ahardly breathe for a good while after. And the Courtier having overcome all that withstood him, threw the ball over the lists, and won the Prize.'

In this story there is, of course, the recurrent theme of the fairy prince, or the all-wise, all-powerful stranger, that covers another theme, of the god that became man. The man of the Renaissance believed in the power of reason, but he did not always disbelieve in the power of the myth. The reverse of this legend as told by Boccalini and retold by the Earl of Monmouth, is that repeated by Sir Frederick Eden.[25] In fact the Scottish theory as expounded by him undoubtedly derived from some former contact between Scotland and Italy.

A further account of *Calcio* was published in 1670 in Richard Lassels's *The Voyage of Italy*, a useful guide-book to Italy, which like many others relied for judgements on painting on the fundamental *Lives of the Most Eminent Painters* by Lazzaro Vasari. A later example of English interest in *Calcio* was recorded in 1766, when the British Consul at Leghorn attended and reported the game played there in that year in honour of the marriage of Prince Pietro Leopolde and Princess Maria Luisa.[26]

Throughout this part of the history of the game there is always some question as to when football is football. *Calcio* clearly resembles Rugby Football in some particulars (which is a matter for the reader to decide according to logic but also according to personal prejudice); but its fundamentals, of design and movement, are common to all

25. See p. 37.
26. *Enc. It.*, loc. cit.

ball-games before the time of subtle definition and modern terminology. It is, therefore, tempting to pick up the Cornish exercise of 'hurling'—to which allusion has already been made—and to discover in one branch of it the influence of Italy. This influence could easily have been imparted by some Cornish gentleman, probably a Catholic, after a visit to Florence.

In 1602 Richard Carew, antiquary, High Sheriff for Cornwall, and translator of Tasso, gave a description of 'hurling' in some detail:

'For hurling to goales,' writes Carew, 'there are fifteen, twenty or thirty players, more or less, chosen on each side, who strip themselves to their slightest apparel and then join hands in ranks one against another; out of these ranks they match themselves by payres,[27] one embracing another and so passe away, every of which couple are especially to watch one another during the play. After this they pitch two bushes on the ground some eight or ten feet asunder, and directly against them ten or twelve paces off other twain in like distance which they term goales, where some indifferent person throweth up a ball the which whomsoever can catch and carry through the adversaries' goals hath won the game.'

In so far as 'hurling' has gravitated towards hockey it would seem that the Cornish preferred an earlier and more general signification. What Carew describes is at least very close to *Calcio*—with the rough and tumble of 'justling' and 'thursting' omitted from the progress of the goal-scorer. One notes the 'indifferent' person—the referee, as Mulcaster would have had him—and the numbers involved

27.   And sometimes Foot-ball for the Men.
                   To try their strength 10 against 10.

This couplet, occurring in a catalogue of sports for August in *Poor Robin*, *An Almanack* (1696), contains, I suspect, some poetic licence in the conveniently rhyming number; but it probably is not to far from actuality.

(which *could* on occasion no doubt equate with the *Calcio* set-up). One further notes the preliminary courtesy of the pairing of rivals—followed, it would seem, by man-for-man marking. This, it must be supposed was the game witnessed by Oliver Cromwell.

In contrast Carew gives a long account of 'hurling over country'—the common folk game-ritual. On its hidden properties he makes interesting comment: 'The ball in this play may be compared to an infernal spirit, for whosoever catcheth it fareth straightways like a madman struggling and fighting with those that go about to hold him; no sooner is the ball gone from him than he resigneth this fury to the next receiver and himself becometh peaceable as before . . .'[28]

So, once again, one is made aware of the civilising influences that were at work in society. During the seventeenth century football became more purposeful, more scientific, and more spectacular. Any account of it is dependent, of course, on a selection of impressions from those few who, seeing the game from different angles, left on record but one or two snapshots. It is proper that a brief piece of near-Impressionism should come from a French writer. In 1698 Henri Misson de Valbourg published in Paris his *Memoires et Observations faites par un Voyageur en Angleterre.*

'*En hiver le Footbal est an exercise utile et charmant. C'est un balon de cuir, gros comme la tête et rempli de vent; cela se balotte avec le pied dans les rues par celui qui le peut attraper: il n'y a point d'autre science.*'

According to precedent the introduction of the word *charmant* into this context is irregular. But it is clear that one may read into the statement a tribute to a subtlety, indeed a science, in pedipulation (if the coinage is permitted), the like of which had not been noted since the days

---

28. Regarding the perpetuation of this tradition of hurling there is an evocative passage in Myrna Blumberg's novel *Two Minutes from the Sea*, London, 1965; see Panther edition (1967), pp. 62–3.

of Little Sir Hugh. Misson de Valbourg was fortunate in finding a group, or groups, of pioneers who, anxious to avoid damage to property (and consequent aprehension and penalisation), had developed to some extent the technique of dribbling. Thus were Renaissance values being introduced at the lowest level.

5

The Georgians

In the surviving part of the prehistory of football—that part that is recorded prior to the nineteenth-century revolution—there is an intricacy and delicacy of pattern that is at once fascinating and frustrating. Notions—including some which are part of the modern game—turn up, and as suddenly disappear. The two main lines, which we are able to follow with some consistency, are football in the country and football in the town. These two lines we may pick up later, for the moment turning aside to make an attractive and by no means unimportant detour.

We are still trying to escape from the nineteenth-century dogma that football is a man's game. The latter-day behaviour of the most raucous of supporters on certain grounds often represents a pathetic attempt to insist on the validity of the dogma. But we have to consider that the influence of women on the game has been an effective, if indirect, one. The modern idea that women's interest should be further stimulated is sound, even though the premises on which it rests are of dubious origin.

In more valorous days girls (apart from those ceremonially set against each other in the Shrove Tuesday rites) were by no means unknown as football players. Sir Philip Sidney allows a glimpse of Elizabethan hoydenry in a *Dialogue between two Shepherds*:

> 'A tyme there is for all, my mother often sayes,
> When she, with skirt tuckt very high, with girls
> at football playes.'

A hundred years later, or thereabouts, Thomas D'Urfey admits a similar picture into the ballad *Of noble race was Shenkin*:

> 'Her was the prettiest fellow
> At Foot-ball or at Cricket.
> At Hunting Chase, or nimbe Race,
> Cots-plus how her cou'd prick it.'

Our concern, however, is less with the direct involvement than with the peripheral activities of women.

Bargoed is in the parish of Llandyssul in South Cardiganshire. At the beginning of the eighteenth century there lived there a farmer named Beynon. His elder daughter Mary married one Thomas Powell, by whom she was taken to America in 1714. Powell had strong Nonconformist convictions, for which reason emigration offered the hope of toleration. The Powells settled in Pencader—then in the County of Newcastle and now in Delaware—on land assigned to Welsh Nonconformists by William Penn in 1684. Left behind in Bargoed was Mary's young sister, Anna, a regular and entertaining letter-writer. It is, perhaps, not putting it too strong to say that that part of Cardiganshire and adjacent Pembrokeshire were a hotbed of football. In Pembrokeshire a game called 'knappan' was practised.[1] This was more akin to the Cornish 'hurling' than to football. In Cardiganshire, however, football as such was specified. Any resemblance to the modern game is entirely fortuitous. But Anna Beynon, joining the crowd of spectators against her father's instructions, had the capacity of a first-rate sports-writer. Thus vividly—in a letter dated October 19, 1720—she brings a match to life:

1. Described in George Owen, *The Description of Pembrokeshire* (1603), ed., H. Owen, Cymmrodorion Soc. Rec. Ser., No. 1, 1892, pp. 270–82.

'The parishes of Llandyssul and Llanwenog had a football match last Christmas Day. They had been preparing for months, and hundreds came together to watch them. It was against my father's will that I went, and he would not allow Siencyn[2] to go. Father is a wonderfully wrong-headed old creature, and I think that he gets more and more and more wrong-headed every day. He nearly drives me to say bad words to him sometimes. Nothing is right in his eyes but what the Bible and Mr. Lewis Dinas Cerdin, say.

'Many had brewed in readiness for the match and took food and drink with them, and what running and kicking and noise there was! Now one side was winning, and then the other, but Llandyssul was winning oftenest. Play ceased for an hour at noon for bread and cheese and beer, and everyone was as merry as a cuckoo.

'Soon after play began again in the afternoon they began to quarrel and swear and kick each other. Some of them were drunk, and the rest had taken too much, and it was a fearful sight to see them fighting, and the girls running and screaming, and trying to rescue their brothers and friends, but in spite of all that could be done they kept on fighting like bull-dogs. I think they were at it for an hour till the Llanwenog men were forced to retire.

'Evan Bwlch Gwyn[3] had drunk too much to be able to defend himself and he would have been half-killed if

2. Anna's brother, who, she said, 'was very indifferent to girls for years, but he is now getting sweet on Mali of the Pant. She is a big girl but she is not a good-looking girl. I am sorry that Siencyn is going after her because there is no love lost between us.'

3. Continuation of above: 'I heard that she said she was surprised I kept company with Evan Bwlch Gwyn, but what difference does it make to her whom I keep company with? Let her look after herself and not trouble about me. I will do my best to make mischief between Siencyn and her. I have already turned mother against her and I think that she will have to look for some one besides our Siencyn. The stuck-up creature had better let me alone. I think that Evan Bwlch Gwyn is quite as good as she, anyhow.'

Sioned, his sister and I, had not dragged him away. It was said that one youth of Llanwenog had been killed. He was insensible for a time but he came to and is now well. Twm Penddol was kicked rather badly because he was too drunk to take care of himself. There is much talk of the battle everywhere, and the two parishes threaten to go at it again with cudgels sometime in the summer. They say that the Llanwenog men are very ugly with the cudgel.

'At supper that night our Siencyn said, "Thanks to you, father, for keeping me from going there. My skin is whole and my head is without an ache now." I was disgusted to hear him. Siencyn is far too much of an old flannel. I wish I were a boy instead of him to fight for the parish. Sali Blaen-y-cwm gave a thorough thrashing to a young man from Llanwenog. His blood was spurting with every blow.

'Lewis, the minister, spoke very severely of the thing in Pant-y-creuddyn afterwards. He cried like a baby, while father and mother and the chief people were crying with him. They have since had a good many prayer meetings to pray for the young people, but I do not see the young people one whit the better after they have been prayed for.

'I must at length finish. It is a week since I began this letter, and I am afraid that you will say, when reading it, I am getting more silly every time.

'Your loving sister,[4]
Anne Beynon'

Anna defied her father for two excellent reasons. First, her boy-friend was playing; second, she was concerned for the honour of the parish. Her wish that she could 'fight for the parish' shows her to be of the true stuff of loyal sup-

4. *N. & Q.* 160, May 16, 1931, p. 349. Cf. G. L. Gomme, *The Village Community*, London, 1890, where there are accounts of matches between the Parishes of Cellan and Pencanay, and between the sections of the Parish of Llanwenog known as the Bros—or the 'Paddy' Bros, from the hills—and the Blaenaus, the lowlanders, seen as survivals of clan feuds.

port. Anna informs us that the teams underwent some sort of training for the match—though the effects were pretty thoroughly obliterated by half-time. She also wields a vigorous cudgel in defence of youth. All in all, a splendid asset to the parish.

It had been surmised that the description of certain Welsh footballer players as 'Paddy' Bros denoted an Irish pedigree for the game. For reasons which have been given the Irish and Welsh games were of common stock; and they proceeded into the eighteenth century on comparable footing. Our Welsh recorder, the sprightly Anna, however, shows a realistic approach in contrast to the Irish football writers of the time.

The first was Seumas Dall Mac Cuarta, who described a match between the Boyne men and the Nanny men—the Nanny also being a river, in Lower Meath—which took place in 1660. Such matches took place, like those in Wales, on Christmas Day, and strong feelings were aroused. This was particularly so in the present case, where the Boyne men abused their Nanny opponents on account of their readiness to adopt the habits of the English settlers. As the next poem to be considered will show, however, the Nanny team enjoyed a fame that was not merely local. There was at this time a certain code of rules. If in this game (played with a small ball, as used in hurling) any was adjudged guilty of foul play during a match he 'had to give satisfaction to his accuser, at the end of the play, by wrestling him'.[5]

In 1720 Matthew Concanen, known for his strictures on Pope and Pope's on him[6] and as an Attorney General of Jamaica in later life, published *A Match at Foot-ball*, an artful piece in three cantos, which parodied Pope and was —so the Preface suggests—praised by Swift. It was pub-

5. *Gaelic Journal*, Vol. 10, Dublin, 1899–1900, pp. 550–1, where Mac Cuarta's poem is given (in Gaelic).
6. *The Dunciad*, II, l. 138.

lished anonymously in London by R. Francklin, of Fleet
Street, who remarked that the author was 'a Youth, under
Twenty Years of Age, and if you will give me leave to add
my Suffrage to that of many others, promises to be very
useful to me and my Brethren hereafter'.

The first canto begins, in conventional manner, but with
a psychological observation indicating the vicarious character of football:

> 'I sing the Pleasures of the Rural Throng,
> And mimick was as yet unknown to song.'

The claim contained within the second line was not quite
accurate, for football had its small place in song. However,
the boast, being a modest one, may be forgiven. The match
on which the poem centres was between Lusk and Soards,
according to an annotation, '. . . Two Baronies in the
County of Dublin, whose Inhabitants are the most fam'd
for Dexterity at this Game, and are always at Variance for
a Superiority of skill.'

The match was played in the evening, for—

> 'The distant Sun now shoots a feeble Ray.'

The pitch, if not prepared, was carefully selected, being 'A
wide Extent of Level Ground'. There was a 'num'rous
Crowd' and

> '. . . Troups of Horsemen throng the varied Scene.'

There were charming preliminaries to the game. The author
footnotes that 'It is customary for the Maids to dance for
Cakes, and have several other sports before the Foot-ball
is begun.' The said maids, it is made clear, had other
sports to attend to once recovered from their exertions.
Just before the kick-off the spectators were addressed by

'Old Hobbinol', who displayed the six beribboned Holland
caps, for the winning team, and the six pairs of gloves, for
the losers. The winning side were also promised a bonus
from the Squire in the form of a 'Cask of humming beer'.

The establishment of a six-a-side football is of interest
from several points of view. It indicated a laudable desire to
encourage an open and fast game, in which individual skill
and enterprise should find opportunity. It was, in contrast
to the frequent free-for-all, an artificial game, and, as such,
apt for the artifacted convention of heroic couplets. Six-a-
side football, which comes up again,[7] is, of course, practised at the present time, as particularly in the annual
Christmas English Schools Competition.

The first team to appear was that of Soards. Each man
was in white, and wearing a cap distinguished by a red
ribbon. The team comprised Terence (in love with Norah,
who, distractingly beautiful, kept her vigil on the touch-
line), a shepherd; the brothers Darby and John, both
locally born, the one celebrated as a singer, the other as a
dancer, 'and both in grappling skill'd'. Next an Alien—
Hugh, from the Wicklow Mountains, whose sinews were
'tougher than the twanging *Eugh*' and whose diet consisted
of strengthening Pignuts and Potatoes'.

The ideal team combines youth with experience. So we
meet Felim:

> 'Though three times Twenty rolling Years have shed
> Their hoary Honours on thy rev'rend Head,
> *Entullus* like, thou couldst not brook to stay,
> A bare Spectator on this glorious Day.
> Practice and Years to thee the Knack impart,
> To shift with Cunning, and to trip with Art.'

Finally Daniel—well known as a player of defensive skill
at Oxmantown Green in Dublin—'frequently the scene of

7. See p. 91.

these kind of Sports'—and Ventoso, the bagpiper. The
tunes of the piper, however

> '... were drown'd in shriller Cries;
> Loud Acclamations fill the spacious Round,
> And distant Rocks repeat the joyous Sound.'

The Lusk players followed, also in white, but with blue
ribbons waving from their caps. They were led by Paddy
(also in love with Norah) a gardener, a vegetarian ('Herbs
were his choicest Fare'), and hitherto something of a dilet-
tante. After Paddy came Kit, a farm labourer, and an
obvious candidate for consideration as the first footballer
to have sought a transfer. He was

> '... near *Nanny-Water* bred,
> But now by Thirst of Reputation led,
> A denizen of *Lusk*.

The Lusk team was exceptional in a preference for imported players, for these came—

> 'Next Neal and Cabe, whom Poverty sent forth,
> From the bleak Regions of the rugged North;
> Wasted with Toils, and starv'd on scanty Oats,
> With tatter'd shirts, and destitute of Coats.'

The Ulstermen found Lusk a veritable Paradise and

> 'With strengthening Turnips fed, and fatning Pease,'

were ready for any exertion. Next came Lenard—

> 'So swift to gain, and firm to keep his Ground.'

Last, Dick the Miller: 'surly' and viewing the scene 'with a
gloomy look'. A strong player,

'Nor fir'd with Pleasure, nor with Danger aw'd,'

than whom none could 'toss the *Foot-ball* with a surer
Aim'. Partisanship ran high, to the disadvantage of the
visiting team:

'Hail'd by no friendly Voice they take their Stand.'

In his second canto Concanen gets down to business.
'Old Hobbinol' produces the ball (a gift from the Squire[8]),
which is

'... three Fold's of Bullock's Hide,
With Leathern Thongs bound fast on every Side;
A Mass of finest Hay, conceal'd from sight,
Conspire at once to make it firm and light.'[9]

'Old Hobbinol'—a wordy fellow—points to the goals
('form'd by sticking two Willow Twigs in the Ground, at a
small Distance, and twisting the Tops, so that they seem a
Gate'), exhorts the players, and then tosses the ball into the
air. Felim caught it and, not surprisingly, dispatched it.
The pass (if it was) went astray and Dick intercepted. At
once he created alarm in the ranks of Soards supporters,
for

'A dextrous Kick with artful Fury drew
The light Machine, with force unerring, flew
To th' adverse Goal; where, in the sight of all,
The watchful Daniel caught the flying ball.'

Daniel ran half the length of the field assisted by Darby
and John (how, is uncertain) until halted by Paddy. After
a fierce episode of in-fighting the gods—or rather the

8. Squire Brown—in *Tom Brown's Schooldays*—was in the habit of
presenting a football for the village game.
9. Cf. use of feathers, p. 31 n. 2.

goddess Flora—intervened. Daniel caught his foot in long grass and dropped the ball.

There followed what might now be termed a period of indecisive play in mid-field. Neal was neatly tripped by Terence; Kit 'drop'd' by Felim; Hugh laid out by Paddy. After Dick was 'toss'd down' by Darby he would appear to have gone off for repairs. At any rate he 'forbore to play'. Cabe had his shirt pull'd by John. Lenard, standing by, considers this the moment for a breakaway. But the watchful Daniel, seeing danger approaching, pulls back the defence. Lenard

'. . . now to kick the rolling Ball prepar'd,'

but Terence, first catching his arm and then tripping him with 'a dextrous Crook', prevented a score. Play, however, was definitely in favour of the visitors. Before long the goddess Flora called in the Zephyrs to aid the Lusk attack. They

'. . . on their Wings (to mortal Eyes unseen)
    . . . bore the light Machine:
Daniel despairing of his promis'd Prize,
Jumps up, and strives to stop it as it flies.
They [the Zephyrs] to avoid his Fury upward soar,
Till past the Goal their pond'rous Load they bore:
At this Advantage all the Forces pause,
And the Field echoes with the loud Applause.'

The practice of having an interval after a goal had been passed[10] persisted until well into modern times. But here in Ireland the interval was protracted (for the benefit of the Poet) in order to arouse a sleeping Pan and to enlist his aid

10. Concanen footnotes thus: 'It is the Method when ever the Ball is drove beyond the Goal, without going through it, for both Parties to change Goals; and this is done, to prevent the sun, or Winds, being for any time on either side.'

for the hard-pressed home team. The drama of the match now takes a new dimension. The humans are seen to be but instruments in the hands of the immortals, and Concanen as a determinist. Pan hates Flora: Flora hates Pan. Or so it seems. But Pan, it transpires, is desolate at the thought of the game being invaded by a woman's whims. He says:

> 'Know then, I first of God or Man was seen
> To toss a *Foot-ball* on your flow'ry Green:
> Apollo taught me, when from Jove he fled,
> And on the Plain Admetus' Cattle fed.'

A Satyr comes and relates to Flora how the willow-twig goals were a monument to 'a girl call'd Sally' who, once chased by a lovesick God, was saved from disgrace by more protective deities who considerately changed her into a willow-tree—hence Sally.

Following this intermission Concanen resumed his proper narrative. After a robust, but unprofitable opening to the second session, Terence got the ball. He ran, but was over-haul'd by Paddy. A manly set-to between Terence and Paddy, Norah swinging from horror to elation, ended in the downfall of the latter and in Terence making some further progress. But Neal obtains possession and frees the Lusk goal from danger.

Just when it seems that a goal-less draw is in sight Terence takes a moment's respite to address a prayer to Pan. To make sure that his prayer is efficacious he promises the god a sacrificial lamb.

> 'The God consents—One Kick he softly stole,
> And with another drove it through the Goal.
> *Lusk*'s Champions droop; loud Acclamations rise.
> And the shrill clamours pierce the vaulted skies,
> Joy smiles in ev'ry Face, all Heads are bare,
> While Clouds of Hats play wanton in the Air.'

Thus the match, but not the poem, ends. Several more lines
are required to tie up Terence and Norah, and to conclude
with a suitable moral couplet:

> 'What Monarch's Envy might not Terence move,
> So crown'd with Conquest, and so pleas'd with love.'

There may have been better accounts of football matches,
but few of such importance. For here is a move-by-move
commentary on a specific match in which due regard is
paid to custom, law and practice. The game described by
Concanen is, beyond dispute, football, and its relationship
to the modern game is close. Closer than anything heretofore to be found. The game at Soards, and where it was
otherwise played in Ireland, during the early eighteenth
century, was not only designed for the benefit of the players
but also of the spectators. And among the spectators, if
lucky, one found the appreciative Norah, before whose
charms, and in anticipation of whose criticism, it was
thought more profitable to play fair.

It would, on the whole, not surprise the Irish to discover
that their football, during the eighteenth century at least,
was both more advanced and more civilised than that of the
English. Nor was it lacking in fervour, a quality also to be
descried in the Welsh village game. The Irish took their
football with them when they emigrated. Thus one of
William Hone's correspondents (one J.R.P.) described how
the Irish used to play on a pitch which had fixed boundaries, between Oldfield's dairy and Copenhagen House,
Islington, the games beginning at three o'clock in the afternoon and continuing until dusk. J.R.P. observed that this
was 'as is usual in the sister kingdom, [where] county-men
play against other country-men'. A little nostalgically, perhaps, the writer recalled how when he was a boy, 'football
was commonly played on a Sunday morning, before church
time, in a village in the West of England, and the church-

piece was the ground chosen for it'.[11]

Lacking such detailed accounts of English football during the same period one is forced back to the generalisations of Addison, Gay, and the strictures of César de Saussure. Addison, in the person of 'The Spectator', went down to Worcestershire to visit Sir Roger de Coverley. A match (in which one Tom Short distinguished himself) was taking place on the village green. 'Having played many a match myself,'[12] said Addison, 'I could have looked longer on the sport had I not observed a country girl.' An Irish or Welsh country girl, no doubt, would have kept him at the match.

In 1716 John Gay issued his *Trivia*, a lively, realistic, Hogarthian account of London life. Thus he wrote of the scene in Covent Garden—where, no doubt, the great portico of Inigo Jones that faced the square from St. Paul's Church, and is referred to by Gay, was used as one goal:

> 'Here oft' my course I bend, when lo! from far
> I spy the furies of the foot-ball war:
> The 'prentice quits his shop, to join the crew,
> Increasing crowds the flying game pursue.
> Thus, as you roll the ball o'er snowy ground,
> The gathering globe augments with ev'ry round.
> But whither shall I run? the throng draws nigh,
> The ball now skims the street, now soars on high;
> The dextrous glazier strong returns the bound,
> And gingling sashes on the pent-house sound.'[13]

It was as well to keep out of the way. So too thought the Frenchman, de Saussure, who wrote a sourer note than his compatriot de Valbourg:

11. Hone, op. cit., II, p. 374.
12. At Charterhouse, where he was at school, or at Queen's College, Oxford?
13. *Trivia, or, the Art of Walking the Streets of London*, Book II, l. 343, 'The Dangers of Foot-ball'.

'The populace has other amusements and very rude ones, such as throwing dead dogs and cats and mud at passers-by on certain festival days. Another amusement which is very inconvenient to passers-by is football. For this game a leather ball filled with air is used, and is kicked about with the feet. In cold weather you sometimes see a score of rascals in the streets kicking at a ball, and they will break panes of glass anl smash the windows of coaches, and also knock you down without the slightest compunction; on the contrary they will roar with laughter.'[14]

The apprentices may have been troublesome with their football. But their enthusiasm for this sport was a good deal healthier than the drinking, gambling, and wenching, that were other popular, and deplored, pastimes. Many serious citizens were shocked at apprentice behaviour, but few did anything to provide congenial facilities for the protection of the morals of the young.

No doubt if a Stuart had been on the throne football would have continued under princely patronage. The Hanoverians had no interest in such activities. Football in England, therefore, declined. Nevertheless there are occasional evidences of a formal game. An illustration of a game in progress in the market-place at Barnet—about the middle of the century—shows a balance of forms and actions that might well have been used to illustrate those defined in Concanen's text. Hertfordshire would appear to have been a nursery of football, for the game 'was adopted by the Free School boys and played with rules, lines and goals in Hitchin. In 1819 there was an attempt to deprive the scholars of their ground, whereupon a meeting was called and Charles Barns, who had been a trustee of the school for seventy years (surely a record service), and Daniel Chapman, who had been trustee for sixty, and

14. *The Letters of Monsieur César de Saussure to his Family*, trs. & ed. Mme von Muyden, London, 1902, pp. 294–5; Letter xii, London, June 1728.

Timothy Bristow, who had been trustee for fifty-two years, all declared that the game had been played on that field (Paynes Park) for as long as they remembered. Nevertheless they did not retain their ground.'[15]

After leaving school, however, the footballers had only the rough and ready community game to look forward to. The process is familiar: '. . . a writer describing a great football match between Gosmore and Hitchin (in 1772), speaks of the ball being "drowned" for a time in the Priory pond, then forced along Angel Street across the Market Place into the Artichoke beer house, and finally goaled in the porch of St. Mary's Church.'[16]

History often bestows respectability. Football built up a balance of credit from its association, with people, with institutions, and places. Thus, as we review that long tradition up to the middle of the Georgian era, we find ourselves in a condition of bemused wonderment. If we are careless we fall into raptures over the archaisms of the game, its folklorist validity, its legends, and its *mise en scène*.

It is overlooked that often the game was a means of temporary relief, from frustration, from boredom, from social injustice. It afforded opportunity for demonstrating personal prowess for many who had no other medium to hand. The whole of that is written into Concanen's poem, of which the darker side is not difficult to discover. Concanen hints at the feudal domination of the Squire—a colonist in that Irish setting; he does more than hint at the condition of life in the province of Ulster; the diet-sheet he details suggests that it was remarkable that the young men to whom it applied were able to undertake the rigours of the game. One suspects that the long history of window-

15. R. L. Hine, op. cit., II, p. 266. Hine goes on to say that the Hitchin Football Club was formed in 1865, under the captaincy of Francis Shillitoe, a well-known local sportsman. This date is confirmed by *The Football Annual* (1873).

16. ibid., p. 244.

breaking was, in fact, an unconscious gesture that stemmed from unspoken revolutionary sentiments.

Football, in one sense, may appear to have stood still. But social conditions did not. During the last quarter of the eighteenth century the Industrial Revolution had changed the face of Britain, and the character of the British. There was a considerable increase in population, more especially in the Midlands and the North, and towns hitherto unregarded had assumed a considerable importance as commercial and administrative centres of territories which had gone over to industrial production. The old masters had been replaced by new: those who controlled the destinies of the labouring classes were owners of the raw materials of industry, those who used such, as well as the resources of the Empire, to manufacture machinery and goods, and those who were able to exploit a situation ripe for large-scale commercialisation. Men, and women, and children, worked long hours; fourteen, fifteen, sixteen hours a day, with relief only on three or four days in the year. In 1807 Robert Southey, in the supposed character of a Spanish visitor, drew attention to the damage brought on the community by not allowing for adequate breaks in the year. '[The English] reproach the Catholic religion with the number of its holidays, never considering how the want of holidays breaks down and brutalises the labouring class, and that where they occur seldom they are uniformly abused. Christmas, Easter, and Whitsuntide, the only seasons of festival in England are always devoted by artificers and the peasantry to riot and intoxication.'[17] There were shifts of population. Indigent Scots and poverty-racked Irish poured into England. The process continued for a century and more.

There is a general truth in Wordsworth's axiom that poetry is emotion recollected in tranquillity. It is applicable

17. Alvarez Espriella, *Letters from England*, London, 1808, II, p. 169.

to all art forms, including, if we accept (as I think we must) that it is a kind of art, football. Football as an activity mirrors the present. Its rituals reflect the more or less immediate past; its symbols, which lie within the ritual, the distant, inaccessible, past.

In the late eighteenth century two phenomena are to be noted: the appearance of fresh names on the map; and a general decline of interest. These two phenomena are interrelated.

Neither Bolton nor Sheffield have hitherto received mention. No doubt there were football players in both towns from time immemorial; but neither their virtues nor their misdemeanours were remarkable, simply because hitherto neither town was remarkable. A collection appertaining to an eighteenth-century clergyman of Bolton, Rev. James Folds, affords a glimpse into the regularised street-game as it was there practised:

'The streets, squares, and thoroughfares, as now comprehended, would only be "few and far between" in 1755 —narrow, mean, and irregular. The shops, dwellings, and most other town outfit, would be uniform therewith. In fact, the town proper would present so slight a distinction as compared with the country, that the juvenile pastime of football kicking (which is now set off by the kickers wearing red stockings in place of trousers, drawn tightly up to the middle quarters of the human body, low shoes, and other "kicky" costumes, and lifted up into such an unmanly way of kicking-time now a day) used to be "purred" out in the main street, even within the memory of people still living. Parson Folds himself, in season, betimes purchased the ball for presentation, and as per custom, pitched it over from the back part of the Swan Inn, or Man and Scythe, into Churchgate, a practice then adopted to hide the pitcher, so that the "kick off" (as per modern phraseology) might not be inspired by personal feeling. At this period the kickers wore clogs (and not low-sandaled shoes, more fitting for a ball-room) when and where the contest began; and those were accounted the best kickers who might kick the bladder of wind, in spite of opposing kickers, either across the River Croal in Churchbank, or at Great Bridge.'[18]

On which one may, perhaps, comment that the modern footballer is back to low-sandalled shoes—which might be thought not unfitting for a ballroom; and also that Parson Folds was a necessary link in the line of apostolic descent which placed the clergy in the responsible position of protecting the rites of football.

The allusion to football in Sheffield is more complex, and, as will be seen, the fact that the reporter was an Irishman is significant. The number of players initially involved compares with that of the Soards *v.* Lusk match already described. The fact that this turned out to be a three-day match,[19] however, necessitated the calling-up of substitutes and reserves, so that what happened in the end is somewhat obscure:

'Football at Bent's Green, in the year 1793, a great football match took place between Norton and Sheffield— There were selected six young men of Norton, dressed in green; and six young men of Sheffield, dressed in red. The play continued for three consecutive days. At the arch which was erected at each end of the place selected, there was a hole in the goal, and those on the Sheffield side would prevent the ball from passing through the hole. Then those of the Norton side (not being so numerous as those of Sheffield) sent messengers to the Peak and other places in the county of Derby; in consequence thereof, a great number of men appeared on the ground from Derbyshire. Then those of Sheffield sent fife and drum through the streets of

18. *Sayings and doings of the Rev. Folds, otherwise Parson Folds,* compiled by J. D. Greenhalgh, Bolton, 1879, p. 33.

19. Matches spread over several days continued to the middle of the nineteenth century. See p. 99.

Sheffield, to collect recruits and sufficient force against the Derbyshire men. (The fashion then was for all respectable gentlemen, tradesmen, and artisans of Sheffield to wear long [pig] tails). Hence, at the conclusion of the third day, a general row or struggle took place between the contending parties, insomuch that the men of Derbyshire cut and pulled nearly all the tails from the heads of the gentlemen of Sheffield. I understand there were many slightly wounded, but none were killed; thus ended the celebrated football match, which aroused the bad passions of humanity for several years afterwards, insomuch that the inhabitants of Norton felt a dread of coming to Sheffield, even about their necessary business.'[20]

The game of football crossed over the Napoleonic Wars (commemorated by the selection of 'French' and 'English' sides in the Shrovetide game at the Jesuit school, Stony-hurst College) and was picked up for castigation by a former scholar of Eton College in 1831. 'I cannot', he wrote, 'consider the game of football as being at all gentle-manly. It is a game which the common people of Yorkshire are particularly partial to, the tips of their shoes being heavily shod with iron: and frequently death has been known to ensue from the severity of the blows inflicted thereby.'[21]

Here is a footnote to add to the 'two-nations' theory; and one on which the most part of this book hinges.

20. [Bernard Bird], *The Perambulations of Barney the Irishman*, Sheffield, 1854.
21. *Eton, by an Etonian* ... 1831, p. 47.

6

Struggle for Survival

The so-called Romantic period had many faces. One has already been revealed, and it is not comely. The more familiar, or more acceptable one is represented by a literary movement. Since the period was one of change it was also one of reassessment. Thus old values, and old traditions, were brushed up and given a new set of clothing. Balladry and Gothic architecture were scrutinised and popularised, and the fast-vanishing vestiges of folk-custom were chased around the countryside by scholars. Conservatism and radicalism clashed on many fronts—internationally at the Congress of Vienna, nationally in the circumstances that led to the Reform Bill of 1832.

In respect of football we are led to the Romantic aspect by the arch-Romantic, Sir Walter Scott. Scottish football followed the general pattern of the Irish-Welsh game; clan versus clan. Scott, a 'rattle-skulled half-lawyer, half-sportsman', as he once described himself, appreciated country-life (provided that he could be relieved of its inconveniences) and was a fervent supporter of the traditional football game.

The most famous and the most historic of Scottish football matches (according to the old dispensation) took place at Carterhaugh, in Ettrick Forest, between the men of Selkirk and the men of Yarrow, on December 5, 1815. The rival teams were respectively backed by Sir Walter Scott (Keeper of the Forest) and the Earl of Home. The Selkirk men were distinguished by 'slips of fir', the Yarrow men by 'sprigs of heath'.

This was a momentous occasion. There was a reported attendance of 2,000—including all the nobility for miles around. A unique distinction was conferred on this contest, for before it commenced two broadsheets were handed out to all the spectators. Each carried a ballad specially written for the day; the one by Scott, the other by James Hogg, the 'Ettrick Shepherd'.

Although banners are liable to be banned on a modern British football ground such prohibition was not in force at Carterhaugh a century and a half ago. So it was that Scott's elder son, Walter (or, familiarly, 'Gilnockie'), a pupil at Edinburgh High School and fourteen years of age at the time, paraded the field waving the banner of the Buccleuchs. The Duke of Buccleuch was present, and did indeed start the game. So far as young Scott was concerned it was reported that his father 'would rather have seen his heir carry the Banner of Bellenden gallantly at a football match in Carterhaugh, than he would have heard that the boy had attained the highest honours of the first university in Europe'. It may be thought that that was taking things rather far—but Sir Walter, like Buccleuch and Home, and the rest of the aristocracy, was deeply committed. A lot of money was laid out in bets on these days.

The game in this instance is to be read as a collective noun, for it comprised two self-contained units. What was described as the 'first game' lasted an hour and a half, and it was won by the Selkirk men. The 'second game' went on for twice as long and, as the Yarrow men prevailed, left the issue even. Since the day was passing, and in view of the fact that there were tents piled high with food and running with drink, it was reluctantly decided that there was no time to play a decider. The whole occasion was written up in the *Edinburgh Journal*, and its echoes come down to us in Scott's heart-warming lines, of which the last two have

furnished a moral theme for many generations of popular
philosophers:

> 'From the brown nest of Newark its summons
>   extending,
> Our signal is waving in smoke and in flame;
> And each forester blithe from his mountain descending
> Bounds light o'er the heather to join in the game.
>
> Then strip lads and to it, though sharp be the weather,
> And if, by mischance, you should happen to fall,
> There are worse things in life than a tumble on heather,
> And life is itself but a game at football.'[1]

The ingenuosity of the conclusion—to be found in the
games philosophy of British education from that time on—
is, of course, an implicit commendation of the *status quo*.

When the American writer Washington Irving visited
Scott at Abbotsford the subject of football came up. Scott
reflected that '. . . it was not always safe to have even the
game of football between villages;—the old clannish spirit
was too apt to break out'. It may be wondered if the same
may not sometimes be true today.

By 1815, however, events had overtaken the *status quo*.
Even in Scotland there was decline. Thus an eminent Edinburgh historian wrote:

'Many of our national games, as handball, football,
ninepins, golf, and curling, though not discontinued, are
less generally practised than when I was a younger man.'[2]

Joseph Strutt, the antiquary, engraver, and novelist—
whose Jacobean romance *Queen-Hoo* was completed by
Scott and inspired the idea of *Waverley*—gave a definition

1. For full details of the 1815 match, and Scott's general interest in
football, see J. G. Lockhart, *Memoirs of the Life of Sir Walter Scott,*
Bart., 7 vol., Edinburgh, 1837, III, pp. 395–9.
2. Thomas Somerville, D.D. (1741–1830), *My Own Life and Times*,
Edinburgh, 1881, p. 345.

of football in his *Sports and Pastimes of the People of England* (1801). But he made it clear that it was all but defunct. 'The game', he wrote, 'was formerly much in vogue among the common people, though of late years it seems to have fallen into disrepute and is but little practised.'[3] As has been seen the 'common people' of Yorkshire displayed a characteristic tenacity in maintaining the game, but against the odds of virtually impossible conditions of labour.

Strutt gives the following definition:

'When a match at football is made an equal number of competitors take the field and stand between two goals placed at a distance of eighty or an hundred yards the one from the other. The goal is usually made with two sticks driven into the ground about two or three feet apart. The ball, which is commonly made of a blown bladder and cased with leather, is delivered in the midst of the ground, and the object of each party is to drive it through the goal of their antagonists, which being achieved the game is won. The abilities of the performers are best displayed in attacking and defending the goals; and hence the pastime was more frequently called a goal at football than a game at football. When the exercise becomes exceedingly violent the players kick each other's shins without the least ceremony, and some of them are overthrown at the hazard of their limbs.'

Strutt may be presumed to have depended on hearsay rather than first-hand experience (which helps to prove his main point concerning the game's obsolescence), but he adds one important piece of information, concerning the size of the field.

In spite of the regional interest shown by enthusiastic gentlemen like Major E. Moore, who wrote of the East Anglian game in 1823,[4] the view of Strutt and Hone tended

3. p. 168.
4. E. Moor(e), *Suffolk Words and Phrases*, Woodbridge, 1823, pp. 63–6.

1966: Presentation of the World Cup to the English captain, Bobby Moore, by Her Majesty Queen Elizabeth. The group also includes H.R.H. the Duke of Edinburgh and Sir Stanley Rous, President of F.I.F.A.

The pride of Scotland, 1967: Celtic (2) v. Internazionale Milan (1) in a fitting setting at Lisbon.

1871: 'A Match at Football—the Last Scrimmage', from *The Illustrated London News.*

MY FIRST FOOTBALL MATCH.

BY AN OLD BOY.

IT was a proud moment in my existence when Wright, captain of our football club, came up to me in school one Friday and said, "Adams, your name is down to play in the match against Craven to-morrow."

I could have knighted him on the spot. To be one of the picked "fifteen," whose glory it was to fight the battles of their school in the Great Close, had been the leading ambition of my life—I suppose I ought to be ashamed to confess it—ever since, as a little chap of ten, I entered Parkhurst six years ago. Not a winter Saturday but had seen me either looking on at some big match, or oftener still scrimmaging about with a score or so of other juniors in a scratch game. But for a long time, do what I would, I always

seemed as far as ever from the coveted goal, and was half despairing of ever rising to win my "first fifteen cap." Lately, however, I had noticed Wright and a few others of our best players more than once lounging about in the Little Close where we juniors used to play, evidently taking observations with an eye to business. Under the awful gaze of these heroes, need I say I exerted myself as I had never done before? What cared I for hacks or bruises, so only that I could distinguish myself in their eyes? And never was music sweeter

"Down!"

'My First Football Match', from *The Boy's Own Paper*, Vol. 1, No. 1, January 18, 1879.

Pioneers: Wolverhampton Wanderers, *c.* 1880.

'A Maul in Goal', from *The Illustrated London News*, 1882.

'The Association Game'. An Engraving for *The Badminton Library* after an 'instant' photograph by G. Mitchell (*c.* 1885).

Queen's Park F.C., Glasgow, 1873–4.

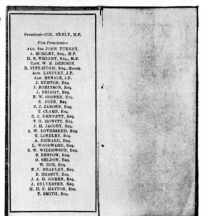

a   b

c   d

Season tickets: (a) and (b) West Bromwich Albion, 1883–4; (c) Notts. Forest, 1892–3; (d) Queen's Park Rangers, 1894–5.

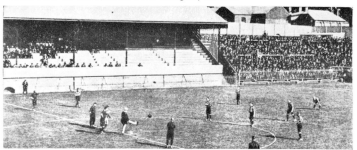

The Mayor of Southampton 'kicks off' to inaugurate The Dell (Southampton v. Brighton, September 3rd, 1898).

Crowd disorder and military intervention at Perry Barr, January, 1888;
Aston Villa v. Preston North End, 5th Round, F.A. Cup Competition.

The end of an era; the last match between Queen's Park (2) and Preston
North End (1) November 12, 1892, at Hampden Park.

Billy Meredith in the 1904 Cup Final at which the Prime Minister (A. J. Balfour) and Dr W. G. Grace were present.

England (5) v. Scotland (2), at Richmond, 1893.

Newcomers to the English League—Newton Heath (later Manchester United) play against Derby County at North Road, Newton Heath, in December, 1892.

Woolwich Arsenal; first League match (Division II) v. Newcastle United at Plumstead on September 2nd, 1893.

to prevail. Football was an antiquity. As late as 1846 a fictitious Tom (not Brown) could apply to his Vicar for information on the subject. 'I long to hear something about foot-ball!' exclaimed Tom. He got the whole of Strutt, word for word, with an excerpt from Stubbs thrown in. The Vicar was a well-read man.[5]

The years between 1835 and 1857 were crucial for British football, for during these two decades the game, saving consequent refinements in detail, was reconditioned and made into an effective instrument for modern use. What is remarkable is that reform when undertaken needed so little time for its accomplishment. In 1835, or thereabouts, Tom Brown—aged thirteen and claiming to have played football 'all his life'—arrived at Rugby, to be introduced to the traditional form of the game as formalised there. In 1857 *Tom Brown's Schooldays* was published. In the same year a football club was seen to be established in Sheffield. Within this period there was also some amelioration brought to working-class life, by the Factory Act of 1847, which freed women and children from Saturday employment: a privilege later extended to men also. The era which saw the transformation of the ancient football game, and its bifurcation into Rugby and Association, also saw the emergence of a new professional class, comprising scholars, physicians, surgeons, the Established clergy, the armed forces, lawyers, and civil servants. Connected to the landed gentry, by family ties, by patronage, or both, this class contrived to build up its own ethos of superiority and to conduct the most important part of the nation's business in a spirit of barely modified paternalism. If anything needed running, then these were the people to do it. By the middle of the century the cachet of a public school education

5. Anon., *Philosophy in Sport made Science in Earnest; being an attempt to illustrate the first principles of natural philosophy by the aid of the popular toys and sports of youth*, ded. to Michael Faraday, London, 6th ed. 1846, p. 163.

D

(with or without a subsequent university career) was the warrant for leadership. Old and well-known schools—Winchester, Eton, Charterhouse, Shrewsbury, Westminster, Harrow—and new foundations, such as Cheltenham (1841), Marlborough (1843) and Wellington (1853), adopted the principles of Dr. Thomas Arnold, and thereby established a compact system for the propagation of quasi-patrician virtues and vices—these in about equal parts. The need for such principles was emphasised by the growth in number of pupils in the more important schools. Thus in 1844 there were but sixty-nine boys at Harrow. Within fifty years this total had increased to more than five hundred.

When the eighteenth-century apprentices (some of good family) disported themselves gracelessly they were, in fact, following the example of their betters. Drinking, gambling, poaching, and other familiar occupations, were neither conducive to the corporate character at which the nineteenth-century 'public school' aimed, nor convenient to accommodate. Sport, therefore, became, and remained, at once a means of sublimation and correction. It also afforded pious headmasters suitable analogies wherewith to imbue their less intelligent charges with a basic moral philosophy.

The Rugby game may be disposed of first. The importance of this game immediately lies less in the character of the game itself than in the fact that it was the first of the games of which the codification has remained; by *The Laws of Football as played at Rugby School, sanctioned by a Levee of Bigside on the 7th of September, 1846*, Thomas Hughes at that time enjoying the honours of the office of 'Captain of Bigside'. By the Laws of 1846 a certain anomaly was dispersed, and the way was made clear for the definition of two distinctive types of football.

In 1823 William Webb Ellis (1807–1872), son of a Manchester gentleman and later Minister of St. George's, Albemarle Street, and Rector of Laver Magdalen, Essex, is said to have startled his friends at Rugby School by catching the ball during a game and *running with it*. In so doing he departed, perhaps, from one accepted code which allowed a player to catch a ball and then kick (as from the modern 'mark') but which disallowed any running. For this act of seemingly improper conduct Ellis was later apotheosised: a monument was erected to his memory at Rugby. Now, as has been seen, handling the ball was part of the folk-football from the earliest times. The pre-1823 game at Rugby was of a familiar pattern. For twenty years after 1823 it was in a state of flux. There were those who condemned Ellis's action; there were others who found the practice of 'running-in' an addition to the skills and attractions of the game. Introduced to the Rugby game by the bolder spirits among Arnold's pupils, 'running-in' was accepted by 1842—the year in which Arnold relinquished his headmastership—and regularised in 1846. At the same time a player could then only run with the ball himself and not pass it to a colleague.

The Rules of 1846 mitigated some of the former severities, but there was still scope for the forceful and determined to wreak havoc among the opposition. 'Hacking' was not allowed above the knee, but not disallowed below. ('Hacking' and tripping seem often to have been synonymous; the technique has, perhaps, not yet been entirely forgotten.) A player in possession of the ball could be held by one arm, but not by two. It was forbidden to stand on the cross-bar to prevent the scoring of goals. It was also forbidden to remove the ball from the area of play—the Close. If a match was level after one day's (afternoon's) play it was continued on the next. The limits were three days,[6] if no goals had been scored; five days if goals had been registered. Much of this defined the kind of the game described in the fifth chapter of *Tom Brown's Schooldays*,

6. Cf. the three games of the Carterhaugh match (p. 94) and the Sheffield–Norton match of 1793 (p. 91). See also p. 108.

and also in 'My first football match'—the first story in the first issue of *The Boy's Own Paper*, of January 18, 1879.

The Rugby game was taken up at schools such as Marlborough and Cheltenham which were the early monuments to the educational principles of Thomas Arnold. This type of football was continued at the universities, especially at Cambridge, as remarked by Venn. An agreed set of rules was issued in Cambridge in 1848. But by this time many other influences were at work.

The history of football is a record of adaptation to terrain and to circumstance. In the confined spaces of towns football occasionally acquired a certain delicacy of style. The more 'dribbling' was encouraged the greater the aesthetic gain; and the less the advantage to the merely tough. It was not, however, until full research was made into the merits of the 'dribbling' game that all this became patent.

Schools in towns, or where the area for play was restricted, evolved their individual variants of the general scheme of folk-football. Certain of these variants, as at Eton, Winchester and Harrow, are occasionally maintained at the present time: ritual offerings to an unknown god, and, at the same time, evidences of a corporate eccentricity.

In London football was enthusiastically practised at Christ's Hospital (the Governors suffered complaints on this account in the eighteenth century), at Charterhouse[7] (where Steele as well as Addison had learned the game), and at Westminster. The poet William Cowper, a pupil at Westminster in the middle of the eighteenth century, sub-

---

7. From a Charterhouse song of 1794:

'I challenge all the men alive to say they e'er were gladder
Than boys all striving who should kick most wind out of the
    bladder.'

quoted from *Association Football*, N. L. Jackson, London, 1900, p. 275.

sequently remembered his prowess both at football and cricket during his school days with satisfaction, in a letter (May 1781) to his friend William Unwin. At these schools football was first played in the cloisters which was finally forbidden at Westminster in 1820.

When cloisters were built in the Middle Ages they were intended for work and not for play. After the Reformation, however, boys immured in formerly monastic foundations, with a natural aversion from work, found the cloisters ideal for other purposes. At the beginning of the nineteenth century the Chapter of Westminster decided that there were better places for playing games. Thus, on November 13, 1810, it was ordered: 'that Jonathan Green's bill of £3 1s. for marking out ten acres of ground in Tothill Fields as a playground for the Westminster scholars, and for the use of his team of horses and plough two days, viz. the 28th and 29th of August last to mark the said piece of ground with a deep furrough, be paid'.[8]

This was a great step forward: it was many years before other city schools were provided with playing fields.

The old, cloistral, football that was a feature of those schools built on the monastic pattern, but which held no possibility of development, is described in a Carthusian parody. The poet, signing himself 'Antiquarian', suggested that he had found it in a tin box during building operations and he proposed 1650 as the date of composition!

Footeballe

Ye boarderes camme downe from ye boaredres base
With victorie gleaminge in evverie face;
For they had lickedde ye gowneboye foe,
Of whom fulle mannie hadde been laide low.

8. N. L. Jackson, op. cit., p. 269.

But a day of vengeance cometh at last,
Ye game it waxeth fierce and faste;
'Go itte, ye crippels!' is ye shoute,
'let's putte ye boaredres to ye route'.

Ye boardere championne rushed with mighte
Into ye thickeste of the fighte;
Ye gowneboye heroe, like a rocke;
Stands firme to meete ye comminge shocke.

'Now shove, ye gowneboys, shove, I praye!
Perchance your valour winnes ye day'.
'Squashe oute!' shoutes evverie boardere fagge,
'Nor lette your droopinge courage lagge.'

But now through cloisteres comes ye crye,
'Ye fagges!' ye fagges come rushinge bye;
And now ye batelle's loste and wonne,
And now ye hurley-burley's donne.[9]

As at Rugby (see *Tom Brown*) and as in the local games at
Shrewsbury and Harrow, and in the other public schools,
many of the smaller boys were offered up to sacrifice in the
inchoate scrimmages that were part of the ritual. This not
so 'friendly fightinge' was, of course, a reduction of the
macroscopic 'folk football'.

In place of a boast of former times it might now be suggested that the World Cup of 1966 was won on the playing
fields of Eton, for it was once written: 'The game of football, as originally played at the Wall at Eton, was the
author of every sort and condition of football now played
throughout the United Kingdom.'[10] The Wall, after which

9. *Papers from Greyfriars. A Selection from the Contributions of Old
and Present Carthusians*, 1860–1, London, 1861, p. 258: See also E. P.
Eardley-Wilmot and E. C. Streatfield, *Charterhouse Old and New*,
London, 1895, pp. 74–6.
    10. *The Etonian*, No. 26, November 27, 1884.

the game is named and by which it is bounded, was built in 1717. The playing area was 120 yards long by one 6 yards wide, the one goal being a door in a garden wall, the other a marked portion of the trunk of an elm tree. A writer who was at school at Eton in the early 1820s said that the Wall Game then was practically the only game played there (other than cricket) and that it was usually conducted by eighteen or twenty a side.[11] The idea of 'fair play' was not then part of the ethos, for the match between

'Collegers and Oppidans had been played for some years, before it came to an end in 1827 owing to a free fight which ensued. There was a loose bully [scrimmage][12] of considerable freedom and vigour in bad calx [area in front of one goal] by the tree-goal. [In front of the door was "good calx".] But Latham, a Colleger in liberty, had shinned Crawshay, a sturdy lower boy, who hit out promptly and knocked him down, and was himself immediately laid out by —— Captain of College.' The oppidans [compare the feuding parties at Charterhouse] vowed vengeance, and 'the fight [became] general, when Big Bethell arrived on the scene from Cloisters, and the fight stopped as the combatants heard the big tones of his "Shameful, shameful!" in the midst of them.'[13]

The Headmaster, John Keate (1773–1852), stopped the Wall Game, which, however, was resumed after a restless interlude of ten years. Side by side with the Wall Game there developed also the Field Game. Here the area for play was more normally proportioned (though not defined

11. [W. H. Tucker], *Eton of Old (1811–22)*, Eton, 1892, p. 221.

12. Cf. 'Then came a hot bully almost under the Tannery crossbar, but at length the ball rolled harmlessly out of play.' Ernest Protheroe, *St. Merville's Scholarship Boys*, London [c. 1906], p. 55. This is an abnormally late use of the word 'bully'. Protheroe's novel of school life, initially set in a Midlands' industrial town, is a timid attempt at social realism: in the two football matches described virtue is seen to be worth at least a goal start.

13. Quotation without ascription published in *Upon St. Andrew's Day, 1841–1901*, compiled R. A. A[usten]-L[eigh], Eton, 1902, p. VI.

until 1897). Like its companion—and in early times the two were barely distinguishable—the Field Game operated mysteriously. In 1841, however, football at Eton, for the first time, received official encouragement:

'Last week a match (11 a side) took place at Eton between the Collegians (Boats and Dry-Bobs), which, after a well-contested game of upwards of an hour, was won by the Boats. This season the game of football, which was not previously countenanced by the masters, has been greatly encouraged, and contributed much to keeping the students within bounds.'[14]

The eleven-a-side principle was an important innovation, although there is some evidence that eleven-a-side had already been introduced at Harrow.[15] In 1845 Eton instituted the office of referee (nearly three centuries after Mulcaster's proposition) and a year later two umpires were adopted as additional supervisors of fair play. Previously these functionaries, one chosen by each team, determined when a goal was a goal, since there was no string, or bar, between the uprights. A year later a set of Rules was promulgated, in which tendencies away from the Rugbeian manner and towards Association football were more strongly marked. While the ball could be stopped with the hand it could not be caught, carried, thrown, or struck. There was also a strict rule against 'sneaking' or off-side. 'A player', it was stated, 'is considered to be "sneaking" when only three, or less than three, of the opposite side are before him and the ball behind him, and in such case he may not kick the ball.' Eton further insisted that teams were to remain constant during a match, no substitutes being permitted.

Before a new wing was added to the old schools at

14. *Bell's Life*, December 5, 1841. The Field Game, after a particularly savage exhibition, was also proscribed for a matter of three weeks by Dr. Edward Hawtrey (1789–1862), Headmaster of Eton, 1834–52.
15. See p. 105 n. 16.

Harrow, football, unorganised, was for the most part played
in the Yard and (under the title of 'fug' football, where
a soft small ball covered with wash leather was used)
in the Cloisters. But a more highly organised game—
played until 1853 on the present sixth-form cricket ground
—emerged,[16] to be regulated by the Philathletic Club as
from 1853, at which time eight-a-side games were undertaken against Old Harrovians.

In 1887 Shearman declared that the Rules at Harrow
then obtaining, subject to very slender modification and
occasional terminological simplification, were those that
had prevailed for 'upwards of half a century'. The Harrow
game was adapted to the fields that lay at the foot of the
Hill. With indifferent drainage the playing area was often
a regular slough in wintertime. A heavy ball was needed,
and also a system which encouraged movement. The goals
were made by twelve-foot-high poles, and were called bases.
Harrow boys had their special football costume: white duck
trousers and sometimes black gaiters.

The Rules of the Harrow Game, by chance, became an
important part of the foundations on which Association
football were erected. They were (and are, insofar as this
type of game is still preserved at Harrow) as follows:

'1. The choice of Bases is determined by tossing: the
side that wins the toss must have the choice of Bases, the
side that loses has the right to kick off.

'2. The Bases must be 18 feet in width, and the distance
between them not greater than 150 yards. The width of the
ground must not be more than 100 yards.

'3. The Ball must be kicked off from the middle of the
ground, half way between the two Bases. A Base may not
be obtained unless the Ball has touched one of the opposite

16. Mr. L. J. Verney informs me that his great-grandfather, Sir
Harry Verney (1801–1894), 'always maintained that he was in the
[Harrow] School XI, 1814–15'. This is the earliest positive information
in respect of organised football at Harrow.

side to the kicker previously to passing between the Base Poles.

'4. When the Ball is kicked, any one on the same side as the kicker is entitled to kick or catch it, provided that at the same time of the delivery of the kick he is not nearer the line of the *opponents'* Base than the kicker. If he is nearer he is *"Offside"*, and virtually out of the Game till the Ball has been touched by one of the opposite side. Nor may he interfere with anyone of the opposite side, or in any way prevent or obstruct his kicking or catching the Ball.

'5. The Ball may only be caught if it has not touched the ground since it was kicked by the leg below the knee, or the foot.

'6. Whoever catches the Ball is entitled to a free kick if he calls *"Yards"*; but whoever catches the ball, and does not call *"Yards"*, is liable to have the Ball knocked out of his hands. N.B. The Ball must be kicked without delay: and the preliminary run must not be longer than Three Yards (i.e. the utmost length to which Three running strides would extend).

'7. When a player catches the Ball, he may take his Three Yards or each of them in any direction he likes.

'8. If a player catches the Ball near the opposite Base, he may try to carry the Ball through by jumping the Three Yards. If he fail in this attempt, no second try is allowed, but he must return to the spot where he caught the Ball, and from there may have a free kick at the Base, none of the opposite side may in this case get in his way nearer than the spot to which his jump brought him.

'9. The Ball, when in play, must never be touched by the hand or arm unless close to the body, except in the case of a catch as stated in Rule 5.

'10. The Ball, if kicked beyond the prescribed limits of the ground, must be thrown in again (at least six yards from the thrower) by one of the opposite side to the player who shall have last touched the Ball, and his throw may be made in any direction, but may not obtain a Base unless the Ball has previously touched one of the players. In making the throw, the thrower may not hold the Ball by the lace, nor may he touch the Ball after the throw, until it has been touched by one of the other players.

'11. From behind his own Base a player must kick the Ball instead of throwing it, the preliminary run not being longer than three running strides from the Base Line. From behind the opponent's Base the throw must be straight in, and may be of any length. In the first case the kicker, and in the second the thrower, must not again touch the Ball until it has been touched by another player.

'Neither in Rule 10 nor in this Rule do Rules 4 or 5 apply.

'12. All charging is fair, but no holding, tripping, push-ink with hands, shinning, or back-shinning, either of the Ball or the players, is allowed.

'13. If the Ball strike the Base Pole and go through, it shall count as a Base, but if, in the opinion of the Umpires, it shall have passed over the Pole, it shall not count as a Base.

'14. If the Ball strike the Base Pole and rebound into the ground play shall continue.

'15. No nails or spikes of any sort are allowed in Football Boots.

'16. There must always be two Umpires in a House Match, and, if possible, in School Matches. Their decision shall be final as to matters of fact, but they are at liberty to refer any question of law to the Committee of the Phil-athletic Club if they feel unable to decide it at the time.

'17. It shall be the duty of the Umpires in all Football Matches to take away a Base or "Yards" unfairly obtained; to award them if clearly and undoubtedly obtained, or stopped by unfair means, and in House Matches to put out of the Game any player wilfully break-ing any of the Football Rules.

'18. If it is necessary to replay a House Match, the distance between the Base Poles shall be doubled, the sides tossing again for choice of Bases. The date of the replay shall be decided by the Committee of the Philathletic Club.

'19. After a tie each House is at liberty to play with any alterations or substitutions in its team that it may wish.

'20. On the second day of a House Match, if a draw be the result, the Umpires must compel an extra quarter of-an-hour to be played, changing ends after seven minutes. The same to apply to Champion House Match on the first day's play if it be a draw, at the end of the hour.

'21. In the event of there being any reason for putting off a House Match it shall be decided by the Committee of the Philathletic Club.'

It will be noticed that the number of players on each side is not presented in these Rules. In fact, as in the Eton games, eleven a side was favoured for important occasions. The kind of ball (described by Shearman) is interesting —'being a kind of irregular oval in shape, and really, in fact, nothing more than a bladder enclosed in three pieces of thick shoemaker's leather, two being circular and the third a broad strip equal in length to the circumference of the ball.'[17] With such a ball they had played at Lusk.[18]

Relics of older football stand in the 'catching' clauses (4–8) and the regulations for more than one day's play. But more significant are those refinements which appear as the vehicles that carried the old game into Association football. There are to be noted the mode of starting a game (Rule 3), the 'throw-in' (Rule 10) and the rudimentary goal-kick (Rule 11), the reduction of methods of assault to one—'charging' (Rule 12). It is also apparent that adequate attempts were being made to ensure a code in which foul play was not only discountenanced but one in which all

17. op. cit., p. 290.
18. See p. 82.

precautions were being taken to ensure that standards of
fair play would be preserved.[19]

These basic Rules were to be found in 1873 in a small
village in Lancashire, as the guiding statutes for a football
club of the new dispensation. The '[Playing] Rules of the
Turton Football Club, Established November, 1872—
Harrow Game' show slender amendation of and addition
to the parent, Harrovian, code. Since these are not in themselves significant and are irrelevant to the main line of
development they do not call for comment. One does
notice, however, that 'The Uniform of the Club shall be
Blue Knickerbockers, White Stockings, and *White Jerseys*'.

In fact Harrow-type football in 1873 in Lancashire was a
curious anachronism. That it existed at all was due to the
determination of a local family of Old Harrovians to infuse
something of what they had expensively learned into provincial life. The phase of football lying between the middle
of the century and the formation of the Turton Football
Club is, in fact, generally characterised by this attempt to
transmute values.

Association football emerged in what for practical purposes was its final form at a time when a new social order
had been established, in which a great part of effective
power rested with the middle class. The middle class at one
end had its contacts with the older landed class, which contacts it tried not to forget. At the other end it touched—
though not more closely than it could help—the working
class. Authority derived from wealth; but also from a
superior education. Authority asserted, below the govern-
mental level, itself either through charity or through

19. Small addenda were made to the Harrow Rules in 1911, 1919
and 1961. Attached to the currently available Rules are some *obiter
dicta*, of which the first is as follows: 'Remember that there are no
penalties (other than those prescribed in the rules) and that the game is
never stopped if it can be helped while the ball is in play. So rules have
to be kept for the sake of conscience, and the benefit of the doubt is
habitually given to the opposition.'

organisation. On the whole, there is nothing that satisfies the ego quite as much as organising other people. Some of this zeal for organisation came from unconscious sources, some from a conscious intention. When the condition of football was debated in the Universities the consequent legislation (of local significance only) was the outcome of an application of abstract principles. When the Football Association was founded in 1863 there were more pragmatic considerations involved. From that point on the story became a conflict of points of view: the points of view of sectional infants.

7

Law-makers

Against the general stands the particular. The doctrine of gradual evolution towards a state of perfection is a respected principle in England, where even a political theory of 'emergence' was unquestioned until quite recently. Football had been evolving and emerging for many centuries before it got entangled with the socio-pedagogic facts of mid-Victorian life. Then it began firmly to be made both institutional and constitutional. Some of the leading schools had been playing their part, and, by extending facilities on the one hand and introducing the element of compulsion on the other, they continued to do so. The universities—that of Cambridge in particular—acting in close collaboration with the schools took matters a stage further; by ratifying the place of football among at least the lesser disciplines the authorities set on it a final warrant of respectability. After centuries of contemptuous disapproval and sporadic interdict a student could begin to take pride in his college's, or his university's, achievement. True, the game was as yet reserved to a minority, but it was an influential minority.

The minority—by no means comprising only Philistines —had to fight against prejudice. Thus:

'Hockey and football were left to boys. I have since been informed that some devotees of what was commonly regarded as a school game occasionally indulged, in obscure places, in the peculiar art that they had acquired at Rugby or Eton. But I am certain that I never saw the game played, and that no friend of mine ever practised it. This is confirmed by my brother, who—tells me that he remembers a friend coming into Hall and relating that he had seen a number of Rugby men, mostly freshmen, playing a new game: that "they made a circle round a ball and butted each other".[1]

The first signs of organised football at Cambridge appear towards the year 1840. Edgar Montague (1811–1902), an Old Boy of Shrewsbury School, and a student at Caius College from 1837 to 1842, who spent the most of his life as rector of a country parish in East Anglia, wrote: 'I was one of seven who drew up the rules for football, when we made the first football club, to be fair to all the schools.'[2]

At this point we may pick up the line of development from Shrewsbury. When Samuel Butler was Headmaster— between 1798 and 1836—football was disparaged as being 'only fit for butcher boys'.[3] There was a playing field in Raven Meadows, but since this lay in full view of the Headmaster's windows, it took a bold spirit to kick a ball there. After Butler came Benjamin Kennedy, who reigned from 1836 to 1866, and with the acquisition of a field on Coton Hill games were taken more seriously. Shrewsbury had its own form of football, known as 'douling' (or, corruptly, 'dowling'), the word being derived from the Greek word for 'slave': this school was strong in classical learning. As complex as most of these private diversions 'douling' showed two features.[4] It was strict on off-side: 'no one might stand wilfully between the ball and his opponent's goal'. It was essentially a dribbling game; 'the game', observed A. F. Chance, 'was admirably adapted for

1. J. Venn, op. cit., p. 280.
2. J. Basil Oldham, *A History of Shrewsbury School*, London, 1952, p. 232, n. 1; Letter of 1899 to E. Tudor Owen.
3. J. M. West, *Shrewsbury* (English Public Schools Series), London, 1937, p. 51.
4. The rules for 'douling' were printed in N. L. Jackson, op. cit., pp. 296–300.

bringing out cleverness in this direction and encouraging the most egregious selfishness'.[5] Apparently this particular technique was well mastered by the more scholarly of Kennedy's Shrewsbury pupils. J. C. Thring (1824–1909),[6] who had also been at school at Winchester, went up to St. John's College in 1843, and caught up with another Old Salopian, H. de Winton (1823–1895).[7] Together with some Old Etonians they formed a Cambridge University team. The date is uncertain, but since Winton graduated in 1846 it was prior to that year.[8] Matches were played on Parker's Piece.

In 1847 Henry Charles Malden[9] was admitted to Trinity College. A keen footballer, he had only been in residence at Cambridge for a year when he was called upon to preside over a meeting, at Trinity, to hammer out an agreed set of football rules.[10] Fourteen men were present, representing Eton, Harrow, Winchester, Rugby, and the 'non-public schools'. After a seven-hour session the 'Cambridge Rules' of 1848 were promulgated. Of these no record survived. In 1856, however, another set, probably containing basic material from 1848, was issued. There is an extant copy, signed by representatives of Eton, Rugby, Harrow, Shrewsbury, and the University, in the Library of Shrewsbury School:

5. For an account of douling see Desmond Coke (at Shrewsbury 1893–9), *The Bending of a Twig*, London, 1906, pp. 116–20.
6. J. C. Thring, a member of a distinguished academic family, was ordained. He was an assistant master at Uppingham School from 1859 to 1869 (see pp. 118–19).
7. H. de Winton (later known as Wilkins), was 3rd Classic in his final year. Also ordained, he spent his working life mostly in Breconshire.
8. See Oldham, op. cit., pp. 232–3.
9. Malden was the son of the proprietor of Windlesham House School, Brighton, at which he was educated and of which he ultimately became proprietor.
10. Letter from Malden (October 8, 1897) quoted by Oldham, op. cit., p. 233.

'Laws of the University Foot Ball Club

'1. This Club shall be called the *University Foot Ball Club*.

'2. At the commencement of play, the ball shall be kicked off from the middle of the ground; after every goal there shall be a kick-off in the same way or manner.

'3. After a goal, the losing side shall kick off; the sides changing goals unless a previous arrangement be made to the contrary.

'4. The ball is *out* when it has passed the line of the flag-posts on either side of the ground, in which case it shall be *thrown* in straight.

'5. The ball is "behind" when it has passed the goal on either side of it.

'6. When the ball is behind, it shall be brought forward at the place where it left the ground not more than ten paces, and kicked off.'

'7. Goal is when the ball is kicked through the flag-posts and under the string.

'8. When a player catches the ball directly from the foot, he may kick it as he can without running it. In no other case may the ball be touched with the hands, except to stop it.

'9. If the ball has passed a player and has come from the direction of his own goal, he may not touch it till the other side have kicked it, unless there are more than three of the other side before him. No player is allowed to loiter between the ball and the adversaries' goal.

'10. In no case is holding a player, pushing with the hands or tripping up allowed. Any player may prevent another from getting to the ball by any means consistent with this rule.

'11. Every match shall be decided by a majority of goals.'

These Rules were, no doubt, the basis of the inter-university matches which are reported to have been played in or about 1855.[11]

At this point there is a fictional throw-back, which, although palpably referring to the 'Rugby' type of game, indicates the growing desire to formalise procedures:

'Football had never been played on any system at Abbeyside School till the Christmas half of 1856. Then, for the first time, a set of rules was issued. I remember with awe the majestic Rawlinson coming round the studies one evening before preparation, and doling out printed cards—one for each boy. On receiving my copy I timidly asked what it was for? "Football rules", he said, "and you have got to learn them by heart."—It was said that we should be examined in the rules in a week hence, and that if we failed in a single clause we should be skinned alive. Poor wretches! How we quivered and quavered and tried to learn them, and how we found to our cost that there were worse things on earth than Greek verbs.'[12]

Just at this time pieces of the jigsaw of football were—somewhat unexpectedly it may seem—falling into place in the north of England. In 1854 the Sheffield Cricket Club proceeded to lease a site of eight and a half acres in Bramall Lane from the Duke of Norfolk. In the following year an inaugural match between 'The Eleven' and 'The Twenty-

11. Shearman, op. cit., p. 276. There are scanty records of early matches. It is, however, known that in 1852 Westminster School played against Harrow. Five years later there was a fixture against Haileybury. In 1858 Westminster played against Winchester, a club known as Dingley Dell, and various Oxford and Cambridge colleges. In 1861 there was a Westminster v. Eton fixture. In that year the game was regularised at Charterhouse and that school undertook its first match against Westminster in 1863, losing by 0–2. See Jackson, op. cit., p. 270.

12. Rev. A. N. Malan, D.D., 'How Risden played for Abbeyside', in *Twenty-five Football Stories*, pub. Newnes. Malan was a prolific writer of 'boys' stories' between 1880 and 1904. Here he sounds autobiographic, and it is significant that he gives a precise year for the issue of the Rules at 'Abbeyside'.

two' was played. Among the members of 'The Eleven' was a young man named William Prest, who had a zeal for football as compelling as that for cricket, and was an all-round athlete. Prest assembled his friends—in the main Old Boys of the Collegiate School in Sheffield—and formed a football club. It would seem almost certain that this club was in effect an Old Boys' club. Claims for its existence in 1855 have been made. These are not improper claims; but the fact remains that the first constitution and set of regulations were issued on October 24, 1857. That a sister club was also officially functioning in the suburb of Hallam in this year lends credibility to existence of football clubs in and about Sheffield before what must now be accepted as the foundation year.

The committee members of the first Sheffield Football Club—with modest, temporary, headquarters in a green-house near Bramall Lane—were typical of the new men of the age; technologists, industrial magnates in the making, merchants, solicitors. Frederick Ward (1825–1908) was the President of the club. In later life he became Chairman of the Sheffield Forge and Rolling Mills Company. T. A. Sorby (1825–1885), one of the Vice-Presidents, was an active partner in the family business and brother of H. C. Sorby, a famous scientist and one of the founders of Sheffield University. Of the committee men T. E. Vickers (1833–1915), son of Edward Vickers of Tapton Hall, became head of the great firm of that name, a Justice of the Peace, and Honorary Colonel of the 1st Volunteer Battalion of the York and Lancaster Regiment. Staunchly Conservative, loyal churchmen, proudly provincial, these young men, of signal ability, laid the foundations of modern football in the north of England. Since tradition affected them at least in a sentimental way it is to be noticed that when the celebrated Sheffield *v.* Norton match of 1793 took place the father of Frederick Ward, Thomas Asline Ward, could, as a boy of twelve, have seen it played.

So far as may be judged the establishment of the football club in Sheffield was the result of indigenous forces and spontaneous action. The Sheffield Rules of 1857 read:

'1. The kick off from the middle must be a place kick.

'2. Kick Out must not be from more than 25 yards out of goal.

'3. Fair Catch is a catch from any player provided the ball has not touched the ground or has not been thrown from touch and is entitled to a free kick.

'4. Charging is fair in case of a place kick (with the exception of a kick off as soon as the player offers to kick) but he may always draw back unless he has actually touched the ball with his foot.

'5. Pushing with hands is allowed but no hacking or tripping up is fair under any circumstances whatever.

'6. No player may be held or pulled over.

'7. It is not lawful to take the ball off the ground (except in touch) for any purpose whatever.

'8. The ball may be pushed on or hit with the hand, but holding the ball except in the case of a free kick is altogether disallowed.

'9. A goal must be kicked but not from touch nor by a free kick from a catch.

'10. A ball in touch is dead, consequently the side that touches it down must bring it to the edge of the touch and throw it straight out from touch.

'11. Each player must provide himself with a red and dark blue flannel cap, one colour to be worn by each side.'

Within a year or two football in Sheffield was well worked into the amenities of the city and neighbourhood, and by 1862 there were fifteen clubs in being. The chief rivals were Sheffield and Hallam, and on February 12, 1861, a crowd of six hundred spectators, from whom donations were subscribed to the Public Hospital and Dispensary, saw Sheffield win by 2–0. On December 29, 1862, the same two teams played another celebrated Charity Match, in aid of the Lancashire Distress Fund.[13] This match was long remembered on account of Major Nathaniel Creswick, of the Sheffield team, being illegally held by two Hallam worthies; whereat the Major punched one of his captors named Waterfall, who, throwing off his waistcoat, retaliated. Soon there was a general fracas, only ended by the intervention of senior spectators. Waterfall was the only one to be reprimanded. In disgrace he was sent back to keep goal.

Although the game had thus far matured it was still subject to considerable variation. So, during this formative period, provision was made for the scoring of 'rouges'—i.e. touch-downs, in an area on either side of each goal—after the Eton fashion. Here the direct influence may be detected. A. C. Ainger, who had played football at Eton (his name appearing in the Wall Game lists), was an assistant at Sheffield Collegiate School from 1864 to 1866.

One of the greatest of Victorian educationalists was Edward Thring (1821–1887), also an Etonian and a scholar and Fellow of King's College, Cambridge. He was the elder brother of J. C. Thring and was appointed Headmaster of Uppingham School in 1853, where he found but twenty-five boys and two masters. Cast in the mould of Mulcaster, Edward Thring held revolutionary views and the assurance necessary to carry them into effect. He laid stress on the teaching of English, unusual in an age which based the curriculum firmly and exclusively on the Classics; he was aware of the importance of the arts in education and therefore appointed Julius David, son of Mendelssohn's friend

13. On June 20, 1862, the Central Relief Committee set up in Manchester, resolved as follows: 'That the existing distress of the work people connected with the cotton trade in Lancashire, Cheshire, Yorkshire and Derbyshire, and the well-founded expectation of its increasing intensity as the winter approaches, warrants the Committee in communicating to the various counties, cities and towns of the country that it is prepared to receive any sum that may be subscribed for the object in view, and will give its best attention to the proper and judicious distribution thereof'. See W. O. Henderson, *The Lancashire Cotton Famine 1861–1865*, Manchester, 1934, p. 75.

Ferdinand David, to be music master; a keen sportsman he was willing to play with and against the boys and regularly opened the innings for the cricket team which he captained annually against the school. He also installed a school gymnasium, said to have been the first in the country. The first instructor was Herr G. H. C. Beisiegel (Thring married a German wife and was extremely Germanophile—hence his keeness for music and physical fitness), who also taught a little music. Thring built the developing activities of the school into a moral framework, of which a symbol was the School Mission (the first of its kind) which he founded for the benefit of the London poor. He was also instrumental in establishing the Headmasters' Conference, a consequence of the Public Schools Act of 1868, in 1869.

As has been stated J. C. Thring was a member of the Uppingham staff from 1859 to 1869. In 1862 he issued the Rules of the 'Simplest Game' for use at Uppingham. The process of streamlining thus produced the following:

'1. A goal is scored whenever the ball is forced through the goal and under the bar, except it be thrown by the hand.

'2. Hands may be used only to stop a ball and place it on the ground before the feet.

'3. Kicks must be aimed only at the ball.

'4. A player may not kick the ball whilst in the air.

'5. No tripping up or heel kicking allowed.

'6. Whenever a ball is kicked beyond the side flags, it must be returned by the player who kicked it, from the spot it passed the flagline in a straight line towards the middle of the ground.

'7. When a ball is kicked behind the line of goal, it shall be kicked off from that line by one of the side whose goal it is.

'8. No player may stand within six paces of the kicker when he is kicking off.

'9. A player is out of play immediately he is in front of the ball, and must return behind the ball as soon as possible.

If the ball is kicked by his own side past a player, he may not touch it, or advance, until one of the other side has first kicked it, or one of his own side, having followed it up, has been able, when in front of him, to kick it.

'10. No charging is allowed when a player is out of play —i.e. immediately the ball is behind him.'

The Rules—noted by the following excerpt as particular rather than general—had a remarkable effect. On the one hand there were developments elsewhere—to be noticed in due course, on the other a great stimulation within the school itself.

'On Saturday, October 10th [1863], the opening game of Football for the season was played, and augured well for the future play, considering the number of those to whom our rules are new.

'Tuesday the 13th, saw one of the first games it has been our lot to join in: both "red" and "white"[14] backed and played up[15] in a manner to leave very little to be desired.

'. . . On Friday, 23rd, the long-looked-for match between the Pickwick Club and the rest of the School was commenced, and was one of the most vigorous games we have played: there were no goals for either side.'[16]

In November this important letter appeared in the school magazine:

'Dear Sir:

I want to make a few suggestions about our Football. Might not we have a Football eleven? Even if we did not play above one or two matches, it would be of great use in stimulating the fellows to play well, so as to try and become members. We might play some school not very far off: or I am sure among the number of "Old Boys" Upping-

14. The symbolic colours red and white, significant at the beginning of time, are still meaningful within the liturgy of football.
15. For further references to 'backing up' see p. 142 n. 14.
16. *The School Magazine*, Uppingham, November, 1863, p. 283.

ham has turned out, eleven would willingly play a friendly game with us.

'Also, with respect to our dress. I think we ought either to have a house cap, each one of a different colour; or else each member of the Upper Club ought to have two caps to wear, according to the side he is picked upon. I think this would greatly improve the general effect of the game.

'I remain, etc.,
A FOOTBALL PLAYER.'[17]

A year later there was a School XI, the captain being F. W. Boys,[18] and on November 16 a set of *Rules for the Football-House Matches* were printed:

'1. That they be played in the Christmas Examination, and if not played out, be continued in the following half-year.

'2. That each game last one hour and a half.

'3. That unless some advantage be gained within that time, the game be continued some other day until some advantage *be* gained.

'4. That each team nominate its own umpire, subject to the disapproval of the other house.

'5. That the number playing for each house be left to the discretion of the captain of the side.'[19]

There will be noted the term of one hour and a half set on the match; and also the discretionary powers reserved to house captains regarding the numbers in a team. In fact, although Boys was captain of 'the Eleven', the school was organised into sets of 'Football Fifteens'.[20]

Meanwhile events were also moving fast at Shrewsbury. So, in 1864, F. Gregory wrote to Henry Taylor: 'There is a regular football eleven now, as I have no doubt you will have heard . . . and they have got a regular uniform,

17. ibid., p. 277.
18. Who went up to Clare College, Cambridge, in 1865 but died in 1868.
19. op. cit., 1864, p. 409.
20. ibid., p. 421. See illustration.

knickerbockers with magenta and black striped stockings, white shirts, and magenta and black cap.'[21]

That disputations over the possible inaccuracy of a referee's timekeeping started early in the history of the modern game became apparent from the account of the first match played by Uppingham against the Old Boys, on December 15, 1865:

'. . . The game for some time was very equal. Bully after bully [as at Eton] was speedily gained; then after some interval the old boys obtained a goal. This advantage they seemed determined to keep. The goal keeping of [W.F.] Rawnsley[22] for our opponents was in excellent style; not so that of the school which was loose and defective in generalship. Both sides played up decidedly better as the game went on, especially the school, and the ball was kept in close proximity to the old boys' goal and, but alas, it evinced a decided repugnance to the space between the two posts.

'Meanwhile the minutes were getting very precious and still the old boys were that envious goal ahead. "Two minutes more", cried the umpire. Now for a last effort. The school led gallantly by [C.] Childs was becoming eager and furious. Rawnsley was cool and observant at the goal. No ball passed his ubiquitous hands and feet. Could nothing be done? Was there no pluck left to deserve and win success? Yes. A sudden rush, a flying ball, a desperate charge, feet well together, enemy after enemy passed, Childs demonstrating the well known proverb, the "right foot in the right place", Rawnsley's eye deceived and quickness frustrated and the goal was won.

21. Oldham, op. cit., p. 237. The first picture of a Shrewsbury XI dates from 1870. The first inter-school match played by Shrewsbury was against Uppingham (temporarily evacuated to Borth) in 1876.

22. Willingham Franklin Rawnsley (1845–1927), a page at Tennyson's wedding in 1850, was the Elder brother of Canon H. D. Rawnsley, of National Trust fame. He was at Uppingham from 1855–64; graduated at Corpus Christi, Oxford, and taught at his old school from 1871–8. In later life he became a J.P. for Southampton.

'It was remarked as a curious coincidence that the goal was gained in the last two minutes and the umpire's watch was carefully corrected to Greenwich time by two minutes. Someone was heard to be cruelly insinuating that the Uppingham clock had just pealed its last note of the hour. But what of that, *if true*? We are not at liberty to attack the sobriety of the clock-winder in a magazine, as this is, of world wide notoriety. Besides, both sides were equally contented—the old boys at having so long held an advantage against our best efforts—the school at not having lost.'[23]

In the following March another Old Boys match took place. In the report there is given a vignette of a true master of dribbling, one who, before his time was thought to be too clever by half:

'Who does not know D'Orsey's[24] play? The slow dribbled ball, the ubiquitous feet, the side to side action, all combine to excite astonishment and amusement. Never was such cunning play . . .

'Can it be that D'Orsey, always playing a crooked game, full of twists and turns, full of contrivances and devices, has lost the power of kicking straight before him? We leave that for men of metaphysical tendencies.'[25]

The Old Boys of Uppingham did not, unfortunately, take their football commitments as seriously as they should have done. On December 16, 1870, for instance, 'they mustered their ranks, and found after close scrutiny that in numbers they were three . . . (they therefore) proceeded to collect stragglers and press any able-bodied men they could find into the ranks till they had swelled to the respectable number of eleven.'[26] One wonders how the press-ganged Herr

23. *The School Magazine*, 1865, pp. 35–6.
24. Lambert Murray D'Orsey, the son of a theologian, was born in Glasgow, graduated at Corpus Christi College, Cambridge, and was ordained. In 1870 he was a member of Clapham Rovers F.C.
25. op. cit., 1866, p. 20.
26. ibid., December, 1879, p. 16.

Beisiegel performed on this occasion, and whether, after his retirement in 1902, he ultimately carried the Faith back to Germany.

If the Uppingham Old Boys' sequence of matches makes attractive marginal reading it was not of great consequence to the main line of development. The enthusiasm and sense of development of the game which characterised the footballers of Harrow, on the other hand, was of crucial significance. What the Harrovians did was of twofold consequence. The university attitude to the game was greatly influenced; but—and this was much more important—the game outside the universities and schools was reconditioned as a result of Harrovian enterprise.

In respect of football at Cambridge the following letter and addendum are of considerable importance. The date of the letter falls into the context of events detailed in the next chapter. The appended rules, more or less contemporary with those of Thring, preceded the better-known Cambridge code detailed on p. 87, and must be seen as a vital link in the legislative chain. The writer was clearly aware of the articles lately published by John D. Cartwright in which he advocated a conference of school and university footballers in order to achieve some uniformity of method:

'Sir,
    As the question of universal Football rules is now under discussion, it may interest some of your readers to know that a match was played at Cambridge, last November [i.e. 1862], between Eleven Harrovians and Eleven Etonians, according to rules drawn up for the occasion by a committee. These rules were observed without any difficulty; no dispute took place: the only unsatisfactory result of the game was that (owing, I think, to the insufficient width of the bases) it ended in a tie, no bases being obtained by either side. I enclose the rules: they may seem over-particu-

lar in details, but it was necessary to provide against the possibility of dispute.

Oct. 9 1863   I remain, Sir, yours,

J.A.C.'[27]

'RULES drawn up for a Match at Football, to be played between Etonian and Harrovian Resident Members of the University.

'(i) That there be eleven a-side; also that a Captain and Umpire be chosen on each side; the Captain to manage his side, and all appeals to the Umpire to be made through the Captain only. The Captains and Umpires shall appoint a neutral person as referee, whose decision upon appeal from the Umpires in every case shall be final.

'(ii) The choice of Bases or Goals, and kick off shall be determined by tossing; the Captains shall also toss for choice of ball; provided that if two matches are played, the side losing the toss in the first match, shall play with their own ball in the second match.

'(iii) The Bases shall be twelve feet between the poles, the poles themselves not exceeding Twenty feet in height and being joined at the top by a string.

'The length of the ground shall be one hundred and fifty yards and the breadth one hundred yards.

'(iv) The game shall last for an hour and a quarter; at the expiration of half the time the Umpires shall call *"change"*, and the sides shall change their Bases.

'(v) The Ball shall be kicked off from the middle of the ground, half-way between the two Bases, at the beginning and change of the Game, and after a Base obtained by either side; the *"kick-off"* being always in the same direction.

'(vi) All charging is fair; but holding, pushing with the

27. J. A. Cruikshank, Harrow, 1854–60, Football XI 1858–9 (Captain 1859), Head of School. After graduating at Trinity College, Cambridge, was a master at Harrow from 1866 to 1891.

hands, tripping up, shinning and back-shinning are forbidden. No nails are allowed in boots unless even with the sole.

'(vii) If the ball shall go beyond the prescribed limits of the Game, whether behind the line of bases, or at the side, it shall be out of play, and must be kicked straight in again to the Game. No player shall intentionally kick the ball behind the line of his own base.

'(viii) The Ball when in play may be stopped by any part of the body, but may not be held or hit by the hands, arms, or shoulders.

'(ix) A base is obtained when the Ball being in play shall pass between the base-poles.

'(x) When there are three or less than three of the opposite side between any player and his opponents' base, and the Ball is kicked to him from the direction of his own base, he shall be considered *sneaking* or *behind*, and is out of play, until another has touched the ball.'[28]

The names of the players in this match, and, therefore, the authors of the Rules, have not been preserved. It does not, however, require an undue degree of speculation to accept a connection between this declaration and that which was to appear a year later.

In the meanwhile certain Harrovians, who had not gone to a university, were busy in the wider world of football. Principal among them were J. F. and C. W. Alcock (1842–1907), sons of Charles Alcock, J.P., of Sunderland. The elder of the brothers was a pupil at Harrow from January 1855 to December 1857; the younger from 1855 until the end of the summer term of 1859. Thus C. W. Alcock had played in the Harrow team with 'J.A.C.' and the public letter of the latter quoted on p. 124 may be seen in the light of events also as a particular communication to Alcock.

28. *The Tyro* (pub. Harrow School), October 1, 1863, no. 1, pp. 52–3.

Alcock is a valuable guide to the critical period of the game now under consideration and (although he ignores Sheffield in this instance) we may pick up his opinion that 'the first club to work on a definite basis with the distinct object of circulating and popularising the game . . . was a club known as the Forest Club'.[29] Founded in 1859, by a group of Harrovians under the captaincy of J. F. Alcock, the Forest Club used a pitch in Epping Forest—near the Merchant Seamen's Orphan Asylum, at Snaresbrook. As well as the Alcocks other founder members were J. Pardoe,[30] the brothers A. and W. J. Thompson, and C. A. Absolom. In broad terms the Cambridge Rules of 1856 were accepted—but, as will be seen, Rules were liable to be accepted on an *ad hoc* basis according to the wishes of the two teams engaged in any match.

Forest F.C., however, added to its private doctrine the following not inconsiderable clauses :

'That Captains be chosen at the commencement of play, who shall have the direction of places, etc., etc., throughout the game.

'That the length and breadth of ground be marked off with flags, and that the distance between the goal-posts do not exceed eight yards.

'That in the event of the bursting of the ball a new one is to be placed in the centre of the ground, and that the side commencing the game have the kick-off.

'That for any infringement of the rules of the game, a fine of Two Shillings and Sixpence be inflicted.'

For four years the Forest Club played against other newly-formed clubs. In 1864, however, since local recruitment had diminished the club was disbanded and re-formed as the Wanderers F.C., with a vivid orange, violet, and

29. C. W. Alcock, 'The Principal Amateur Clubs of the Past' in *The Book of Football*, 1906, p. 255.

30. Pardoe played a large part in establishing Association football in Hitchin and Hertfordshire.

black costume, and headquarters at the Oval.[31] Throughout this period the connection with Harrow School, as will
be shown, was strong. Partly because of this, and the
enthusiasm generated, football began to lose its parochial
quality. A new potential world-game came into view.

The year 1863 was an *annus mirabilis*. As was Rome in
relation to the institution of Christianity, so was Cambridge
to that of football. In October, 1863, a committee of
Trinity men was convened, to draft yet another syllabus.
The senior member was Robert Burn (1829–1904), Tutor
and Praelector of Trinity College, a Salopian.[32] Eton was
represented by Robert Harvey Blake-Humfrey (1847–
1927), who had played 'Walls' for the Oppidans in the Wall
Game of 1860. Blake-Humfrey entered Trinity College in
1861.[33] William Thomas Trench (1843–1911), 'Walls' for the
Oppidans in 1861, also acted as an Eton delegate. Trench,
however, may be said to have represented another tradition,
for he was a member of a distinguished Irish family, belonging to Roscrea, Tipperary.[34] If Ireland was represented, so
too was Wales; in the person of Henry Lewis Williams
(1862–1911), who, although born in Manchester, was the
son of John Williams, of Highfield Hall, Northop, Flint. A
Harrovian, Williams was ordained, becoming curate at
Whitchurch (Salop), and Bebington (Cheshire), and Vicar
of Bingley (Yorks) and Bleasby (Notts). Williams was

31. The Forest Club (under different management) was revised in
1869 and played 'modified Association' football. The jerseys, caps, and
stockings then were 'scarlet in front and black behind', the 'knicker-
bockers' white. There was also a Forest School XI.

32. Burn, the son of a clergyman, was born in Wellington, Salop.
The senior classical scholar at Cambridge in 1852 he subsequently
enjoyed a quietly distinguished career, publishing many learned works
on classical Rome. He was given an honorary Doctorate at Glasgow
University.

33. In some books Blake-Humfrey is named as Blake. In fact Blake-
Humfrey became de-hyphenated, and finally adopted the name Robert
Harvey Mason. He was in later life a prominent agriculturalist in
Norfolk.

34. Trench became a member of the Irish Bar.

joined by another Harrovian, and another future barrister, John Templer Prior (1841–1922), on the 1863 Committee.

One other member represented a 'dribbling' school: William Shaw Wright (1843–1914), the son of Sir William Wright, a landowner in the East Riding of Yorkshire, an old boy of Westminster and a classical scholar.[35] Since there was as yet no official division between the two codes the committee included two Rugbeians,[36] and a Marlburian.[37]

The deliberations of this *ad hoc* body were brought to these conclusions:

'The Cambridge Universities Rules, 1863

'1. The length of the ground shall be not more than 150 yards and the breadth not more than 100 yards.

'The ground shall be marked out by posts, and two posts shall be placed on each side-line at distances of 25 yards from each goal-line.

'2. The *goals* shall consist of two upright poles at a distance of 15 feet from each other.

'3. The choice of goals and kick-off shall be determined by tossing and the ball shall be kicked off from the middle of the ground.

'4. In a match when half the time agreed upon has elapsed, the sides shall change goals when the ball is next out of play. After such change or a goal obtained, the kick-

35. After leaving Cambridge Wright returned to his native county, where he became in due course Chairman of the Hull and Barnsley Railway Company, Chairman of the Humber Conservancy Board, and a Justice of the Peace. Knighted during the last year of his life Wright always maintained his sporting interest, latterly concentrating on tennis and golf.

36. Marcus Trevelyan Martin (1842–1908), who entered Trinity in 1859 and gained a Cricket Blue in 1862. A barrister, he later played cricket for both Middlesex and Warwickshire.

William Robert Collyer (1842–1928), barrister, and a colonial judge.

37. William Parry Crawley (1842–1907), born in Monmouthshire. Crawley became a priest, serving in the Chichester Diocese, and as a Chaplain to the Forces.

off shall be from the middle of the ground in the same direction as before.

'The time during which the game shall last and the numbers on each side are to be settled by the heads of the sides.

'5. When a player has kicked the ball, any one of the same side who is nearer to the opponents' goal-line is *out of play* and may not touch the ball himself nor in any way whatsoever prevent any other player from doing so.

'6. When the ball goes out of the ground by crossing the side-lines, it is out of play and shall be kicked straight into the ground again from a point where it is first stopped.

'7. When a player has kicked the ball beyond the opponents' goal-line, whoever first touches the ball when it is on the ground with his hand, may have a *free* kick bringing the ball straight out from the goal-line.

'8. No player may touch the ball behind his opponents' goal-line, who is behind it when the ball is kicked there.

'9. If the ball is touched down behind the goal-line and beyond the line of the side-posts, the free kick shall be from the 25-yards post.

'10. When a player has a free kick, no one of his own side may be between him and his opponents' goal-line, and no one of the opposite side may stand within 15 yards of him.

'11. A free kick may be taken in any manner the player may choose.

'12. A goal is obtained when the ball goes out of the ground by passing between the poles or in such a manner that it would have passed between them had they been of sufficient height.

'13. The ball, when in play, may be stopped by any part of the body, but may *not* be held or hit by the hands, arms or shoulders.

'14. All charging is fair, but holding, pushing with the hands, tripping up and shinning are forbidden.

'These Rules were first put into operation at Cambridge on November 20, 1863.'

As in the case in all previous statements of similar kind, this is a synthesis and a compromise. Here, for the last time, is a game which, although bearing the marks of sophistication, would have been recognisable in the terms set down by Concanen during the reign of George I. But the shape of the game as it now is may also be recognised.

The authors of the Cambridge scheme (indeed of all the Cambridge schemes) lined up with the football-players of the seventeenth century. They were (or were to be) parsons and lawyers, and to some extent they wore an aristocratic look. But the future of the game now lay in the hands of a more broadly based community of interest. Valiant work had been done in the schools and universities for hundreds of years and generations of scholars had moulded a gamesman's *lingua franca*. This was now ready for general use.

8

The Football Association

Up to date the development of football has appeared to have been largely fortuitous. This, of course, is in the line of the growth of any form of folk-art. We have now, however, arrived at the point of take-off towards a deliberate cultivation of the art. Just as the arts and sciences were shaped for modern times by groups of inspired and informed enthusiasts in the sixteenth and seventeenth centuries, so were the ultimate doctrines and philosophy of football hammered out by 'Academies' (to use an effective and apt Renaissance term) in the nineteenth century. Like the Florentine academicians of earlier times so did the members of the significant football committees of Victorian England know what they were talking about—from first-hand experience. Perhaps there is a lesson in this.

The most important date in the modern history of football is Monday, October 26, 1863. On the evening of this day a meeting of representatives of certain football clubs was convened at the Freemason's Tavern, in Great Queen Street, London. The purpose of the meeting was to form a Football Association. Those attending the meeting were:

J. F. Alcock and A. W. Mackenzie (Forest); Arthur Pember (N. N., Kilburn); E. C. Morley and P. D. Gregory (Barnes); E. Wawn (War Office); H. T. Steward (Crusaders); G. W. Shillingford (Perceval House, Blackheath); F. Day (Crystal Palace); F. H. Moore and F. W. Campbell (Blackheath); W. J. Mackintosh (Kensington School); H. Bell (Surbiton); and W. H. Gordon (Blackheath School).

There were also present some 'unattached' footballers and B. F. Hartshorne, of Charterhouse School, attended as an observer.[1]

Of the clubs represented, apart from Forest, these are the salient facts so far as known. The Kilburn Club N[o]. N[ames], with a ground in Kilburn, existed only for a few years, Pember being captain. Its membership overlapped that of Forest and Wanderers and an association with Harrow was maintained through fixtures against the Old Boys of the School. One or other of the Alcocks turned out for the N.N.s from time to time.[2] The Barnes Club, wearing dark blue and white stripes, absorbed a number of oarsmen (of whom Morley was one) and had the use of a field belonging to J. Johnstone, near the White Hart. The Club was formed in 1862. Although the War Office team as such did not survive for long its influence spread into the regiments. Presumably Wawn was also holding a watching brief

1. B. F. Hartshorne 'could not consent to present [*sic*] to put his name down as a member of the association, as he thought it desirable that the public schools should be adequately represented, and take a prominent part in the movement. It was certainly desirable that some definite set of rules for football should be generally adopted, yet, as the representative of the Charterhouse School, the only public school represented, he could not pledge himself to any course of action until he saw more clearly what the other schools did in the matter. Speaking on behalf of Charterhouse School, he would be willing to coalesce if the other public schools would do the same, and probably at a more advanced stage of the association the opinion of the generality of the other great schools would be obtained. It certainly would be advisable, if possible, to obtain the co-operation of Rugby, Harrow, Winchester, Eton, Marlborough, Cheltenham, and other public schools.'

Pember observed that 'their silence [i.e. of the schools] probably arose from no one in particular liking to take the initiative, and put himself prominently forward'. *Bell's Life*, October 31, 1853.

Bertram Fulke Hartshorne (1844–1921), son of the Rector of Holdenby, Northants, was at Charterhouse from 1857 to 1863. He was in the cricket and football teams in 1862 and 1863. In his last year he was Captain of Football. Subsequently he went to Oxford, became a civil servant in Ceylon, and, after being called to the Bar, Local Government Auditor for Middlesex and Herts.

2. Harrow Chequers (the O.H. team) played against N.N. at Kilburn on December 30, 1865. One Alcock appeared in each team.

for the Civil Service F.C., founded in 1862, which played according to a variety of codes (uniform, blue and orange), first in Battersea Park and then at the Oval and also Lillie Bridge. The Crystal Palace team was a year older than the Civil Service. All these clubs were strongly in favour of Eton-Harrow-Cambridge principles; that is of the 'dribbling' game. The Blackheath Club, which erupted from Old Rugbeian interest in 1858, on the other hand regarded itself as the custodian of the true, Rugby, faith. Blackheath School, in regard to policy, was in all crucial matters to be regarded as a satellite of the Blackheath Club, even though its football team was formed two years before that of the club. The two Blackheath Schools and Kensington Schools were cramming institutions, and were represented at the inaugural meeting by their captains.

It is easy to be wise after the event. The conveners of the famous meeting of October 26 had the good of the game at heart, but lacking diplomatic finesse they had failed properly to negotiate with the chief football-playing schools and with Cambridge. Nor was any account taken of provincial interest, especially in Sheffield. These omissions in fact resulted in a long time-lag. It was almost a decade before any reasonable uniformity of procedure was generally adopted.

The Chairman of the meeting was Pember. Morley proposed, and Steward seconded, a motion that 'the clubs represented at this meeting now form themselves into an association to be called "The Football Association".' The annual subscription was fixed at one guinea a club.[3] Then came consideration of the main problem—the Rules. Reference to the Sheffield Rules of 1857 and to the Cambridge Rules of 1862 and 1863 shows that there was a strong body of opinion in favour of civilising the game by banning one of its more objectionable features. The majority of the F.A. delegates determined at the first meeting to follow this

3. See *Bell's Life*, October 31, 1863.

body of opinion. But there was opposition from a strong and vocal minority. Draft rules were considered at a sequence of meetings in the hope of reaching an agreeable conclusion. For the time being, 'the chief provisions of the rules in force at Rugby were inserted with a view to a probable compromise. The goal was that in use at Harrow, without any cross-bar; but there was a clause to admit of a free kick (place or drop) in the event of a touch-down by the attacking side, as well as to allow a fair catch.'[4] But whatever attempts at compromise were made one item proved to be non-negotiable. The original draft of the F.A. Rules included these clauses:

'9. A player may be entitled to run with the ball towards his adversaries' goal if he makes a fair catch, or catches the ball on the first bound; but in the case of a fair catch, if he makes his mark, he shall not run.

'10. If any player shall run with the ball towards his adversaries' goal, any player on the opposite side shall be at liberty to charge, hold, trip or hack him, or wrest the ball from him; but no player shall be held and hacked at the same time.'

While the two clauses were considered together, either both were in—in which case football would have been for practical purposes of the manner of Rugby—or both were out. The Blackheath group were for retention, the rest of the delegates for excision.

On December 1 matters came to a head. Morley pointed out that while 'hacking' sounded worse than it often was its legalisation would do irreparable danger to the game in that 'men in business—to whom it is of importance to take care of themselves'—would be unwilling to take up the game. Campbell put the contrary point of view saying, 'I'm much afraid that there are many of the clubs who will not join the Association because they fear that our rules will do away with the skill shown in the game at Harrow and Eton,

4. Football, *The Association Game*, C. W. Alcock, 1890, p. 5.

and the pluck so necessary in the game as played at Rugby.

'Hacking is the true football game, and if you look into the Winchester records you will find that in former years men were so wounded that two of them were actually carried off the field, and they allowed two others to occupy their places and finish the game. Lately, however, the game has become more civilised than that state of things which certainly was, to a certain extent, brutal.

'As to not liking hacking as at present carried on, I say that they had no right to draw up such a rule at Cambridge and that it savours far more of the feelings of those who liked their pipes and grog or schnapps more than the manly game of football. I think that the reason they object to hacking is because too many of the members of clubs began late in life and were too old for that spirit of the game which was so fully entered into at the public schools and by public school men in after life.'[5]

Morley, not a 'public school man', was unsympathetic to Campbell, whose attitude now changed to one of arrogance. Finding that the Committee as a whole was against him he moved as an amendment that the meeting be adjourned 'until the vacation so that representatives of the schools who are members of the Association may be enabled to attend'. Defeated by 13 votes to 4, Campbell and his supporters withdrew from the Association. On December 8—to which date the previous meeting had been adjourned—the rules as agreed by the Association and evolved from those of Cambridge—which were specifically stated to 'embrace the true principles of the game'—were formally accepted. In 1871 a Rugby Football Union was formed. Within a year this body had also outlawed hacking and tripping.[6]

The Rules finally approved in 1863 show the descent of

5. *Bell's Life*, December 5, 1863.
6. The dangers of Rugby football had by now become a public scandal, and there were even moves to have the game put down by Act of Parliament. Thus it had been in the Middle Ages!

the game, and the refinements of successive stages of development. They are also, being as it were the Law of the Prophets, the foundation of the game as it now is. They read as follows:

'Laws

'1. The maximum length of the ground shall be 200 yards, the maximum breadth shall be 100 yards, the length and breadth shall be marked off with flags; and the goal shall be defined by two upright posts, eight yards apart, without any tape or bar across them.

'2. A toss for goals shall take place, and the game shall be commenced by a place kick from the centre of the ground by the side losing the toss for goals; the other side shall not approach within 10 yards of the ball until it is kicked off.

'3. After a goal is won, the losing side shall be entitled to kick off, and the two sides shall change goals after each goal is won.

'4. A goal shall be won when the ball passes between the goal-posts or over the space between the goal-posts (at whatever height), not being thrown, knocked on, or carried.

'5. When the ball is in touch, the first player who touches it shall throw it from the point on the boundary line where it left the ground in a direction at right angles with the boundary line, and the ball shall not be in play until it has touched the ground.

'6. When a player has kicked the ball, any one of the same side who is nearer to the opponent's goal line is out of play, and may not touch the ball himself, nor in any way whatever prevent any other player from doing so, until he is in play; but no player is out of play when the ball is kicked off from behind the goal line.

'7. In case the ball goes behind the goal line, if a player on the side to whom the goal belongs first touches the ball, one of his side shall be entitled to a free kick from the goal line at the point opposite the place where the ball shall be touched. If a player of the opposite side first touches the ball, one of his side shall be entitled to a free kick at the goal where the ball is touched, the opposing side standing within their goal line until he has had his kick.

'8. If a player makes a fair catch, he shall be entitled to a free kick, providing he claims it by making a mark with his heel at once; and in order to take such a kick he may go back as far as he pleases, and no player on the opposite side shall advance beyond his mark until he has kicked.

'9. No player shall run with the ball.

'10. Neither tripping nor hacking shall be allowed, and no player shall use his hands to hold or push his adversary.

'11. A player shall not be allowed to throw the ball or pass it to another with his hands.

'12. No player shall be allowed to take the ball from the ground with his hands under any pretext whatever while it is in play.

'13. No player shall be allowed to wear projecting nails, iron plates, or gutta percha on the soles or heels of his boots.'

Up to Law 8 there is common ground with Rugby Football, even as now understood. It is beyond that point that the distinctive features of legislation occur. In addition to issuing the Laws—the term Rules now, be it noted, discarded—the Association also published a glossary of definition of terms. Since these terms are intelligible to the modern reader it is not necessary to reprint this glossary.

When the F.A. set out its Laws (which had been given publicity by being printed in *Bell's Life* on December 5) they were incumbent only on a few clubs—those in the London area that acknowledged and belonged to the Association. It is at this point that the activities of footballers on the field became decisive. And Harrow School, although independent of the Association, remained a focal point.

Shortly after the formation of the F.A. Harrow played a match against a Cambridge XI, and won by 3 bases to 1. The Cambridge XI consisted in fact of fourteen players.[7] On January 16 Harrow beat R. Crompton's Esq. XI by 1—0, and on February 25 defeated J. W. Greaves' Esq. XI by the same score. Greaves's team included several famous players who were members of the Forest Club. This club played against the school in between the two last-named fixtures, the team consisting of the two Alcock brothers, C. M. and A. M. Tebbut, C. A. Absolom, A. K. Finlay, E. W. Burnett, — Gillespie, J. W. Greaves, R. Colton, and C. Adams.[8] At the end of that same year a Harrow 'scratch eleven' set an important precedent by taking part in Christmas holiday matches. Two games were played against the Civil Service, the School winning the first by 5—0, and the second by 3—0.[9]

In the meantime the Forest Club had been transformed into The Wanderers. On the last Saturday of the Christmas quarter, December 9, Harrow School XI took on its greatest task to date. But 'The Wanderers, hitherto invincible, were defeated by four bases to none. The first was obtained by Tupper with a capital "three yards". The next two were both kicked by Montgomery, off the ground, and the last by Noyes.'[10] One of the Alcocks (no initial given) was in the Wanderers team on that occasion.

Now the effect of football indoctrination at school was beginning to be felt in the world at large. Harrow Chequers

7. *The Tyro*, March 1, 1864, p. 123. No date is given, but according to the dates of other matches this must have taken place in December 1863 or in the first part of January, 1864. At that time Cambridge still played on Parker's Piece and were distinguished by broad blue and white stripes.

8. ibid., p. 154.

9. *The Tyro*, February 1, 1865, p. 112.

10. *The Tyro*, February 1, 1866, p. 111.

—comprising Old Boys—came into being and on December 14, 1865, played against the Civil Service, in Battersea Park. Other fixtures followed: against Crystal Palace, at Penge, on December 22; against Reigate, at Reigate, on January 4; against F. Lucas's XI (Old Westminsters?) at Vincent Square, on January 10; and against Crusaders, at the West London Cricket Ground, on January 25.

By now football at Harrow was on a high pedestal of esteem. Thus three football prizes were offered at the end of 1865, 'for the greatest number of bases in the Christmas quarter'. No nonsense here about ethical values, but a highly competitive approach. Montgomery, the hero of the match against the Wanderers, won the first prize having scored 9 bases in 4 games and 5 matches [*sic*]. A fiercely competitive spirit was further stimulated by the house matches, as is indicated by the following letter on that subject:

'Sir,
The idea of challenging has apparently been taken from the plan adopted at Rugby; but House Matches at Harrow, and House Matches at Rugby, are very different. At Harrow, the Champion Football Match is *the* match of the season; and in cricket the Champion House Match is only surpassed in interest by the match at Lord's; while at Rugby very little interest is taken in the House Matches.

A Conservative'[11]

The 'Cock House' competition was soon to inspire another, and greater, competition. A keen eye on what was happening at his old school was kept by C. W. Alcock, who in 1866 was elected to the committee of the F.A. Four years later he became its honorary secretary.

Once or twice a year Alcock captained the Wanderers in matches against Harrow. The Wanderers XI of November

11. ibid., p. 109.

24, 1866, which again lost to the School, by 1—0, comprised: C. W. Alcock, W. O. Hewlett, E. E. Bowen, J. A. Cruikshank, C. F. Reid, J. Bulter, C. M. Tebbut, W. Thompson, C. W. Willis, J. Thomas, and F. Fryer (of Carlisle).[12] There was a strong Harrovian influence in this Wanderers team: Hewlett—son of the school doctor and to become Master of the Supreme Court; Bowen—a master at the school since leaving Cambridge in 1859; Cruikshank, as well as Alcock, all being Old Boys. Alcock made these pilgrimages until 1872, and from the beginning of 1870 he was invariably accompanied by A. F. Kinnaird lately down from Cambridge.

By 1869, however, the rigours of the game and its cult were coming in for criticism. A correspondent had the temerity to write to *The Harrovian* of October 16 that compulsory football was 'positively detested'. Letters in support of this point of view flowed in for the next twelve months until an 'Old Harrovian' stated, on October 8, 1870, that ' "compulsory Football" is objectionable on two grounds: it is not *popular* and it is not *compulsory*'.

However, the athletes saw it another way: the honour of the school was at stake. Those who took football seriously now took it even more seriously. The object of the operation was to win. So:

'If any Eleven wishes to be at all effective, they must "follow up". Each player must feel that the game depends upon *his* own exertions. All *laissez aller* feeling must be banished and trampled under foot ...'[13]

And there were special duties for special players. For instance, backs '... must remember that it is not their office to "dribble". They must remember that there is nothing

12. *The Tyro*, December 15, 1866; which also gives the names of the Cambridge team which played at Harrow on an unstated date: R. C. Moncreif, H. W. Lawrence, E. Porter, G. G. Kennedy, C. L. Mason, T. E. Peel, R. N. Russell, H. H. Montgomery, Hon. G. O. Bridgeman, J. S. Holmes, Sir W. ffolkes, and E. E. Bowen.

13. *The Harrovian*, October 22, 1870, pp. 25–6.

between them and their base. If once the ball is past them, there is small chance of their preventing a base being got. Why then risk all this simply from a desire to "dribble"? The "backs" are not chosen for their "dribbling" but for their kicking powers.'[14]

The principles thus defined remained in constant use for three-quarters of a century.

To encourage a general enthusiasm subtle means were employed. E. E. Bowen was footballer and poet. His musical colleague—very popular in the school—was John Farmer. Between them they knocked up songs designed to nourish a proper corporate spirit. The most famous, indeed, centres on the injunction 'follow up', as quoted above. 'A football Song' puts these admirable sentiments into its chorus:

> 'Cease! cease! cease! now foes are foes no longer
> Brothers climb we the miry slippery clay:
> Football fights make friendship's ties the stronger,
> Football defeats pass with the passing day.'

All in all it is not difficult to see within the maturing football tradition of Harrow School the shape of many things to come.

Once established the F.A. could look out on the world

14. ibid. cf. C. W. Alcock's introductory essay to *The Football Annual*, 1870, p. 10: 'To play for his side and not for individual fame and glory, as is too often the case, even with the most popular performers, ought to be the North Star of the young player's aspirations.' and: 'Second only, perhaps, in importance to the mainspring of football, as I consider "playing up", is the grand and essential principle of "backing up". By "backing up" of course I shall be understood to mean the following closely on a fellow-player to assist him, if required, or to take on the ball in case of his being attacked, or otherwise prevented from continuing his onward course.' Players especially commended for their vigour in 'backing-up' were J. B. Martin (Wanderers and London Athletic), A. F. Kinnaird, W. K. Dixon (Flying Dutchmen—a club which quickly flew into non-existence), A. Baker (N.N.) and R. G. Graham (Barnes).

at large and contemplate the problems which, if its founder's hopes were to be realised, would need to be resolved. The major problems were interrelated. Clubs were springing up like mushrooms, each determining its own playing rules; some clubs, prizing independence, resisted the claims of the F.A. to be regarded as an authoritative body while those in Yorkshire preferred to take protection under the Sheffield F.A. which was set up in 1867. That there was a division between London and Sheffield was no fault of the northerners, for the Secretary of the Sheffield Club had contacted London as early as November 30, 1863. But his overtures met with muted response.[15]

Some of the clubs of early foundation preferring the Association type of game have been detailed. Others, of more or less importance in the home counties, included the following:

Aldenham School (1825),[16] Amateur Athletic (West Brompton (1866), Brentwood School (1865), Brondesbury (1871), Clapham Rovers (1869), 21st Essex Rifles (1868), Gitano (1864), Great Marlow (1871), Hertfordshire Rangers (1865), King's School, Rochester (1866), Leyton (1868), Maidenhead (1870), Pilgrims—formerly Clapham Pilgrims (1871), Rochester (1848), Royal Engineers (1867), St. Alban's Pilgrims (1869), South Norwood (1871), 1st Surrey Rifles (1869), Trojans, at Leyton (1869), Upton Park (1866),[17] Wey-side (1870), and Windsor Home Park (1870).

As for the provinces the chief pioneers (after Sheffield) were: Bramham College, near Tadcaster, Yorks (1855), Burton-on-Trent (1870), Bury St. Edmunds Grammar School (1550), 8th Cheshire Rifles, based on Macclesfield

15. See Percy M. Young, *Football in Sheffield*, 1962, pp. 20 f.
16. Dates of foundation were supplied to C. W. Alcock's *The Football Annual* (1873) by club secretaries. Attention is drawn to the claim of Bury St. Edmunds Grammar School.
17. From which, by devious routes, derived West Ham United in due course.

(1872), Chesterfield (1866), Congleton Rovers (1860), Hampton Common, near Stroud (1869), Holt, near Trow-bridge (1864), Horncastle (1866), Hulme Athenaeum (1863), Kettering (1872), Lancing College (1867), Leam-ington College (1867), Leeds Athletic (1864), Lincoln (1861), Milksham (1865), Newark (1868), Norwich (1868), Nottingham Forest (1865), Nottingham Law (1869), Ock-brook School, Derby (1867), St. Andrew's, Derby (1869), Stoke-upon-Trent (1867),[18] and Whitchurch, Salop (1865).

The location of some of these clubs hints at continuity from ancient times. The names often provide evidence of middle-class interest, of social function, and educational purpose. One or two names still endure; of these the most striking is that of Nottingham Forest.[19]

In the course of a hundred years a good deal of gaiety has passed from the game, not least in the matter of wardrobe. Clapham Rovers, for instance, wore cerise and French grey; Gitano, red, white, and violet; Wey-side, scarlet and white (harlequin) with a black Maltese Cross mounted on a white ground on the left breast. The army teams in full football dress were magnificent: the Royal Engineers with jerseys, 'night-caps' [*sic*] and stockings, horizontally striped in regi-mental red and blue, and with 'dark blue serge knicker-bockers'; the Surrey Rifles with scarlet caps and a gold bugle to embellish each blue jersey. Some of the provincial headquarters were poetically situated. Thus the Congleton Club played, by the winding waters of the Dane, in 'Congle-ton Meadows', and Horncastle 'on the Wong'. Chesterfield,

18. Information provided by Edward T. Gardner, Butterton Hall, Newcastle-under-Lyme, Staffs, Honorary Secretary in 1873. It has been suggested that the Stoke Club was formed in 1863—by Old Carthusians employed in the extensions of the North Staffs Railway then taking place. The later date should, however, be taken as authoritative, since the names given in *The Book of Football* (1905?), p. 87, as of the 1863 Old Carthusians supposed to have been involved do not appear in the 1879 Register of Old Carthusians. The Club (colours crimson and blue) had a ground 'a quarter of a mile from Stoke-upon-Trent Station'.

19. See p. 145.

on the other hand, took advantage of a new amenity in the town and played, as Chesterfield F.C. does at the present time, on the 'New Recreation Ground'. Hulme Athenaeum had their ground at Moss Side, Manchester.

A minority of clubs, Clapham Rovers, for instance, sponsored both Association and Rugby football. Otherwise there was considerable variation within the former code. Wey-side and Burton-on-Trent played according to Association Rules 'slightly modified'; Chesterfield followed Derbyshire F.A. practice; Kettering preferred the Uppingham Rules; Norwich modified both F.A. and Cambridge University principles; Nottingham had its own way of conducting affairs; while clubs within a twenty-mile radius of Sheffield plumped for the Sheffield F.A.

After Sheffield and London the next most significant centre of activity was Nottingham, and by January 2, 1865, skill and enthusiasm had been so effectively blended that a local team (playing according to Nottingham Rules, with eighteen a side) could entertain a Sheffield team and lose by no more than a single goal. After the game both sides had supper at the George Hotel.

From ancient times a game known locally as 'shinney' (otherwise shinty) had been played in Nottingham. The traditional playground was the long tree-less 'Forest', between the Mansfield and Alfreton Roads—the top of the slope formerly lined with windmills—where the race-course was, with a grandstand erected in the eighteenth century. Young men (Major Hack, F. C. Smith, Bernard Bradly, W. Patterson, A. Blake Baillon, the brothers Hodges, and the cricketers George Parr and Richard Daft) played football there in 1862. A year later, now uniformed in black and amber, this group moved to the cricket ground in the Meadows, in Bath Street. As the result of a meeting called by J. S. Scrimshaw at the Clinton Arms Hotel a new club—of which founder members were Charles Daft (brother to Richard), T. G. Howitt, J. H. Rashell, T. Gamble, J. G.

Richardson, R. P. Hawkesley, W. Brown, and W. R. Lymberry[20]—was formed: Nottingham Forest. During 1865 Sheffield took the Forest on to their fixture list, playing two games, as also against the vigorous Lincoln club. In 1866 the Forest played against Notts County for the first time. The kind of the game may be understood from the contemporary account of its conclusion: After a long, negative, scoreless, afternoon, and 'close upon the call of time, there was a sort of steeplechase across the goal-line and over the railings nearest the grand stand between a player named Hugh Brown, of Notts, and W. H. Revis, of the Forest. The latter touched down the ball, and the place kick, which was taken fifteen yards at right angles to the goal-line, being successful, the Forest were proclaimed winners of the first great match between the rivals. There was no cross-bar used, the ball had merely to go between the posts.'[21]

Diplomatic relations of a cautious nature were in the meantime maintained between Sheffield and London. On February 28, 1866, captains of the London clubs belonging to the F.A. were called to a special meeting in E. C. Morley's Chambers in the Temple, to consider a letter from W. Chesterman, Honorary Secretary of the Sheffield Club. The letter contained a challenge to the Londoners to play against the ambitious Yorkshiremen. Having determined, according to custom, on a mutually agreeable set of rules for this one match[22] arrangements were made to play it in

20. Who succeeded J. S. Milford as Hon Sec.

21. Pickford, op. cit. II, p. 111. cf. *The Tourist's Picturesque Guide to Nottingham*, Nottingham, 1871, p. 90: 'Football and other athletic sports have recently been revived in Nottingham, and clubs formed, who contend between themselves except on gala occasions, for the honour of winning, or a supper at the expense of the losers'. It is to be noted that the first Nottingham *v.* Sheffield cricket match took place in 1771, and that between Nottingham and Leicester in 1789 (ibid., p. 98).

22. See Percy M. Young, op. cit., pp. 22 f.

Battersea Park on March 31. The London team[23] won by 2 goals and 4 touch-downs to nil.

This match aroused great interest. The F.A. took two hints. The precedent of 'representative' matches was followed up. The Old Etonian *v.* Old Harrovian engagement became rather more public, while on November 2, 1867, Middlesex (with a strong group of players from who to choose) played a combined Surrey-Kent team in Battersea Park.[24] A few months later Surrey played against Kent at the West London Running Grounds, in Brompton. In that same year the rigours of the off-side rule were modified, the principles observed at Westminster and Charterhouse, now members of the F.A., being adopted. Most important, however, was the enlargement of the F.A. Committee. Yorkshire, with representatives on this body from Bramham College, Hull College, and Sheffield, was now in at the centre.

'The objects of the Association', wrote C. W. Alcock, 'are to still further remove the barriers which prevent the accomplishment of one universal game. To this end the Committee has been judiciously strengthened by the introduction of a provincial element into their body; and yearly, by slow degrees, recruits from all parts of the country have been led to rally round the standard of the legislative assemblage.'[25]

One universal game! A glimpse of what might have been, but for the split over 'hacking and tripping', is given in a recent account of a St. Patrick's Day Rugby football match between Notre Dame and Fordham played in Central Park,

23. C. W. Alcock, R. D. Elphinstone, Quintin Hogg, J. A. Boyson (Wanderers), J. F. Barnes, R. G. Graham, R. W. Willis (Barnes), A. J. Baker, A. Pember, C. M. Tebbut (N.N.), and Alec Morton (Crystal Palace) in goal.

24. The grounds of Beaufort House had been offered; but the offer was withdrawn by Lord Ranelagh on account of disagreement with the Amateur Athletic Club.

25. *The Football Annual*, 1873, p. 53.

New York. 'The game they were having was not the same that the Fighting Irish and Michigan State played to a tie score last fall. Nor was it the game of soccer that Princeton and Rutgers played in the first inter-collegiate football contest in this country in 1869. It was the English game of "rugger", from which American football stemmed by a process of innovations conceived largely by Walter Camp after Yale and Harvard had begun "The Game" in a hybrid contest of rugby and soccer in 1875.'[26] If indeed the Princeton-Rutgers match was (roughly) after the Association principle, the score was a remarkable one. Rutgers, according to a placard still displayed with some pride in the Faculty Club of Rutgers, at New Brunswick, won the match by 29—0.

26. *New York Times*, March 18, 1967.

9

Expansion

Of the three public parks that existed in Glasgow in the 1860s Queen's Park was the one most favoured as a recreation ground. Towards 1867 there were frequently to be seen there three groups of sportsmen: a company of casual footballers, following no particular code; some enthusiasts for hammer-throwing and caber-tossing, who had come from the northern counties; and a number of members of a newly formed branch of the Y.M.C.A. As a result of pooled ideas a merger was proposed. A report of the inaugural conference to determine the form of the merger—an epoch-making document—exists, and reads as follows:

Glasgow, 9th July 1867

'Tonight, at half-past eight o'clock, a number of gentlemen met at No. 3 Eglinton Terrace for the purpose of forming a "football club". After Mr. Black was called to the chair, a good deal of debating ensued, and ultimately the following measures were voted for and carried, viz:—

'*First.* That the club should be called the "Queen's Park Football Club".

'*Second.* That there should be four office-bearers, viz:— A president, captain, secretary and treasurer.

'*Third.* That there should be thirteen members of committee, including office-bearers, seven of whom to form a quorum.

'The following gentlemen were then duly elected as office-bearers and members of committee, viz:—

'Mr. (M.) Ritchie, president; Mr. (L.) Black, captain;

Mr. (W. M.) Klinger, secretary; Mr. (R.) Smith, senior treasurer; Messrs. (J. C.) Grant, (R.) Gardner, sen.; R. Davidson, (J.) Smith jun., (D.) Edmiston, P. Davidson, (A.) Gladstone, (R.) Reid, and (J.) Skinner.

'The secretary then gave intimation that the committee would meet on the 15th inst. for further deliberation, and to draw out a code of rules for the guidance of the club. The business for the evening being now finished, the members retired, after awarding a hearty vote of thanks to Mr. Black for his able conduct in the chair.

W. M. Klinger, *Secretary*

Lewis S. Black, *Chairman*'

Thus was born the premier football club of Scotland, and with it the great tradition of Association football in Scotland.

Mungo Ritchie vacated the Presidency after one year (on account of his marriage) and was succeeded by Lewis Black. Klinger, German by birth, lodged at the house of the brothers Smith, with whom he made a useful pressure group. In 1868 Klinger became captain, taking an active part in drafting the club Rules, and played for the club until he moved to London in 1870. There were three brothers Smith (all being members of Queen's Park)— Robert, James, and John, of whom the first two were original committee members. Robert and James went to London in 1869 and 1871 respectively (Robert eventually emigrating to Canada) where they joined the South Norwood Club. Both took part in the deliberations of the London F.A., where, in fact, their presence was invaluable in that it soon became apparent both in London and Glasgow that some kind of relationship needed to be worked out between England and Scotland. There was yet another Smith—not of this family—who was an early and influential member of Queen's Park. This was H. N. Smith, who became President in 1871-2, having already proved an effective agent in the realm of public relations. He contributed notices of football matches to the *North British Daily Mail* and the *Glasgow Herald* at an early date. Nor was he averse from balladry in the grand tradition, and on June 2, 1869, he (it is supposed) contributed a poem on a match between Queen's Park and Hamilton Gymnasium (May 29, 1869) to the *Herald*.

Grant achieved distinction as a goalkeeper. Between 1867 and 1872 no goal nor touch-down was scored against Queen's Park in any official match. His successor was Gardner, formerly a forward, who remained with the club until 1873, when, dissatisfied with the club's representation in the newly formed Scottish F.A., he joined Clydesdale. The Davidsons and Alexander Gladstone belonged to the club only for a couple of years; Robert Davidson went to West Africa, and the others found the pressures of business too heavy. Reid and Skinner were also early defectors, leaving the committee after one year and the club after five. Edmiston, an Aberdonian and an expert in various Highland games, however, remained a tower of strength, both as player and official, to exert a considerable influence in respect of the connection with England.

At first Queen's Park played football in the summer, and early fixtures were against Thistle (August 1, 1868), Hamilton Gymnasium (as above) and Airdrie (June 23, 1870). The Rules were still somewhat indeterminate. In the autumn of 1870, however, events conspired to stimulate the desire to rationalise them and also to open up wider vistas for Scottish football.

On November 3, 1870, C. W. Alcock, lately elected Honorary Secretary of the Football Association, wrote to the *Glasgow Herald* announcing that the Association proposed to select teams of English and Scottish players to compete against each other at the Oval on November 19. He invited nominations from Scotland. 'In Scotland,' he wrote: 'once essentially the land of football, there should still be a spark left of the old fire, and I confidently appeal to Scotsmen to aid to their utmost the efforts of the committee to confer success on what London fondly hopes to found, an annual trial of skill between the champions of England and Scotland.'[1]

There was an immediate response from Queen's Park, who assumed membership of the F.A., and elected Robert Smith—now based in London—as their representative player. Smith was also asked to report on the proceedings.

The 'Scottish' team for 1870 was: J. Kirkpatrick (Civil Service), A. F. Kinnaird (Old Etonians), G. E. W. Crawford (Harrow School), H. W. Primrose (Civil Service), C. E. Nepean (University College, Oxford), Quintin Hogg[2] (Wanderers), G. F. Congreve (Old Rugbeians), R. Smith (Queen's Park), G. G. Kennedy (Wanderers), J. F. Inglis (Charterhouse), A. K. Smith (Oxford), and W. H. Gladstone (Old Etonians). 'England' won by 1—0.

The Scots, it will be noted, were strongly patrician. Some names have already been encountered in southern contexts. One or two call for special comment. A. Kirke Smith (to become a clergyman) belonged to a well-known Sheffield family, and his right to appear in these fixtures derived from the family tenure of property in Scotland. He will be found also to have appeared as an English international. During his football career he rendered yeoman service to the cause of the game particularly at Oxford and as a member of the Sheffield Club. William Henry Gladstone (1840–91) was the eldest son of W. E. Gladstone. A student of Christ Church, Oxford, he entered politics and was M.P. for Chester (1865–8) and for Whitby (1868–86). Thus he was a Member of Parliament when he played for England. This precedent has not been followed, although

1. Robinson, op. cit., p. 42.
2. Quintin Hogg (1845–1903), an Etonian, was a philanthropist, best known for his inauguration of the polytechnic movement. He encouraged football and athletics in the polytechnic institutions.

the Minister responsible for Sport (Dennis Howell) in 1967 was active as referee while an M.P. The most resonant name on the list, however, is that of A. F. Kinnaird. He and C. W. Alcock must be regarded as the founder-fathers of the game as we now know it.

Arthur Fitzgerald Kinnaird (1867–1923), only son of the 10th Baron Kinnaird, of Rossie Priory, Inchtone, Perthshire, entered Trinity College, Cambridge, from Eton, in 1864. Five years later, having captained his college football team, he graduated and went into the profession of merchant banking. A tough, fearless, footballer, he played on every possible occasion, and kept going until into middle age. A member of the committee of the F.A. from 1868 he continued to serve that body—becoming Treasurer in 1877 and in 1890 President[3]—for the rest of his life. Kinnaird was a many-sided man. He enjoyed a successful professional career; he fulfilled the social requirements laid on him when he succeeded to the Barony in 1887, and he worthily filled the honourable office of Lord High Commissioner of the Church of Scotland from 1907 to 1909.

Kinnaird came from a family known for its Liberal views and practices, his father having taken a deep interest in the social problems of Scotland. He himself is known to posterity for his influence on football; and a great, and beneficial, influence it was. Kinnaird had a vision, if not of a classless society, then, at any rate, of a classless game; of a game which could bring together all kinds of men. Equality of opportunity was hinted at by the seventeenth-century aristocracy: two centuries later Kinnaird helped to give a wider significance to the term. 'I believe', he once said, 'that all rightminded people have good reason to

3. He succeeded Sir Francis Arthur Marindin (1838–1900). Marindin, of a Shropshire family and son of a vicar, was also an Etonian. He helped to form the R.E. Football Club. He enjoyed a distinguished military career and subsequently became an Inspecting Officer of Railways to the Board of Trade.

thank God for the great progress of this popular national game.'

The Anglo-Scottish match of 1870 set a precedent. There were further fixtures of similar nature on February 28 (1—1), and November 18, 1871 (England 2, 'Scotland' 1), and on February 24, 1872 (England 1, 'Scotland' 0). Overlapping this sequence was another London-Sheffield encounter, which proved to be the start of a complete, and fruitful, series. On December 2, 1871, Sheffield beat London, on the Bramall Lane ground, by 3 goals to 1.[4]

But by now another acorn had been planted. The growing competitiveness of football and the unquenched rivalries that existed threw Alcock's mind back to Harrow. At his old school there was a Football Championship, based on a knock-out system. How sensible it would be if this idea could be translated. On July 20, 1871, a resolution was passed at the F.A.: 'that it is desirable that a Challenge Cup should be established in Connection with the Association for which all clubs [belonging to the Football Association] should be invited to compete.'

On October 16 a meeting at the office of *The Sportsman* attended by delegates from Royal Engineers, Barnes, Wanderers, Harrow, Chequers, Clapham Rovers, Hampstead Heathens, Civil Service, Crystal Palace, Upton Park, Windsor Home Park, and Lausanne approved the resolution.

A silver cup was purchased at a cost of twenty pounds—towards which Queen's Park gave a guinea, approximately a sixth of the then annual income.

In the first year of the competition there were entries from Barnes, Civil Service, Crystal Palace, Clapham Rovers, Hitchin, Maidenhead, Marlow, Hampstead Heathens, Harrow Chequers, Reigate Priory, Royal Engineers, Upton Park, and the Wanderers, from the home coun-

---

4. For details and *Sheffield Independent* report, see Young, op. cit., pp. 24 ff.

ties; Donnington School, from Lincolnshire; and the intrepid Queen's Park, from Glasgow. On account of distance the latter club was exempted from competition until the semi-final.

Behind this story lay another. For some little time Queen's Park had been anxious to play against the London Wanderers. They had gone so far as to suggest that the southerners should live up to their title and, in defence of their by now formidable reputation, go north to meet the Scotsmen on technically neutral territory at Carlisle or Newcastle. The winners should have as a memento a silver cup (priced at eleven guineas) or a set of eleven silver medals. Alcock, on behalf of the Wanderers, showed some reluctance to undertake such an engagement, but kept the lines of communication open by counter-proposing home and away matches in London and Edinburgh.

The new F.A. Competition proved its own solution to this dialogue, for when it came to the semi-final round Queen's Park found themselves drawn against the Wanderers—in London. The money already collected in aid of a fixture on the Border was re-allocated; and Queen's Park (helped by the Smith Brothers, now resident in London), went to the Oval on March 4, 1872. The result of the match was a draw. Queen's Park, lacking J. J. Thomson, who had been previously injured, and with Edmiston hurt during the match, covered themselves with glory and their opponents with confusion. But, having enjoyed a convivial evening with the Wanderers at the Freemason's Tavern, to replay the tie was impossible. There were no funds available to cover the costs of travel. After the enforced withdrawal of Queen's Park, the Wanderers went on to beat the Royal Engineers in the final.

For the first time, but not for the last, the favourites lost the final. Royal Engineers had been firmly tipped, not having conceded a goal in three previous rounds. In the event the Wanderers won by a single goal, scored by 'A. H.

Chequer'. The match took place at the Oval on March 16 before almost 2,000 spectators.

The teams were:

Wanderers: C. W. Alcock, A. G. Bonsor, 'A. H. Chequer' (i.e. M. P. Betts), W. P. Crake, T. C. Hooman, E. Lubbock, A. C. Thompson, R. C. Welch, R. W. S. Vidal, C. H. R. Wollaston, and E. E. Bowen.

Royal Engineers: Captain Merriman, Captain Francis Marindin, Lieutenants Addison, Mitchell, Creswell, Renny-Tailyour, Rich, A. G. Goodwyn, Muirhead, Cotter, and Boyle.

The rules concerning this competition at this time required captains to toss for choice of ground in the first two rounds. Subsequent rounds to the semi-final were to take place at the Oval, or on such ground as the committee might select. In the final the cup-holders—only required to appear at this point in defence of their title—were allowed the choice of ground. The Wanderers won the Cup again in 1873, 1876, 1877, and 1878.

Having successfully launched the competition, the logical step was to formalise the Anglo-Scottish international fixtures. Accordingly,

'The first match of any importance that has taken place over the border according to the rules of the F.A., was played at Glasgow on Saturday, November 30, 1872. Though both elevens did all they knew no decision was arrived at, neither side being able to force their opponents' lines.'[5]

5. *The Football Annual*, 1873, p. 48. Long accounts of the match appeared in the *North British Daily Mail* and *Glasgow Herald*, for December 2. Both accounts are given in full in Robinson, op. cit., pp 49–52.

The teams were: *Scotland:* R. Gardner (capt.), goal; W. Ker, J. Taylor (backs); J. J. Thomson, James Smith, half-backs; Robert Smith, R. Leckie, A Rhind, W. M'Kinnon, J. Weir, and D. Wotherspoon. *England:* R. Barker (Herts. Rangers), goal; E. H. Greenhalgh (Notts) three-quarter back; R. C. Welch (Harrow Chequers) half-back; F. Chappell (Oxford Univ.), fly-kick; C. J. Ottaway (Oxford Univ.), Capt.

The gate on this occasion was close on 4,000, including many ladies. The Scottish team comprised only players from Queen's Park—there being but a few clubs in existence in Scotland[6]—who promptly began to look around for a private ground on which future matches of comparable importance might be played.[7]

On March 8, 1873, a return match was played at the Oval.

'The play was chiefly remarkable for the rapidity with which the respective goals were lost and won; as, when time was called, the English team had placed 4 to their credit '(Capt. Kenyon-Slaney, 2, A. G. Bonsor, G. J. Chenery), while the Northerners claimed 2 (H. W. Renny-Tailyour, W. Gibb). No less than 3,000 passed the turnstiles during the afternoon.'[8]

Nine days later another step forward in the popularisation of the game was taken when 'the London Eleven paid their first visit to the Trent Bridge Ground (Nottingham) to meet their new opponents. The immense size of the ground operated greatly to the disadvantage of the visitors; and thus it came about that no decisive result was arrived at, neither party obtaining a goal.'[9]

C. J. Chenery (Crystal Palace & Oxford Univ.); J. C. Clegg (Sheffield), and A. Kirke Smith (Oxford Univ.), middles; J. Brockbank (Oxford Univ.), right side; W. J. Maynard (1st Surrey Rifles), and J. F. Morice (Barnes), left side.

6. In addition to Queen's Park the following clubs helped to lay the foundations of the Scottish game: Ayr Thistle (1872), Clydesdale (1872), Dumbrech (1872), Eastern (1873–4), 3rd Edinburgh Rifle Volunteers (1874), Kilmarnock (1872), 1st Lanarkshire Rifle Volunteers (1874), 3rd Lanarkshire Rifle Volunteers (1874), Oxford Glasgow (1869), Rangers (1873), Renton (1873), Rovers (1873).

7. On October 21, 1873, it was reported that the Town Council had agreed to let 'Hampden Park, Mount Florida' to the club. Ten years later the construction of the Cathcart Railway made it necessary to move to another site in Hampden Park. The new ground was opened on October 18, 1884, Dumbarton being the visiting team.

8. *The Football Annual*, 1873, p. 48.

9. *The Football Annual*, 1873, p. 48: *Nottingham:* E. H. Greenhalgh

Representative matches now became general. At the end
of 1874 Surrey, captained by C. W. Alcock, drew 1—1 with
Middlesex, captained by Kinnaird; London, as usual, twice
played Sheffield—once according to London and once
according to Sheffield Rules; the Royal Engineers, pioneers
in extended touring, played against Sheffield, Derbyshire,
and Nottingham Forest; the Oxford *v.* Cambridge match
(won 2—0 by Cambridge) was ranked as a national sporting occasion. Early in 1875 Surrey beat Berkshire at the
Oval, and Berkshire drew with Bucks at Maidenhead.

Crowds varied in size, but sometimes they were very large.
When, for example, Sheffield went to Glasgow (where
they lost 0—2) the gate was 10,000. There was also a
change in the mood and character of spectators, particularly in Scotland. The record of Queen's Park had so far
been a glorious one. The club was, in fact, undefeated until
February 5, 1876, when the team lost to the Wanderers in
London. There still, however, remained an unblemished
home record. This was destroyed on December 30, 1876,
in a Scottish cup-tie against Vale of Leven. The crowd—
2,000 only, for it was an unpleasant day—was driven to the
edge of hysteria, and the hidden parts of vocabulary were
clearly and luridly exposed.

'Yelling, hooting, and calling out the players by cog-
nomens were nothing compared to the coarse and vulgar
pleasantries indulged in. Happily no ladies were present in
the vitiated atmosphere.'[10]

As was said at the beginning of this book the basic *idea* of

(captain) and W. H. Revis, half backs; A. Bright, A. W. Cursham, G.
Hayes, F. Marriott, W. Mason, G. M. Robinson, S. W. Widdowson,
C. T. Spencer, back; J. Parr, goals. *London:* A. F. Kinnaird (captain);
G. G. Kennedy (Wanderers), A. G. Benson (Old Etonians), C. J.
Chenery, A. J. Heath (Harrow Chequers), H. Heron (Uxbridge), G.
Holden (Clapham Rovers), R. K. Kingsford (Old Marlburians), R. C.
Welch (Harrow Chequers), half-back; Conrad Warner (Upton Park),
back; H. Williams (Wanderers), goals.

10. Quoted by Robinson, op. cit., p. 89.

football has remained constant. In the 1870s one part of this idea came into particular prominence because of one course of the general development of a game within an altered social framework. From the earliest times football offered opportunity for heroic performance on the part of the individual, who was able to prevail either by virtue of superior strength or by access to private resources of skill or cunning. The classic theme is of one player who takes the ball, against massed opposition, from one end of the playing area to the other—to score the winning goal. (In one of the early games in Nottingham a player scored a touch-down by reaching the opponents' line after breaking through the hedge and taking his route through the adjacent field.) The cultivation of 'dribbling' in the public schools helped to emphasise individual excellence. That this practice was encouraged may be seen as a derivant from the 'leadership' philosophy of those institutions. The style of football played at the time when the F.A. came into being was clearly described by C. W. Alcock:

'The arrangement of an eleven . . . was directed rather to strengthen the attack than to procure a stout defence. The tendency was certainly to favour the forwards rather than to encourage the backs. The formation of a team as a rule, indeed, was to provide for seven forwards, and only four players to constitute the three lines of defence. The last line was, of course, the goal-keeper, and in front of him was only one full-back, who had again before him but two half-backs, to check the rushes of the opposite forwards. Under the old style of play this formation was not so dangerous as it might appear to anyone of the modern school of football. Dribbling had been chiefly encouraged at the schools, from which the Association game really sprung, and it remained for a long time one of the chief features of an Association match. There was some little attempt at passing, of course, but a good dribbler stuck to the ball as long as he could, especially if he saw a good chance of outrunning the three backs, who formed the only obstacle he had to overcome. Long runs were frequent, and as a consequence individual skill was in a great measure the source of a football reputation.'[11]

Among the classical masters of this type of forward play were W. S. Kenyon-Slaney,[12] of Eton, the Household Brigade, and England, and R. W. S. Vidal, of Westminster and Oxford—'one of the fastest and best dribblers of the day, and well known for his sideshots at goal'. Under the conditions of occasional, friendly, and spectator-less football this method was no doubt as good as any other. Within the context of the more highly organised and competitive game, however, the accent on simple individualism often led to stalemate. For spectators—now beginning to assemble in thousands on greater occasions—the monotony of the processes was frustrating.

The credit for adding more sophisticated methods of passing goes to the Royal Engineers, to Sheffield, and to Queen's Park. 'The strong point with the home club', it was written after the Anglo-Scottish match of November 30, 1872, 'was that they played excellently well together.'[13] It is noteworthy that the Scots on this occasion employed two full-backs, which formation was adopted by the English for the next encounter, with satisfactory results, for England won by 4—2. W. E. Clegg claimed that it was the Royal Engineers who 'were the first football team to introduce the "combination" style of play'.[14] Alcock was impressed by the short passing of Queen's Park and Sheffield.[15] The seal was set on the new style by Cambridge University. In 1874 the

11. *Football, The Association Game*, p. 30.
12. 1847–1908; a prominent politician, and the subject of a memoir by W. Durnford, 1909. See pp. 8–10 for an account of football at Eton from 1860 (when John [later Bishop] Selwyn was Captain) to 1865 (House Cup-Final). For Kenyon-Slaney's later career as footballer and cricketer, see pp. 116–18.
13. *Glasgow Herald*, December 2, 1872.
14. Young, op. cit., p. 30.
15. *The Football Annual*, 1878.

team was set out in the older form for the university match; in the next year, however, the second full-back had become indispensable in order to cope with the complexities of Oxonian passing.

Although the history of football may sometimes appear as a sequence of fortuitous incidents its final emergence as a national and then a fully international game can convincingly be read as the result of disparate but interlocking circumstances outside football itself. Between 1863 and 1878 greater changes took place in respect of the game than in any comparable period of time either before or since. These, indeed, were the climactic years. 'What was ten or fifteen years ago', wrote C. W. Alcock in 1878, 'the recreation of a few has now become the pursuit of thousands—an athletic exercise, carried on under a strict system and, in many cases, by an enforced term of training, almost magnified into a profession.'[16] The last words, in 1878, were prophetic.

One of the main reasons for the quickened rate of development was transport. Inter-town, inter-regional, and inter-national matches were one consequence of the railway age. The fact that Britain was far advanced in this mode of transport is one reason for the early supremacy of the nation in football. A close relationship between the Church and the game has already been demonstrated. After the middle of the nineteenth century sporting parsons had new worlds to conquer. By now every industrial town had one or more newly built, neo-Gothic, churches, many hopefully set in working-class districts. The curate, and often the vicar, inspired by his own early education, frequently set out to claim souls with a Bible in one hand and a football in the other. The most evocative and familiar of terms used in this connection actually appeared—albeit under disparagement —in the records of Queen's Park, for April 1874. In his report for that year A. Rae, Honorary Secretary, said: 'The

16. *Football, The Association Game*, p. 33.

F

muscular Christianity to which we owe our existence—for we were evolved (that's the scientific term) from the Young Men's Christian Association—was not always in favour.'[17] The footballing (or cricketing) parson, none the less, was able to exert influence through his secular interests, and particularly in working-class districts. (This I learned at first hand.) He also became the hero figure in a new mythology invented by inferior writers of fiction, of whom A. B. Cooper (see p. 203) was one of the most prolific.

At this point a triangular pattern of church, education, and organised football takes clearer shape. As the Church of England revitalised itself during the Victorian era, so it extended its educational activities. Church schools were built, some for the rich, and some—the 'National' schools —for the poor. In 1870 the Education Act of W. E. Forster brought into being the concept of universal, elementary, education, of which the visible token was the Board School. Because of the abiding principle that aspiration is fed by imitation, schoolmasters on the lower level—often prompted by the curate or the vicar—took up the football enthusiasm of those on the higher. In 1877 there was football at Eton, but there was also football at the Black Country school of St. Luke's, Blakenhall. On November 10, 1876, the First General Meeting of the Goldthorn Football Club was held there by permission of the Vicar. On March 15 following the then headmaster wrote in his log-book: 'Let boys out earlier on Friday afternoon and they had a Football Match.' From such a beginning sprang Wolverhampton Wanderers.

In an age of progress the railways represented one facet of technological advance: electric lighting another. On October 14, 1878, a match was played at Bramall Lane, Sheffield, under electric lights.[18] On November 16, at the

17. The Y.M.C.A. of Glasgow found it difficult to accommodate itself to the fact that club meetings were held on licensed premises.
18. Reported in *Sheffield Independent*, October 15, 1878.

Oval, the Wanderers played Clapham Rovers under similar conditions.[19]

Under these circumstances football clubs multiplied, and the hegemony of the middle-class began to be questioned.

Aston Villa came into being through the energies of young Wesleyans in Birmingham in 1874. The birth of this famous club was assisted by a couple of migrant Scots— members of Queen's Park. A year later Small Heath Alliance (later Birmingham City) was formed by cricketing members of Holy Trinity Church. Football was established in Blackburn by Old Boys of the grammar school and a number of Old Malvernians. The foundation year for Blackburn Rovers was 1875. The outline of football at Turton, by Bolton, has already been seen.[20] In 1874 Christ Church, Bolton, promoted a team; within three years this had become known as Bolton Wanderers. For their inauguration Everton F.C. have the Congregational Church to thank; the germ of the present club was the St. Domingo's Sunday School team of 1878. In that year a team was started by the workers at the Newton Heath depot of the Lancashire and Yorkshire Railway; the name of this club in due course was changed to Manchester United. In 1879 the north-east was irradiated by the zest and zeal of the Sunderland School Teachers, who formed their own club, which seven years later was known as Sunderland F.C.

Other still familiar clubs which originated before 1880 are those at Crewe, Doncaster, Grimsby, Mansfield, Middlesbrough, and West Bromwich. To the same decade belonged the now defunct Accrington Stanley. In character all were different from the prominent and powerful London clubs.

For each one of these clubs there were some ten or twenty others. Thus some kind of devolution was necessary. Under

19. See *Illustrated London News*.
20. See p. 109.

the general cover and protection of the F.A.[21] local County Associations were set up—each with its own Championship Cup. The foundation of the Scottish F.A. has already been noted, and in 1874 the first Scottish Cup competition took place between Queen's Park (2) and Clydesdale (0). In 1876 a Welsh F.A. was set up; Wrexham (1) winning the first Welsh Cup Final against Druids (0) in 1878. In 1882 the establishment of an Irish F.A. followed missionary excursions from Scotland, and in 1881 Moyola Park (1) won the Irish Cup by defeating Cliftonville (0). In 1876 Wales played against Scotland. A match with England took place three years later. Ireland's first fixtures were in 1882, against England and Wales. Two years later Ireland played Scotland for the first time.

The final comment on the changing order during this era may be deduced from a scrutiny of the records of the F.A. Cup. Until 1881 the final was regularly contested by London clubs. In that year Darwen came out of Lancashire with a semi-final tie with the ultimate winners of the trophy —Old Carthusians. A year later the Old Etonians won the Cup. Their opponents were unfamiliar on the London scene. They were Blackburn Rovers. A year later the crowd of 8,000 at the final did not need to ask where Blackburn was. What they wondered at was that such a town could send another team to the Oval. This team, Blackburn Olympic, beat the Old Etonians, after extra time 2—1. The next year Blackburn Rovers came back, to defeat Queen's Park, Glasgow, also by 2—1. Blackburn won the Cup in the next year, and the next. So was a revolution accomplished and symbolised.

21. See p. 145 f.

10

Social Stresses and the Emergence of the Professional

As had been seen, what had previously been a matter of Football within an astonishingly brief period—of six or seven years—had achieved a wide popularity. In a sense this was by way of being a return to first principles: the pastime of the masses was in process of being restored to the masses. There was, however, this difference: it was, relatively speaking, now both refined and scientific. The game was an art, and as such was invested with artistic properties, which brought it into a particular relationship with spectators, who now had their own part to perform.

Under such circumstances certain conditions are constant. The spectator, who pays to see a spectacle, wants to see the best rather than the worst. Indeed he is entitled to expect a reasonable return on his investment. This, in turn, adds responsibility to the performers—a responsibility which is not lessened or increased by their status. Secondly, but conjointly, the spectator, already fired by parochial loyalties and prejudices, wants to see his own team win.

It is always easy to be wise after the event. Beforehand it is difficult to determine what ought to be done even when certain consequences are foreseeable. The legislators of football would have been saved many headaches if they had stood back in the 1870s to study the pattern evolving from their own actions. On the whole they suffered from the inescapable difficulties inherent in their own antecedents. The 'two nations' of Disraeli, though deplored by him, were accepted by the majority of Victorians. The gentlemen, it was axiomatic, knew best. So, on the football field, they did, until the Old Etonians were compelled to surrender the F.A. Cup to Blackburn Olympic. This was not only a blow to the *ancien régime* but also to the South of England. It was soon made apparent that there was another interpretation of a two-nations theory: there was the south, and there was the north. Football intensified this division.

The factor of the spectator has been noticed. We now begin to see how organisers responded. On the legislative side recognition of the absurdity of variations in playing rules brought Sheffield and London into harmony. In 1866 the London F.A., under pressure from Sheffield, accepted the need for a tape[1] between the goal-posts. Six years later the London F.A. agreed to the replacement of its existing Rule 7 by the following clause, proposed from Sheffield:

'When the ball is kicked over the bar of the goal, it must be kicked off by the side behind whose goal it went, within six yards from the limit of their goal. The side who thus kick the ball are entitled to a fair kick-off in whatever way they please; the opposite side not being allowed to approach within six yards of the ball. When the ball is kicked behind the goal-line, a player of the opposite side to that which kicked it out shall kick it from the nearest corner flag. No player to be allowed within six yards of the ball until kicked.'

Meanwhile the F.A. Cup Competition was quickening acceptance of uniformity. The duration of a match as one and a half hours was finally determined. Neutral referee and umpires were installed as indispensable officers. Handling the ball while in play was absolutely reserved only to the goalkeeper. Infringements were made liable to free-kicks (as at Sheffield). In 1871 the size of the ball was specified—in circumference not less than twenty-seven inches and not

1. In fact the Secretary of the Sheffield Club had proposed a *cross-bar*. This was permitted in 1875, but not made obligatory until after a conference held in Manchester on December 6, 1882.

more than twenty-eight inches. In 1877, as a result of letters from representatives of the Manchester Football Club and Marlborough College, the overriding authority of the F.A. Rules was generally acknowledged. Thereupon the Sheffield Rules passed into history, but not before they had materially affected the structure of the modern game.

The acceptance of a common code—with as few opportunities for inventive interpretation as possible—meant, of course, that all spectators in England were now able to think in common terms. In Scotland independence in certain particulars was maintained for some years to come.

An important point of dissension between the Associations had been the method of throw-in permitted. According to English usage one-handed throwing had been in order. Specialists of the long throw, particularly when allowed a preliminary run, had been able to reach almost any part of the field. In Scotland, on the other hand, two-handed throwing, with the ball first taken back over the head, was compulsory. In 1882 the Scottish method was adopted at a conference held in Manchester in order to remove obstacles in the way of a tolerably peaceful coexistence. Prior to such a settlement the future of football on an international level had been at hazard.

The status of international football—within the British Isles—was ensured when in 1885 the four national Associations together formed the International Football Association Board.

Meanwhile other developments were in process. We go back to Blackburn. The Rovers who played against the Old Etonians in the Final of 1882 were initially influenced by the public school game. Three notable members of the team, Fred Hargreaves, John Hargreaves, and D. H. Greenwood, had all learned the game at Malvern College. In the formative years of the club the Harrow strain had been introduced by A. N. Hornby. Hornby played for the Rovers when in 1878 they undertook an engagement against Partick

Thistle, for whom at full-back was a player of particular excellence. His name was Fergus Suter. In the Rovers' first Cup Final team there, partnering Hugh McIntyre at full-back, was Fergus Suter, who came to Blackburn by way of Darwen. As for Hugh McIntyre, he too had come from Glasgow. So too had J. Douglas and J. Brown among the forwards.

Examination of the constitution of the principal teams of Lancashire at this time would lead to conclusions from which deductions could easily be made. Most of the clubs had a core of Scottish 'professors'. Immediately, the reason is not far to seek: the Scotsmen came to improve the teams. Why they really came, however, is another matter, intelligible in economic terms. During the 1870s a serious decline in agricultural prosperity coincided with an industrial boom. The manufacturing industries of the North and the Midlands needed every man on whom hands could be laid. Expansion of communications also meant vacancies for labourers on the railways and in the docks. Such conditions encourage immigration. The Irish, the Welsh, and the Scots poured into England. Enterprising football clubs saw in what way this form of brain-drain could be turned to their advantage.

Advertisements in the Glasgow newspapers drew attention to jobs in Darwen, Bolton, Blackburn, Preston, Accrington, and so on.

'The Scots crowded every football team in Lancashire, and in one particular case only a single Englishman was included in the team, who was said to have felt lonely.'[2]

Scottish clubs were alarmed, but not even the surreptitious remuneration of players could staunch the flow.

From one angle the situation—exacerbated by the competitive efficiency of the Lancashire teams—was scandalous. There were inducements. There were under-cover subsidies. There was even a tendency to take football seriously. In

   2. Robinson, op. cit., p. 224.

1883 the Blackburn Olympic team[3] prepared for their Cup
Final by training at Blackpool. In the same year Blackburn
Rovers and Darwen, finalists in the Lancashire F.A. Cup,
went into pre-match retreats at Morecambe and Blackpool
respectively.

One may smile wryly at this point. The amateur credentials of many European teams have been suspect from time
to time, particularly those of army players, who, it was con-
tended, were at least given special privileges in respect of
training and time for training. One may entertain suspicions
that the Royal Engineers of the 1870s owed some of their
success to such advantages.

As this transition took place polite eyes were averted.
When it was too late to do anything effective moral strictures were applied. There was much muddled thinking. The
Simon-pure line was that since football was a game it should
be its own reward. All right, but what about those whose
skill was not supported by ample private funds, and what
about the spectators and their rights? Everyone in Lancashire knew that many footballers did not go unrewarded.
No one admitted it.

A committee of the F.A., consisting of A. F. Kinnaird,
J. H. Cofield, T. Hindle, J. R. Harvey, N. L. Jackson,
M. P. Betts, and C. W. Alcock, was set up to examine the
matter of professionalism. In 1881 the Lancashire F.A. for-
bade absolutely the signing-on of Scottish footballers,
whether drawn south by industry or football. In 1883
Accrington were expelled from the F.A., having been found
guilty of giving an inducement to one Beresford—
'formerly of Staveley, now of Church'—to join them. On
January 19, 1884, 12,000 spectators turned up at Preston

3. Hacking, dentist's assistant; S. A. Warburton, plumber; J. T.
Ward, cotton operative; W. Astley, weaver; T. Gibson, iron-moulder;
J. Hunter, Scotsman of single-minded purpose in respect of football;
T. Dewhurst and J. Yates, weavers; A. Matthews, picture-framer;
J. Costley, spinner; G. Wilson, formerly of Sheffield and of no particu-
lar occupation.

to see a cup-tie against Upton Park. After a drawn game the London club lodged a protest against the inclusion of un-disguised professionals in the Preston side. Preston were thrown out of the competition, but William Sudell, a cotton manufacturer and a man of substance and influence, who had founded the North End, put the cat among the pigeons. Professionalism, he said, was known to be common; more-over, he protested that it was in no way injurious to the best intentions of the game.[4]

The crisis heightened. Great Lever, with six Scotsmen and a Welshman in their team, and Burnley, with seven Scots, were suspended. Meanwhile the Birmingham F.A., having looked at the local situation, disqualified certain players of Walsall and Birmingham St. George's. By now, of course, events had moved too fast for any reversion to what had been. In any case, conditions had so altered that reversion would have been impossible. The hand of the F.A. was forced.

On October 10, 1884, Sudell of Preston convened a meeting of Lancashire representatives at the Commercial Hotel, Bolton. There was also a meeting in Blackburn. Meanwhile the Scottish F.A. was having to fight on two fronts. Not only was it necessary to prevent players from going south but also to put down the evil at home. In a Puritan land ideological principles were at stake. Those who offended against dogma were punished. On October 21 Heart of Midlothian were expelled from the Scottish F.A., it having been proved that two of their players, McNee and Maxwell, were in fact professionals. The two players suffered a two-year suspension.[5]

As this was transpiring, Sudell and his accomplices were collating their views and formulating resolutions. A third

4. Sudell brought 'Nick' Ross, captain of Hearts, to Preston, where he was given employment as a slater. There followed G. Drummond, S. Robertson, D. Russell, J. Graham, S. Thomson, J. Ross, J. Gordon, excellent players whose teaching inspired apt local pupils.
5. See Albert Mackie, *The Hearts*, London, 1959, pp. 77 f.

meeting therefore took place in Manchester on October 30, at which it was proposed to form a break-away union to be known as the British Football Association—'which shall embrace clubs and players of every nationality'. Support for the proposed B.F.A. came from twenty-eight clubs, with the exception of Sunderland and Aston Villa all from Lancashire.

The F.A. meanwhile sent out forms for its member clubs to complete and sign. These forms required statements detailing the circumstances of imported players in considerable detail. They were, to say the least of it, inquisitorial and as such unlikely to be given conscientious attention. At a sub-committee of the F.A. held in Manchester in November, 1884, C. W. Alcock, taking the bull by the horns, moved:

'That it is expedient to legalise professionalism under stringent conditions, but that no paid player shall take part in the Association Cup Competitions.'

The *Manchester Guardian* saw this as the beginning of the end. But it misread the basic points at issue. What, it may be asked, was—or is—equality?

'The admission into amateur ranks of professional football players is possibly the beginning of the end in an important social movement with which everybody must sympathise. The idea has been to bring together all classes in football and athletics on terms of perfect equality. With the introduction of professionals a new departure is taken. The first effect of the change will be to make the Rugby game the aristocratic one, and the Association game will probably almost die out in the South of England, where it is already declining in favour. Again, a fresh excuse will be given for a tendency to exclusiveness which is even now sufficiently apparent. The Universities of Oxford and Cambridge have for some time past picked the clubs with which they deign to compete, and an example of this kind may be widely followed. So also in athletics; I notice that the Oxonians do not allow all athletes to compete at their "open events", but confine these to members of the Army and Navy, the Civil Service, and the London Athletic Club. Perhaps this disruption in both football and athletics was inevitable, and perhaps it may turn out to be slight and unimportant; but the indications of failure in a really great experiment should not pass unnoticed.'[6]

The fact that the *Manchester Guardian* could thus accurately foretell the shape of things to come reflected a social division that was inevitably intensified in the high noon of capitalism. The fight for the recognition of the professional footballer was part of a larger fight: behind it lay the activities of the increasingly important Trades Union organisations, and political manifestations such as those of the Parliamentary Committee of the Trades Union Congress, the Labour Representative League, and the developing philosophy of Liberal Socialism. All these characterised the period under review. In the course of time Association football, its roots spreading in democratic soil, became a symbol both of aspiration and emancipation.

The F.A. Council of the 1880s was composed of honourable men, but often they were men of prejudice. They were, or regarded themselves, as patricians, heirs to the doctrine of 'leadership', and so law-givers by at least semi-divine right. They acted according to their rights. The matter of professionalism had been brought into the open. The Scottish F.A., having already declared itself, stayed adamant until 1893, in which year—after purges, pardons, and recriminations worthy of a central European ideological revolution—the inevitability of professionalism was accepted. The County Associations expressed horror when they saw what they recognised as a not very thin end of the wedge. On January 19, 1885, a special General Meeting of the F.A. took place in London. The proposals brought for-

6. November 30, 1884.

ward by Alcock were rudely rejected. They were rejected again in March.

By now the condition of the game was farcical. The offending clubs continued blatantly to offend. Some, un-certain as to the consequences of their actions, withdrew from the F.A. Competition.

For the second year running Queen's Park were in the final of the English Cup.[7] For the second year running they were beaten by Blackburn Rovers. Brown and Forest scored the goals in Blackburn's 2—1 victory in 1885. Queen's Park complained that on neither occasion had they a full side, and that in the first match there had been some indifferent refereeing by Major Marindin. A good deal of feeling was being generated. Behind it lay the unresolved contention.

On July 20, 1885, another Special General Meeting of the F.A. was called at Anderton's Hotel. The Committee en-trusted with the task of putting recommendations on the question of professionals set out its terms. Proposed by Dr. E. S. Morley (strongly backed by R. P. Gregson, Secretary of the Lancashire F.A.), the following clauses were carried by a majority of 35—5. A number of delegates remained neutral.

'Professionals shall be allowed to compete in all Cups, County and Inter-Association matches, provided they be qualified as follows:

'(a) in Cup matches by birth or residence for two (2) years last past within six (6) miles of the ground or head-quarters of the Club for which they play.

'(b) In County matches as defined in Rule XI, which

7. Since Queen's Park had been regular candidates for the F.A. Cup since its inception a number of ties had taken place on their territory. On December 1, 1883, the Manchester Club were beaten by 15–0. A year later Aston Villa were defeated by 6–1. So far as the Scottish Cup was concerned Queen's Park were the holders from 1874 to 1876, 1880 to 1882, and in 1884, 1886, 1890 and 1893.

applies equally to all players whether amateur or professional.

'(c) In Inter-Association matches by *bona fide* membership for the two (2) years last past of some Club belonging to one of the competing Associations.

'No professional shall be allowed to serve on any Association Committee or represent his own or any other club at any meeting of the Football Association.

'No professional shall be allowed to play for more than one Club in any one season without special permission of the Committee of the Football Association.

'All professionals shall be annually registered in a book to be kept by the Committee of the Football Association, and no professional shall be allowed to play unless he has been so registered.'

That this bears a close relationship to the provisions of cricket is hardly surprising. Alcock had been Honorary Secretary to the Surrey County Cricket Club since 1882. The Scottish F.A. heard the news and noted that sixty-eight players were professional footballers in England. The list was published and a *pronunciamento* issued: none of these players should play in Scotland without special permission. The spirit of John Knox walked again and in that year's report of the Scottish F.A. it was written: 'Taken altogether a good work has begun, a good foundation laid, and if the matter is properly followed up the evil will be kept out of the Association.'

Inflexibility in this dogma was to be found also in Sheffield. Pierce Dix, of the Sheffield Club, summarised the feelings of his associates when he opposed the F.A. proposals: 'Professionalism in football', he thundered, 'is an evil, and as such should be repressed.'

The legalisation of a situation that in any case was not to be altered represented a victory for common sense, and was a reflection of ideas that had begun to bear fruit elsewhere as a result of the Reform Acts of 1884 and 1885, and Joseph

Chamberlain's 'New Radicalism'. At the same time it placed the English F.A. in an unassailable position. That is to say, the Committee assumed powers of ultimate control over the conditions of employment of a body of men that was increasing in number year by year. The professional footballer was dependent on the committee of a club—usually controlled by a local worthy with funds at his disposal—for employment. Without any security other than that afforded by the preservation of both skill and health, and conditioned to an acceptance of social inferiority, he was placed in a state of subordination. Since he was also subject to control by a local Association as well as by the F.A. a deep sense of inferiority was built into his calling. A long catalogue of literature exists to emphasise the doctrine of the 'proper station in life' as applied to football. The player could only assert himself by a direct appeal to the crowd. The story of the professional footballer is that of every other entertainer. Minstrels, waits, actors, performing musicians, at various times all had to struggle to get off the ground. In each case they were helped by a generous measure of support from their wider public.

The crowd, to whom football was a means of protest and of emotional release, a sublimation of group consciousness and local patriotism, applauded skill on the one hand and vigour on the other. If in doubt, however, the preference was for the latter: it was, being more elemental, easier to understand. The interaction of crowd and players under the pressure of strong partisanship and the hidden discords left as a legacy of the debate on professionalism are all illustrated by an Anglo-Scottish match of October 30, 1886. This was a Third Round (First Series) match in the F.A. Cup, between Queen's Park and Preston North End, and was played at Hampden Park.

Preston North End,[8] normally exponents of cultured and

8. Between 1883 and 1889 Preston won 294 games and lost only 35, scoring 1,502 goals against 385.

delicate play, forsook their normal style and battered their way to a 3—0 victory. Five minutes before the end of the match, the issue already settled, Jimmy Ross brought down the Queen's Park centre-forward, Harrower, from behind. Harrower was considerably dazed and was taken into the pavilion.

'Then the game was finished. The indignant crowd now surged into the field, maddened with passion, shouting, waving sticks, umbrellas, and such like weapons, and the North End team were at once engulfed by a living sea, which rolled round them in angry surging waves that threatened to engulf them at any moment. Ross was the centre of attraction . . .'

Disguised in a long ulster and with a hat pulled well down over his face, Ross was spirited through the demonstrating crowd, dressed, and then pushed through a back window into safety.

'When the crowd learned how they had been baulked, they dispersed sullenly, and the ground, which that day had held fifteen thousand precious souls, was soon hushed in the stillness of the night, and there was nothing left to tell of the great battle that had been fought and lost, or of the mighty upheaval of public spirit which had characterised the close of the game.'⁹

A comic turn was given to the occasion by the fact that before the match Preston had thought of objecting to the validity of the tie on the grounds that Queen's Park, an amateur team, had, in apparent contravention of the rules, employed a professional trainer, or 'rubber-down', one Fairley. It was pointed out that Preston had no trainer, each man looking after his own fitness.

The upshot was that after that season Scottish clubs withdrew from the English competition.¹⁰ On May 10, 1887, the Scottish F.A. decreed 'that clubs belonging to this Asso-

9. Robinson, op. cit., p. 171.
10. Scottish entries for 1886-7 were: Third Lanark, Heart of

ciation shall not be members of any other National Association'.

If the arrangement of participation in English football had been maintained for another year it is just conceivable that a British League (a topic for discussion in recent years) might have come into being.

The progress of the F.A. Cup Competition over the years had demonstrated two things: that professional players in general were superior to non-professional; that some few clubs were markedly better than others.

With the wages of professionals to meet budgets needed planning. The main source of income was gate-money (supplemented already, but only to a minor extent, by 'prize draws'), and this, obviously, depended on 'gates'. A cup-tie, whether national or local, drew a generally good attendance, so did a local derby, or a fixture against a good club. But there was no design in the fixture-lists. It took a Scotsman to rationalise the irrational.

William McGregor (1847–1911), a native of Perthshire, arrived in Birmingham in the 1870s with a love of games in general and a scrupulous mind. Established as a draper, he was persuaded by a fellow Scot, George Ramsay, to identify himself with the then nascent Aston Villa club. Under McGregor's guidance football in Birmingham prospered. McGregor, recognised as a logician in the classic Scottish mould, was invested with regional authority and became the spokesman for the Birmingham F.A. In 1885 he spoke to effect on the crisis in football affairs and put his weight behind the proposal to legalise the professional. Quite simply, this was a matter of honour McGregor found the subterfuges obtaining intolerable.

That business settled McGregor refused to assume that thereby everything else was in order. His thinking took posi-

Midlothian, Renton, Queen's Park, Rangers, Cowlairs, Partick Thistle. Rangers reached the semi-final, to lose (1–3) to Aston Villa, at Crewe.

tive shape, and on March 2, 1888, he despatched a circular letter. This, a historic document, read as follows:

'Every year it is becoming more and more difficult for football clubs of any standing to meet their friendly engagements, and even arrange friendly matches. The consequence is that at the last moment, through cup-tie interferences, clubs are compelled to take on teams who will not attract the public.

'I beg to tender the following suggestion as a means of getting over the difficulty. That ten or twelve of the most prominent clubs in England combine to arrange home-and-home [*sic*] fixtures each season, the said fixtures to be arranged at a friendly conference about the same time as the International conference. This combination might be known as the Association Football Union, and could be managed by a representative from each club.

'Of course, this is in no way to interfere with the National Association, even the suggested matches might be played under cup-tie rules. However, this is a detail. My object in writing to you at present is merely to draw your attention to the subject, and to suggest a friendly conference to discuss the matter more fully.

'I would take it as a favour if you would kindly think the matter over, and make whatever suggestion you may deem necessary. I am only writing to the following: Blackburn Rovers,[11] Bolton Wanderers,[12] Preston North End,[13] West Bromwich Albion,[14] and Aston Villa, and should like to hear what other clubs you would suggest.

I am, yours very truly,
William McGregor

11. Cup-winners in 1884–5–6.
12. Winners of Lancashire Cup (defeating Blackburn Rovers in the Final), Bolton Charity Cup, and Derbyshire Charity Cup, 1886.
13. Semi-finalists, F.A. Cup, 1887; losing finalists, 1888.
14. Defeated by Blackburn Rovers in F.A. Cup Final, 1886, and by Aston Villa, 1887. Cup-winners, 1888.

'P.S. How would Friday, March 23, 1888, suit for the friendly conference at Anderton's Hotel, London?'

McGregor's letter, of course, was, if unintentionally, a provocation. The main point of provocation was picked up by the astute J. J. Bentley, the able and energetic Secretary of Bolton Wanderers. To the preliminary list he asked that these other clubs should be added: Wolverhampton Wanderers, Accrington, Burnley, Halliwell, Notts County, Mitchell St. George's (of Birmingham), Stoke, and Old Carthusians. But the gesture to the South and to the amateur side of the game was not taken up. On the eve of the Cup Final representatives of the two finalists, and of Accrington, Burnley, Wolverhampton, Stoke, Notts, Bolton, Blackburn, and Aston Villa, came to Anderton's Hotel in answer to a summons.

McGregor's suggestion was approved in principle. The proposed title of the organisation-to-be was rejected on the grounds that it could cause confusion with the Rugby Football Union. McGregor, haunted by old memories of the Solemn League and Covenant and disturbed by the activities of Irish patriots in the National League and the Land League, demurred when the word 'League' was mentioned. Bowing to majority feeling, however, he buried his prejudices and accepted the definition. He became first President of the Football League, remaining in office until 1894, with Harry Lockett, of Stoke, as Honorary Secretary.

On April 17 a further meeting took place in Manchester. Although there were numerous applicants for membership of the new League, it was determined, in view of the fact that the maximum number of available Saturdays appeared to be twenty-two, that there should be only twelve founder-members. These were:

Accrington, Aston Villa, Blackburn Rovers, Bolton Wanderers, Burnley, Derby County, Everton, Notts

County, Preston North End, Stoke, West Bromwich Albion, Woverhampton Wanderers.

That made six midland and six Lancashire clubs, all with professional players.

The first League matches were played on September 8, 1888. Some things were left to work themselves out—at the risk of some confusion. It was not until November 21 that details of the points system were finalised. By then, however, it was clear that whatever the mathematics one particular team would emerge as *primus inter pares*—which alliterates with 'proud' and also with Preston.

At the end of the season the table showed this final summary:

	P	W	D	L	For	Goals Against	Points
Preston North End	22	18	4	0	74	15	40
Aston Villa	22	12	5	5	61	43	29
Wolverhampton Wanderers	22	12	4	6	50	37	28
Blackburn Rovers	22	10	6	6	66	45	26
Bolton Wanderers	22	10	2	10	63	59	22
West Bromwich Albion	22	10	2	10	40	46	22
Accrington	22	6	8	8	48	48	20
Everton	22	9	2	11	35	46	20
Burnley	22	7	3	12	42	62	17
Derby County	22	7	2	13	41	60	16
Notts County	22	5	2	15	39	73	12
Stoke	22	4	4	14	26	51	12

11

The Power Game

Football came into the closing decade of the nineteenth century with a number of well-marked lines, independent, but for ever crossing and inter-acting. There was one line, of the Football League, increasingly making a stronger mark on the plan of the game. The League was controlled by realists—men like Sudell, of Preston; Lockett, of Stoke; J. J. Bentley, who had a controlling influence in more than one Lancashire organisation; William Allt, the shoemaker, of Wolverhampton; and, of course, McGregor. Of lower middle- or working-class origin, these men, who had lifted themselves into positions of relative prosperity, and local respectability, had few illusions. They were, therefore, tough in negotiation, and rigorous in principle and method. Fired by one overriding ambition—not to fail in any under-taking—they steered the League to stability and security.

Men like these controlled the professional clubs. The Presidents and Chairmen understood the players under their control because, for the most part, they had themselves emerged from not dissimilar backgrounds. Certainly they spoke the same earthy language. Despite this, or because of this, they ruled autocratically. The relation of the profes-sional player to his employers was well defined: as of man to master.

But committees did not only have their staffs to con-sider. There were the spectators. On the whole the midland and northern clubs did well in improving amenities. The grounds were levelled and terraced; refreshment facilities were provided; and the stands that went up in the middle of industrial communities were often not of less splendour than any other buildings within a radius of several miles. Assisted by generous reporting in the provincial papers, as well as special Saturday-night issues, and such helpful supplementary guides as *The Sporting Chronicle* (started in (1888) and, later, *The Athletic News* (1896), a communal interest was warmed with committed partisanship. The football ground, where weekly clashing loyalties were resolved in dramatic crises, and where favourite players were invested with the mystical aura of great actors, was a theatre—sometimes the theatre of cruelty.

In the spring of each year the annual epic was put on for the benefit of a London audience. From the time of the institution of professional football the southern clubs fell out of serious consideration in the later stages of the F.A. Cup. In 1889 Preston North End defeated Wolverhampton Wanderers, at the Oval, by 3—0; in the year following Blackburn Rovers defeated Sheffield Wednesday by 6—1. In 1891 Blackburn came once more to win. This time their victims were Notts County, who lost by 1—3. The next year saw West Bromwich Albion beat their near neighbours, the Villa, by 3—0. Crowds had gone up each year, reaching 25,000 in 1892. When in the season following the venue was moved to Fallowfield, Manchester, the spectators officially numbered 45,000, although there were probably twice as many present. Wolverhampton Wanderers beat Everton in this match by a single goal.

These successful teams blended skill with endeavour, personalities with honest craftsmen. Sternly trained, they based achievement on method and resolution.

Running through all this complex of football activity were the lines of north and south. Professional football showed England as a divided country, and regional antipathies were readily brought to the surface. There was, of course, also a separate and significant line of Scottish independence written into the game.

Within the texture of football the line of amateurism was deeply imbedded. By the end of the 1880s, however, this definition was something of a paradox. For the amateur had in many cases become a kind of vocational, if not indeed professional, amateur.

As has been suggested on many occasions in this book, football was more than 'a thing in itself'. It was, from the earliest days, a mirror of the times, a reflection of society. The Renaissance ideal of the all-round man, with its corollary of the élite of such men to act as rulers, filtered through the educational system to come out in parody in the 'public school' concept of the later nineteenth century. All-rounders fitted well into the political structure, with this reservation: that lack of expert knowledge in any one field qualified the majority of the upper middle class to superintend operations in all. Amateurism became, therefore, a virtue in itself.

So far as games were concerned, this allowed much indulgence in the national vice of hypocrisy. The amateur cricketer, or the amateur footballer, was viewed as one sustained by a moral superiority. Players who were paid were inferior as people to those who were not paid. There is a deep symbolism wrapped up in this axiom. Money, 'an extreme and specialised type of ritual', as Dr. Mary Douglas puts it in *Purity and Danger* (1966), represents a kind of disorder, and disorder a kind of uncleanness. Nowhere is this psychological truism more apparent than in the field of sport. The professional was dirty, the amateur was clean. The feeling that this was true was enhanced by circumstances. Professional football, in the eyes of an influential minority, belonged exclusively to industrial Britain. The muck that made the money rubbed off on to the game and its practitioners. Thus when the English national side travelled, the amateurs were, for virtue's sake, kept apart in superior accommodation.

The amateur is dead: long live the amateur. The Old Etonians and the Old Carthusians passed from the F.A. Cup. Lament for the passing of the old order provoked some hardy spirits to fight a rearguard action. In 1883 N. L. Jackson canvassed the leading public schools and university footballers with a view to establishing a new club—an exclusive club. The aim was twofold. Of the twelve international matches played against Scotland since 1872 England had won only two. Two had been drawn. In 1881, at the Oval, Scotland scored 6 goals against England's 1. In 1882 the score at Glasgow was 5—1 in Scotland's favour. On the national level, backed by the purposefulness of Queen's Park, the Scots held the mastery in combined play. Jackson was convinced, not without reason, that England could improve were matters dealt with in a more logical manner. More opportunity for the best (amateur) players to play together should yield dividends.

The club that was Jackson's brain-child was christened the Corinthians. The basis of the team was the current university sides. Thus it was a prelude to the latter-day short-lived Pegasus. From 1883 to the end of the century the Corinthians proved a match for the best professional sides. In 1884, for instance, they were able to defeat Blackburn Rovers by 8—1. Two years later the England team, with nine Corinthians, beat Scotland 5—0. Eight years later a complete team of Corinthians represented England against Wales and won 5—1. In the following year an all-Corinthian combination drew 1—1 with Wales. With one exception—when Queen's Park took their place—Corinthians played as 'the best amateur team' against 'the best professional team' in the annual match for the Dewar Cup (instituted 1898). Their most celebrated feat was to extinguish the talented Bury side of 1904 by 10—3.

Why, then, were these amateurs—now part of the legend of football—supreme? The answer is not far to seek. First, the Corinthians were not without consistent teaching in the principles of the game, from youth up. They had enjoyed organised football long before the majority of the professionals of that era. Second, they were better fed, better housed, and protected by proper medical advice.[1] Third, they were in the happy position of being eligible for praise whether they won or lost. The professionals were taught that to play against the gentlemen-amateurs was a privilege.

'When one is at school, there is the feeling that the sense of pride in one's school can never be surpassed; when the schoolboy goes to the 'Varsity, he finds that love of his school is swallowed up in an altogether stronger feeling—a sentiment almost of reverence—towards his University; it is a feeling which nerves him to do all things for the honour of alma mater. Then the 'Varsity name goes down, and the feeling is carried on with regard to the Corinthian F.C. They know that they have the honour to be members of a club without rival, and their one desire is to help it to retain that position.'[2]

No doubt the unreasoning loyalties thus described (of the same order as the cults of nationalism that have destroyed half the world) are commendable in that in some cases they act as sublimation, but they contain palpable hypocrisies, and set in motion a train of analogous protestations that have in recent years wrought havoc on the football fields of Britain (and the world). The 'one-eyed' club loyalist, unconsciously the heir to the negative side of the so-called Corinthian spirit, has turned out to be a menace.

There was, of course, a positive aspect of Corinthian endeavour. So long as the members of the club regarded football as an occupation that allowed an equality of talent (and not all of them looked at it in this way), and

1. Cf. passage concerning football and social environment on pp. 207 f.
2. Stanley S. Harris, 'The Famous Corinthian Football Club, 1883–1906', in *The Book of Football*, 1906, pp. 206 f.

not as a subtle means of achieving advancement within profession or business, all was well. At their best the Corinthian footballers brought to the game a sense of style and, unaffected by the attritional battles of the League system, a touch of abandon. The names of the outstanding Corinthians of the nineteenth century still stand in a haze of romantic glory: L. C. H. Palairet, H. K. and R. E. Foster, S. M. J. Woods, Captain E. G. Wynyard, and C. B. Fry (the *beau ideal* of the scholar-sportsman), who also excelled as cricketers; A. M. and P. M. Walters, W. N. Cobbold, and G. O. Smith, all bred in the football tradition of Charterhouse.

In the days when full-back play was generally destructive the Walters brothers—big men and unafraid of physical contact—introduced new ideas. Being fast runners they could, when things were going well, play up-field, almost in the modern manner, and yet have time for retreat under the threat of pressure. The way out of an impasse for those with fewer talents was generally through vigorous kicking, the ultimate destination of the ball being left to chance. A. M. and P. M. Walters were pioneers of defensive interpassing and a talent for holding the ball perplexed opposing forwards brought up on more direct methods. P. M. Walters went to Oxford, A. M. to Cambridge University. In 1884 they played against each other in the university match. Both gave up the game after their younger brother died as the result of an accident at football in 1890.[3]

Cobbold, also a Cambridge footballer, preserved the individualist traditions of the old days and shone as a

3. A Minute of the Queen's Park committee meeting of November 28, 1890, ran as follows: 'Reference was made to the sad death of Mr. H. M. Walters, resulting from an accident on the football field, and, considering the close and friendly intercourse that had so long existed between our club and Messrs. P. M. and A. M. Walters and the Corinthian club, it was moved that we send a wreath to the funeral, and a letter of condolence, extending our sympathy to the members of the family in their sad bereavement.'

'dribbler'. Forceful enough to deter the unwelcome attentions of a defender who believed in attacking the man rather than abstracting the ball, Cobbold rarely made use of his physical strength. He combined patience with cunning and believed in working his way towards goal. He was a fine shot, 'and if only he had two feet of day-light to aim at, he seldom missed the mark'.

G. O. Smith, of slighter physique, was compelled to think his way into the front rank. As it was he became the *nonpareil* of Victorian centre-forwards—a position as difficult satisfactorily to fill as now. Although a dangerous shot, Smith commanded the offensive by his skill in distribution. Unconvinced by the need to score all the goals himself, he was expert in drawing the opposing defence around him and then sliding the ball with unerring accuracy to an unmarked colleague. In 1898 Smith played in the Corinthian team that drew with Sheffield United, who that season were champions of the League, for the Dewar Shield. Both Smith and C. Wreford-Brown (later one of the notable legislators of the F.A.) of that Corinthian team signed amateur forms for Sheffield United in case the United ran out of players before the end of the season. A. M. Walters played for England on nine occasions, his brother on thirteen; Cobbold also won nine caps, while Smith earned nineteen. Few professionals could better the record of these men, only Ernest Needham, of Sheffield United, matching them for consistency. And he represented England no more than sixteen times.

During the last decade of the Victorian era the pressure of popularity necessitated both technical and administrative changes. In 1889 although the umpires were 'to decide all disputed points when appealed to' the referee was allowed greater powers. In addition to adjudicating, if need be, between the umpires, he was now expected to caution players of 'violent conduct' (which had increased as a result of the competitiveness of League matches), if necessary to order them from the field, and to report them to the appropriate national Association. In 1891 the penalty kick, proposed by the Irish Association, was introduced and the sole judge of whether an offence merited this sanction was the referee. In this same year the umpires' powers were reduced and their function was now to act as 'linesmen'. Also in 1891 goal-nets were added to the properties of the game. They were the invention of J. A. Brodie, City Engineer of Liverpool, and were first used in the North *v.* South match played at Nottingham in January. J. J. Bentley, of Bolton, approved the innovation, and soon afterwards introduced goal-nets for a league match between the Wanderers and Notts Forest. The F.A. gave its consent to the principle in February, making nets compulsory when an agreement was reached with the patentee concerning the price to be paid by clubs. In 1892 goal-nets were installed at the Oval for the Cup Final between West Bromwich Albion and Aston Villa.

During 1891 one of those meetings took place which might have been a turning-point in history but was not. On April 20 there was a match at Olive Grove, Sheffield, between the Football League and the Football Alliance—a combination of already established or newly formed and aspiring clubs that, having no opportunity of finding places within the exclusive League, formed their own competition in the autumn of 1889. The Alliance demonstrated that the aspirations of the clubs in membership were not without some justification by playing a 1—1 draw with a powerful League side. After the match it was proposed at a League committee meeting that a new disposition of English clubs should be made; with three classes, each comprising twelve constituent clubs,[4] and among them southern nominees. Had

4. The clubs were: Notts Forest, Newton Heath (f. *c.* 1878, now Manchester United), Small Heath (formerly Small Heath Alliance, f. 1875, now Birmingham City), Sheffield Wednesday, Burton Swifts, Crewe Alexandra (f. 1877), Ardwick (formerly West Gorton, f. 1880, and reconstituted as Machester City, 1894), Bootle, Lincoln City,

this been adopted, it is possible that the subsequent frenzies of congested fixture-lists might have been avoided—to the great benefit of the game. In the event the proposal was rejected, the necessary three-fourths majority not being forthcoming. However, a Second Division of fourteen clubs was established (the First Division had been enlarged to accommodate the same number prior to the 1891–2 season), so that there were now twenty-eight clubs taking part in high-level and national League football in England.

The weakness of the then League was that it was almost entirely exclusive of the southern clubs, who formed their own Southern League in 1894.

Pari passu the Irish League had been formed in 1890, and the Scottish League a year later. The Irish League at first for practical purposes was a Belfast association. The leading participants, then as now, were Linfield (1887), who competed in the English F.A. Cup in 1890, Distillery and Glentoran. Ulster, Old Park, Clarence, and Milford—now no more—were also members. The amateur club, Cliftonville, the *fons et origo* of Irish soccer, unlike its Scottish counterpart, Queen's Park, did not stand out against the League system but was a founder member.[5] In the course of time Derry City and the Dublin clubs of Bohemians and Shelbourne came into the Irish League, which in the end became two leagues in accordance with the political provisions of the country after the First World War.

The original members of the Scottish League were Rangers, Celtic, Third Lanark, Heart of Midlothian, St.

Grimsby Town (from Grimsby Pelham, f. 1878), Walsall Town Swifts, and Birmingham St. George's. Of the Ardwick players of that generation five were induced to go to the U.S.A. in 1895, for a fee of £10 and a weekly wage of £4–£5 each. They went, but quickly came back.

5. The first game played in Ireland under Association Rules took place on the Ulster Cricket Ground, on October 24, 1878. It was an exhibition match between two teams selected from Glasgow Caledonian and Queen's Park players, and was sponsored by the Ulster and Windsor (Rugby Football) Clubs.

Mirren, Dumbarton, Renton, Cowlairs, Cambuslang, Vale of Leven and Abercorn. Of these clubs the last five have passed into oblivion. The first two names, on the other hand, are world-famous.

The Scottish League found itself in its early days in frequent conflict with the national Association The *casus belli* was the subject of professionalism and at the beginning of the inaugural season Renton were expelled from membership of the S.F.A., and therefore from the League, through engaging already vetoed players. None the less League football flourished, crowds accumulated, and feelings ran high.

The symbol of partisanship in British football is Rangers *v.* Celtic. On one level this compares with the blind devotion implicit in the English 'public school' or 'Corinthian' tradition of the nineteenth century. On another it epitomised the ancient tribal animosities by now wrapped up in religious colours. On yet another it stood for the virtues of efficiency on the one hand and inspiration on the other. As outsiders we remain content with the stylistic contrasts maintained across the years by these two great foundations.

In 1894 there was a crowd of 30,000 to watch the Scottish Cup Final. This, for the first time, was between Rangers —with nine internationals—and Celtic—with five internationals. On this occasion the Cup was convincingly won by Rangers, by 3—1. Celtic, however, were League champions.

Rangers enjoyed an income that year of £5,227—a fourfold increase on that of some five years previously. Football in general was now becoming relatively big business. One by one clubs were turning themselves into limited liability companies and raising capital through share issues. After a number of attempts Celtic, originally formed with the intention of accumulating funds for Catholic charitable organisations, became one of them. Many supporters of the club, and many who though not interested in particular charities, were disappointed with the fact that although Celtic prospered, their contributions to good causes decreased. Football was its own good cause. By the time the limited company was instituted the annual income of Celtic was in the region of £16,000—more than that of any other British club.

The purchase of Celtic Park, for £10,000, enabled Celtic to put in its bid for staging international matches, for the Scottish F.A. had no settled venue for these until Hampden Park was enlarged in 1903.[6] The 1898 match against England was played at Celtic Park, and, before 'a battalion of Pressmen, many Kodak-fiends and a cinematographer', England won by 3—1. Two years later Celtic Park was again selected for the occasion. This time the Scots, led by Alex Smith (a Rangers player from 1894 for some twenty years), won a dashing victory by 4—1. In the presence of the Earl of Rosebery the Scots wore the Earl's racing colours, of primrose and pink hoops, in honour of his Lordship and his horse Ladas, the previous year's Derby winner.

Those, as they say, were the days of Scottish soccer. Especially were they great days for Rangers. Between 1898 and 1902 they were League Champions in every season. In 1898–9 they did not drop a single point in achieving this distinction.

For obvious reasons the power in English football was shared more widely than in Scotland. But there was an élite. Preston North End were champions in the first two seasons and runners-up in the three succeeding years. Sunderland, a 'team of all the talents', displaced them in 1893 and 1895. But it was, in truth, the golden era of Aston Villa, who dominated the scene until the end of the century,

6. The 'new' Hampden Park was opened on October 31, 1903, by Sir John Ure Primrose, Lord Provost of Glasgow—in his private capacity a Rangers supporter. The opening match was between Queen's Park and Celtic, the amateurs winning by 1–0.

winning the League five times. In 1895 the Villa had their
revenge for 1892 and beat West Bromwich Albion to win
the F.A. Cup. Two years later they were successful again in
this competition, their victims on this occasion being
Everton.

In the final of 1895, before a record crowd of more than
42,000, the determining goal was sensational—it came
within thirty seconds—a ricocheted shot of Bob Chatt
striking John Devey's knee and thence returning past an
astounded Albion goalkeeper.[7] The sensation that followed
the final was, however, greater. On the night of September
11 the Cup was on the premises of William Shilcock, boot
and shoe manufacturer and sponsor of a local *Football
Annual*, who had borrowed it for exhibition. On the morning of September 12 the Cup had disappeared. It was never
found and the F.A., fining the Villa £25, used that sum to
purchase a new one from Vaughton's Ltd., of Birmingham.[8]

Success depended on two things: on good players and on
sufficient funds and, possibly, fringe benefits to attract and
maintain them. Within a decade of the legalisation of professionalism the situation in essentials was as it is today,
with this reservation—that the individual player, un-
supported by any organised association or union, was in
a less good bargaining position than he is today. Even the
greatest of the professional players belonging to the era that
ended with the First World War often sank into obscurity

7. The goalkeeper was Reader, whose name had been prominently
in the news a year earlier. Injured in a match against Newton Heath he
was said by a reporter of the *Birmingham Gazette* to have been the
victim of foul play. Newton Heath brought an action for libel which
was heard in the Manchester Civil Court on March 2, 1894, by Mr.
Justice Day. The Judge found for the plaintiffs, awarding damages of
one farthing.

8. In 1958 one Harry Burge confessed to having stolen the original
Cup. Whether his confession, at the age of eighty-three, was genuine
would appear doubtful. See Peter Morris, *Aston Villa*, London, 1960,
pp. 45–6.

A section of the crowd at The Dell (Southampton v. Reading, April 13, 1913) on the day of Mrs. Pankhurst's release from prison—as advertised on the newspaper placard.

BURLINGTON CAME IN WITH A TREMENDOUS RUSH.

'St. Merville's College' v. 'Wilchester Grammar School': illustration by J. Finnemore, R.I., from *St. Merville's Scholarship Boys*, c. 1906.

F.A. Cup Final at Crystal Palace on April 21st, 1906: Everton (1) v. Newcastle United (0).

Musical tribute to Tottenham Hotspur on leaving the Southern for the Football League, 1908.

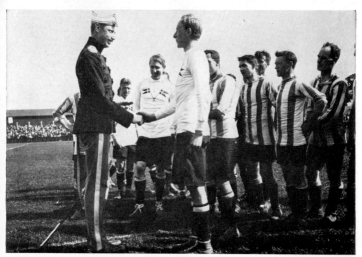

Ambassadors of football: Sheffield Wednesday F.C. welcomed in Copenhagen by the Crown Prince of Denmark, 1913.

THE REDS' RECOMPENSE

F.A. Cup, 6th Round, 2nd replay, 1926; Bolton Wanderers v. Notts. Forest.

"We're pleased to meet you at last, Mr. Fat-Gate"
(And, on top of the big receipts at Bolton. there should be another fine attendance on Monday.)

The dignity of management: E. Buckley (the Major), left, and J. W. Tinn, right, precede their teams (Wolverhampton Wanderers and Portsmouth) at Wembley for the F.A. Cup Final of 1939.

Manchester United F.C., 1958.

Red Star, Belgrade v. Manchester United, at Belgrade, February 5th, 1958.

Record gate? Northwich Victoria v. Stalybridge Celtic, Cheshire League, *c.* 1964.

F.A. Cup (3rd round), 1967, match at Swindon: the anxiety of West Ham, and the jubilation of Swindon Town, winners by 3–1.

Ashbourne in Derbyshire, a home of British Football; West German team end a training session in preparation for the World Cup, 1966.

Presentation of the painting of Vasco Lazzolo to Sir Alf Ramsey, supported by West Ham members of the English World Cup team, Bobby Moore, Martin Peters, and Geoff Hurst, 1966.

Street football, 1967. The Welsh Under-23 team train in Belfast under difficulties, the Windsor Park ground being waterlogged.

Boots of genius: Denis Follows, Secretary of the F.A., inspects the former property of Sir Stanley Matthews, now exhibited in Hitchin Town F.C. Football Museum.

and relative or absolute indigence once their playing days were done.

Since football is less immune to change in fundamentals than is sometimes thought the qualities looked for when recruiting players were much the same eighty years ago as now: strength, speed, and skill. Naturally one had an eye also for genius, but this, being extraordinary, may for the time being be left on one side. Beyond the basic qualities the wise manager, aware that ultimate success reposes on corporate as well as individual endeavour, considers traits of character. The ideal footballer is one who disciplines himself to adjust himself to, and to belong to, the group. Thus we arrive at team spirit, but by a rational and not (as, say, on p. 123 an irrational approach.

It is, of course, not possible to compare players of different generations. One can, however, aver that, relatively speaking, the notable players of the past were as dominant in their own environment as their successors. They also seem to have been more durable—although the more stringent economic circumstances of the times had some influence on this.

It is always hoped that a defence will prove impregnable. Among the accumulated myths that are not the least of football's attractions stands the legendary Stoke City trio of Rowley, Clare, and Underwood. Despite the indifferent results achieved by that club in its early days it has long been maintained that nothing ever passed this triumvirate. Local boys, then a matter of major pride, Rowley (in goal), Clare and Underwood (full-backs) were large and solid men. If they had a fault it was that they overworked themselves, but maybe they had to. This they did in the simplest manner, for since—as it was charmingly put—'charging was no foreign article in the creed of the two backs', when 'they found a forward in their way [they] cleared him out of the path'.

These were sound rather than brilliant players, local

G

craftsmen with few ambitions and fewer illusions. They enjoyed the game and were content with the applause and consolidated affection of their townsfellows. The 'old' game—as we may now call it—depended on such stability.

Qualitative full-back play, however, was not unfamiliar and had been determined principally by Nicholas Ross, who came to Preston in 1883, having played for Hibernians and Hearts (of which he was captain). He became the chief architect of Preston's pristine glory. In 1888 he moved to Liverpool, being appointed captain of Everton. Ross—and here one remembers Herbert Smith once writing that a good footballer required some of the skills of a chess player —dominated the game not by physical force but by a delicacy and assurance in execution. He had prevision; could read the course of an action, as well as the thoughts of an opposing player. Thus he generally knew where best to make his interception. Because he was analytical he sensed where he should be at any moment; and he was not afraid to be an attacking full-back. In Scotland, indeed, he had been a forward; hence his versatility.

After Ross the next eminence among full-backs was Howard Spencer. Birmingham-born, Spencer joined the Villa from a junior club at the age of seventeen. He played for fourteen years and then became a director of the club, an office he held for twenty-nine years. The facts are as eloquent as Spencer's play is said to have been. Like Ross he depended on quickness of movement and mental reaction, and he had the capacity to be able to recover a situation apparently lost. Spencer was the quiet inspiration of the Villa in its golden years, and played in the Cup Finals of 1895, 1897, and 1905. Yet he was a connoisseur's full-back. At Villa Park the less informed used to complain that he did not 'get stuck in'. On one occasion it is even reported that the England selectors turned him down on account of his renunciation of violent methods.

Ernest Needham, the great master of wing-half-back play

and for long a member of Sheffield United, had similar qualities of artistry. His principle was simple, and explains a good deal of the then general style of play: 'Keep an eye', he wrote, 'on your wing men, and lend what help you can to the centre-half now and then.' Needham, like Ross, watched the ball and was adept in interception and in cutting down his opponent's freedom of manœuvre. He by no means disliked an attacking function when conditions allowed.

It will be seen that strength is more than mere physical strength. Needham, even though a small man, could dominate a game. So too could Stephen Bloomer. Derby County long ago were one of the leading clubs. Between 1896 and 1903 they appeared in four semi-finals and one final—without, in fact, winning any. (Those interested in the black arts will like to know that since Derby County established a headquarters where once there had been a gipsy encampment it used to be said that they carried a witch's curse.) The master of Derby County was Bloomer, who came to Derby in 1892, when he was paid 7s. 6d. a match. To what extent is testified by his record of 352 goals in League football and twenty-eight in international matches.[9] Pale, slight of build, apparently indolent, Bloomer knew all about time and motion study. He played at inside-forward and was unpredictable. An individualist, he sought those moments when his speed and shooting-power could be used to greatest effect. He was, it might seem, the Greaves of his day.

These, and many others, were idolised by crowds and (occasionally) fêted by municipalities. What did they earn? When professionalism was first allowed, wages were nominal—in 1885, for example, West Bromwich players were paid 10s. a week. A League club in the 1890s paid what it thought it could afford—between 30s. and 40s. a

9. Dean of Everton destroyed the first record (see p. 252), the second fell to Lofthouse, of Bolton, who passed the twenty-eight mark in 1956.

week for a first-class player.[10] An unknown, like the young Bloomer, as has been seen, received much less. When Ross went to Everton he was given the princely wage of £10 a month all the year round. If Ross's terms were exceptional in English League football those offered to Charles Athersmith, the great outside-right of Aston Villa, were more so: it was reported that he was paid at the rate of £6 per week. But Villa at that time was a wealthy organisation. In 1894 Everton tried to re-sign Dan Doyle, who had returned to his first club, Celtic. It was reported that he was offered £5 a week and the tenancy of a public house (the management of which represented a highish rung on the social ladder); but he remained content with the licence he already had acquired in Glasgow and a weekly wage of £2 from Celtic. Like other clubs Celtic dispensed occasional bonuses. After success in the 1892 Scottish Cup Final, for instance, each player received a special award of £3 and a new suit of clothes. In 1893 the Celtic committee were prepared to offer bonuses of not more than £5 a man if the season's results justified this. A year later a League match won brought an extra 10s. to a man, a draw 5s. When in 1894, the manager of Celtic, William Maley, had an offer to go to Sheffield his employers suggested a new five-year contract worth £150 per annum. It took three years for this to be approved by the committee, but at the end of the negotiations Maley was still there and, in fact, was appointed Secretary of the newly constituted limited liability company.

The transfer of a player from one club to another was

10. Compare with: 'In 1900 a skilled fitter or turner got 38s. in London, and 36s. in most other large towns, and an ironfounder 42s. and 40s. A London compositor on time rates got 38s., which was in fact the commonest rate for a highly skilled London craftsman. In agriculture, over the country as a whole, average weekly wages rose by about 1s. between 1874 and 1900—from 14s. to 15s. . . .' G. D. H. Cole and Raymond Postgate, *The Common People 1746–1938*, London, 1938, p. 430.

part of the system of professional football from the outset. At first the F.A. supervised transfers in a general sort of way, and it was not until 1904 that the whole matter came within the jurisdiction of the League(s). Early transfer transactions were of a relatively modest order (whether players made anything on the side is a moot point, and it was not until 1958 that a proportion of a transfer fee was legitimately assigned to the subject of the transfer). As has been noted, Aston Villa were the big spenders of long ago (the habit has died of late years) and when Willie Groves and John Reynolds moved from West Bromwich Albion to the Villa after the 1892 Cup Final their transfers cost £100 and £40 respectively. In 1895, coveting one of the best wing-halves of the day, the Villa approached Burnley in regard to the brilliant, local, international, Jimmy Crabtree. The cost was prodigious: the Villa paid £250. When Fred Wheldon came to the Villa from neighbouring Small Heath, however, the fee was £350. The process of inflation has gone on from that point—the early landmark being Alfred Common's move from Sunderland to Middlesbrough in 1905 at the then fantastic figure of £1,000.[11]

Football managements often chase mirages. The game itself is part of the British romantic tradition. Each minor club that goes into the F.A. Cup competition fancies itself as in the final before the first qualifying round has taken place. Realism is not the strongest point in the intellectual equipment of the average director.

Who now has heard of Bootle? Yet there they once were, the Merseyside rivals of Everton, inducing Welshmen from the Druids, southerners from Essex, and Lancastrians from distant parts of the county to join their ranks long before any form of transfer system was regularised. In 1882 Everton claimed a Liverpool cup-tie on account of the unruliness of the Bootle supporters who invaded the pitch during play. In due course Bootle went into the new

11. See comments on this on pp. 247, 254.

Second Division. In 1892 it was a case of now or never.

'The permanent wholesale disqualifications of Davies, Kilner, Burns (late of Builth), and Law, by the Bootle F.C., has been freely and unpleasantly commented on in Liverpool football circles during the last few days. We have it officially that in each case the action was justifiable, and that the Directors were actuated by no other motive save the improvement of their team, which, unfortunately, has not been blest this season, either with a happy arrangement of the fixtures, or with that share of luck which naturally enters into the successful workings of a football club.

'Ere this point sees light, it is expected the registration of Bootle F.C. as a Limited Liability will be sealed, settled, delivered. The Directors have already spent £120, and have received as yet but very scanty support. Let us hope their supporters will prove themselves worthy of the name by rallying round Hewthorne enclosure once more.

'A certain ex-Celtic forward offered himself to Bootle for the modest sum of £8 down, £3 a week, and 25s. during the close season. Bravo!'[12]

In 1893 Bootle passed away. Their place in Division II was allowed to the Liverpool F.C., champions of the Lancashire League.

12. *Out of Doors*, October 29, 1892, p. 3.

A Matter of Rights

Thus far the pattern of professional football is seen to have been established in the North; an extension and amelioration of the general manner of life in grimly industrial societies. By the time League football was established the northern English and the southern Scots were an urban people with new cultural traditions. Football, in its revised form, was written into these traditions at an early stage; this was the cause of the parochialism that still obtains. The rigours of League football—increased by the introduction of relegation and promotion in 1898[1]—were viewed by influential southern footballers with relative distaste. The philosophy that one should 'love the game beyond the prize' is one of the most specious ever smuggled into English ethics; not because it is in itself bad, but because it is unworkable. The snobbery that tended to run through much of amateur sport (more, perhaps, in cricket than in football) became inverted when the doctrine of the less the reward the greater the glory was preached, but the doctrine was overturned when the F.A. Amateur Cup was instituted in 1893.

The Sheffield Club had proposed such a competition in 1891. It took three years for the idea to be approved and put into effect by the F.A. The first Amateur Cup Final, then, was played in 1894 between the Old Carthusians and the Casuals, the former winning the trophy by 2—1. Old Carthusians played in the next year's final, only to be beaten

1. From 1893 to 1898 promotion was determined by end-of-season 'test matches'—a series of games between the last two of the First and the first two of the Second Divisions.

by Middlesbrough. This established a precedent. Northern clubs—Bishop Auckland, Stockton, Crook Town, among them—monopolised the Amateur Cup until 1906, in which year it was won by Oxford City.

The organisation of a separate competition for amateurs, although the outcome of a suggestion from the North, was thought of as something of a panacea for bruised southern pride. It did not quite work that way, but the new competition did serve to detach the gentlemen from the players. It was a recognition of the professional quality of professional football, and even though a reasonable number of non-vocational players continued to take part in League football this was a steadily decreasing percentage of the total top-class playing resources.

Among amateurs capable of holding their own in first-class professional company at the beginning of the century were Herbert Smith, the determined leader of Reading, Vivian Woodward, an incisive centre-forward for Spurs, and cast in a mould still retained by that club, Harold Hardman, of Everton and other northern clubs, and later the distinguished Chairman of Manchester United, and Rev. K. R. G. Hunt, of Wolves. Perhaps, as an unconscious reflection of the latter's prowess (Hunt had played for Oxford University) P. G. Wodehouse made reference to football in a short story, 'Petticoat Influence'.[2]

' "They're playing Bob at half for Oxford, Joan," he said, "against Wolverhampton Wanderers."

' "Oh, father!" I said, "are they really?" '

In the general set-up of the game, however, a sequence of interrelated developments gave to it a new dimension. In, and shortly after, the middle of the nineteenth century football missionaries had gone from south to north. The then professors had been academics with strongly developed social instincts. At the end of the century the direction of proselytism was reversed. Now it was a case of the experts

2. See *Twenty-five Football Stories*, London 1908, p. 6.

coming from the North to the South. In many cases this resulted from what would now be termed a redeployment of labour. In the last decade of the nineteenth and the first of the twentieth centuries the threat of redundancy was constant, and skill at football was one kind of insurance against industrial unemployment. The symbol of the overall industrial situation was the passing of the Unemployed Workman Act in 1905; a political consequence of general distress was the Liberal landslide of 1906.

In 1895 the Crystal Palace became the venue for the F.A. Cup Final, and it remained as such until 1914.[3] Londoners looked on the annual invasion of northern and midland clubs and their supporters with awe and some apprehension. In 1900, however, their attitude was modified, for in that year Southampton appeared in the final—to be beaten, by 4—0, by Bury. *Eheu fugaces!* Three years later Bury won the Cup again, defeating Derby County—the Chelsea of that time, with talent but, it seemed, not the capacity to get beyond the second place in any major competition— by what still stands as a record score for a Cup Final: 6—0. Southampton, too, enjoyed a reversion of fame, if of a lesser order. In 1902 they drew in the final against Sheffield United at Crystal Palace, but lost in the replay by 2—1. On this occasion Sheffield United (the tradition of clubs making a concentration of final appearances, although more or less fortuitous, is a lasting one) redeemed themselves. For in 1901 after drawing 2—2 at the Crystal Palace they had lost in the replay at Bolton, by 3—1, to Tottenham Hotspur.

Here we reach a double climax. The attendance at the first of these two matches was 111,815—a record up to that point in time: the Spurs were the first southern professional team to capture the Cup. To keep the record straight, and to indicate the mobility of football labour, it should be noted that the Spurs team of that year comprised one Irish-

3. Burnley 1, Liverpool 0.

man, two Welshmen, five Scots, and three northern Englishmen, who had just broken Southampton's three-year monopoly of the Championship of the Southern League.

The credit for encouraging professional football in the South goes first to the Arsenal Football Club, and then to the Hampshire F.A., of which the Southampton Club was a member.

The (Woolwich) Arsenal Club was formed in 1886, the first captain being David Danskin, a Scotsman from Kirkaldy. At the end of the year the name Royal Arsenal Football Club was adopted.

The team was conscripted in the first place from workers in the shops of the Royal Arsenal; in the second place they were conscripted, and then allocated to jobs that were sometimes created for them. As well as Danskin other Kirkaldians included Peter Connolly, MacBean, and Charteris; the latter was renowned for his irrepressible urge to argue with referees. Wolverhampton Wanderers shed Bob Crichton and Jimmy Hill (not the well-known TV sports personality), and both tried their luck with Arsenal. In token of a connection with Nottingham through a number of players the team wore red shirts, the first set being a gift from the Forest. At first Arsenal were members of the London F.A., but in 1891, agreeing to adopt professionalism at a public meeting at the old Windsor Castle Music Hall, the committee withdrew from this organisation. The difficulty of obtaining a fixture-list from among southern clubs led the Directors to choose opponents from the Midlands and North. In 1893 the club joined the Second Division—the first member elected from the South. Eleven years later promotion to the First Division was gained.

Football in Southampton developed when a number of immigrant Scotsmen took up employment in the Woolston Shipyard. The experience of seeing qualitative football played in the town proved an inspiration to the football-playing youth of the place. Out of the ruck of minor sides that founded by Rev. A. B. Sole[4] in connection with St. Mary's Church emerged as the most effective. Sent into the world with the blessing of Canon A. B. O. Wilberforce (Rector, 1871–94, and then Canon of Westminster), first President of St. Mary's F.C. (hence the later and lasting sobriquet, the Saints), the team won the County Junior and Senior Cups. Looking for fresh worlds to conquer the St. Mary's Club decided to adopt the professional game. They signed a number of Stoke players who—having played a friendly fixture there—preferred the balmy air of the Solent to the silicosic atmosphere of the Potteries. On the formation of the Southern League, in 1894, St. Mary's (renamed Southampton F.C. in 1897) were elected to membership after a preferred candidate had withdrawn.

The idea of the Southern League was thought up at Millwall, where a local works team had followed the lead of Arsenal and embraced professionalism.

Apart from Southampton and Tottenham the only other southern clubs to make their mark in the wider world of Cup Football were Bristol City, beaten by Manchester United in the final of 1909, and Chelsea, who lost to Sheffield United, at Old Trafford, Manchester, in the muted match played under wartime conditions in 1915.

In 1909 Manchester United had shown signs of beginning to arrive. Reconstituted, and floated as a new company on the investment of a large capital sum by a local plutocrat, in 1907, a certain restlessness was showing itself. Of major importance, the United made a European tour in the summer of 1907, consolidating the good work done by other clubs with continental aspirations, such as the

4. Arthur Baron Sole (1853–1903), son of William Sole, F.R.C.S., was born at St. Neot's, Huntingdonshire, and educated at Wellington School, Jesus College, Cambridge, and Leeds Clergy School. His Curacy at St. Mary's lasted from 1878 to 1886.

amateur Corinthians and Pilgrims.[5] They played matches in Prague and Budapest. In 1908 the United won the League Championship, and preparations were made to move from a dismal ground at Clayton to Old Trafford, where, it was announced, there was the possibility of 'seating nearly 100,000 people'. The inspiration of the Manchester United of those days was William Meredith, one of the very few players to rank as an immortal. A slight, often lackadaisical, player, Meredith, whose career lasted until he was fifty years of age, was the master outside-right. He was subtle in motion, economical in energy, and a tease to any opposition. A Welshman from Chirk—a nursery of fine footballers—Meredith played for Manchester City, with whom he won a Cup-winner's medal in 1904 by scoring the only goal of the match (against Bolton Wanderers), for Manchester United, and again for Manchester City. He retired in 1925, having played fifty-one times for Wales.

As town after town developed its football club—some more profitably than others—interest widened. As this happened so too did crowds increase. This gave rise to problems concerning public order. As far back as 1888 the possibility of chaos occurring when star-studded teams met was demonstrated. In that year Aston Villa were at home at Perry Barr to Preston North End in the first round of the Cup. The interest was tremendous, and more than twice as many people for whom there was room got into the ground. Naturally those who could not see (more than those who could) pushed forward, with the result that many spectators encroached on the field of play. In desperation, the match having been stopped many times by trespass, the authorities mounted two troopers, who had come to see the game, on horses and persuaded them to patrol the

5. F.I.F.A. was established on May 21, 1904. British coaches were prominent on the Continent at this time and international football was beginning to appear in Europe. The pilot match—between Austria and Hungary—took place in 1902.

goal-lines. The Press, then as now alive to any whiff of sensation, headlined: 'Military called out.'

The Villa were admonished by the F.A. for failing to take adequate measures to deal with the situation.

In 1904 the Villa were involved in a similar incident when playing a cup-tie against Tottenham Hotspur at Tottenham. This time the match was abandoned and the home team fined £350, which sum was dispensed among various London charities. The 1893 Cup Final at Fallowfield, won by Wolverhampton Wanderers, was a fiasco for the same reason, and numerous among the spectators were injured. The famous 1901 final at Crystal Palace was also oversubscribed, but there being breathing-space at Sydenham there was discontent but not disaster.

What had long been threatening took place at Ibrox Park, Glasgow, on April 5, 1902.

On that day Scotland, led by R. S. McColl, of Queen's Park, Newcastle, and Rangers, played England. Rangers had lately built a new stand which, approved by engineers and architects alike, promised to be a magnificent amenity. The stand was constructed on wooden terraces supported by pillars. The gate was upwards of 60,000, and the ground, therefore, packed to capacity. As excitement—centred largely on the grace and conscious showmanship of the Scottish outside-left Bob Templeton (Villa, Newcastle, Arsenal, Kilmarnock)—mounted the structure of the stand weakened. Eventually a large part collapsed. The scenes below were indescribable: twenty-five people were killed, and more than five hundred injured. Unaware that anything untoward had happened, however, the referee allowed the match to continue. It was declared unofficial by the National Associations.

The Rangers were liable for thousands of pounds in respect of damages, but sporting organisations all over Britain contributed to a fund which should relieve the host club of some considerable part of this financial responsibility. One outcome of this disaster was an interesting fund-raising scheme arranged by Rangers.

The holders of a cup awarded at the Glasgow International Exhibition, Rangers renamed it the 'British League Cup' and staged a quadripartite competition between themselves as Scottish Champions, Celtic, runners-up, Sunderland, Football League Champions, and Everton, runners-up in that competition. The English clubs were eliminated, leaving Celtic and Rangers as finalists. Celtic, the eventual winners, took the cup and have it to this day. Thus out of disaster there was born a British League, which, however, was but a nine days' wonder. The British League—a 'super-league'—which might have been, which has been mooted on many occasions and in many quarters in later years, now, perhaps, will never be.

During the formative period of British football—signified by the stabilisation of League and Cup competitions, the separation of amateur from professional, and, most of all, the codification of its commercial structure—the position of the individual footballer underwent a change. Four aspects of the professional footballer came under constant review. On the whole this is still the case. Thus we may consider the footballer as craftsman, the footballer as hero, the footballer as a moral force, and the footballer as an economic unit. Behind this consideration lies the premise that the footballer comes from modest, working-class, origins. The career of the great professional footballer, then, more often than not in former days represented an unconscious protest against privilege, and the urge to reach the top in the only way practicable.

The craftsman-footballer, conscientious, stable, unquestioning, and content to accept conditions as they are, is the mainstay of the game. His value to a team is an inverse ratio to the amount of noise he makes. Often one is conscious of the indispensability of such a player on the field precisely because he does not appear to be present.

The player of this type exerts influence not only because of what he does but also on account of what he is able to prevent his opponents from accomplishing. The craftsman-player goes out from the game as he comes in—quietly. Typical of this class was J. R. Auld, of Queen's Park, 3rd L.R.V., Sunderland, and Scotland: 'the chief features of his play are, his power in "bottling up" the opposing centre forward, incessant feeding of his forwards, his grand shooting and . . . his beautiful headwork. What can a half-back be more?'[6] What indeed?

Another, contrasting, type of half-back is represented by Kelly Houlker, once of Blackburn, Southampton, and England. Here is football's Prometheus, *c.* 1900:

'He bewilders with his activity and omnipresence, and yet out of the chaos he appears to move in he directs the storm with a subtle brain. In the fire and heat of the game he becomes the embodiment of perpetual motion. He prances, whirls, and bounces. He feints, attacks, and runs away—and when he runs away there is the greater danger. In the exuberance of sheer delight in the game he drops his hands and kicks double shuffles in the air.'[7]

The extravagance of the prose while absolutely hardly warrantable is so at least relatively. The drama of football for the British is an image of the world, the sublimation of real issues to the plane of the symbolic. 'And now,' said Lord Derby after the Cup Final of 1915, 'having fought a great fight, gird yourselves for a greater: for England.'

Credited by public and critics with knightly virtues the more extrovert among early twentieth-century footballers became heroes. And afterwards? The pub, the small shop, the factory, or oblivion. That was the pattern. The rules of society as it was did not permit limits to be over-stepped. The footballer had his place.

6. *Out of Doors*, Ap. 15, 1893, p. 6.
7. Pickford, op. cit., IV, pp. 29–30.

The two categories described above represent the plain man's index to the Faustian divisibility of human nature. The conservative (and all Britons are basically conservative) envies the man who touches the stars—or becomes one of them. But prudently he extols virtuous obedience. The honest toiler in the football field is the theme of a good deal of Edwardian literature.

In a short story, characteristically entitled *Only a Footballer*, A. B. Cooper dealt with the time-honoured theme of the local Derby. The rivals in this case were 'Barton Ramblers' and 'Nighbury', two Midland clubs. The suspension of the Ramblers' strong man (on account of over-emphasis on his strength in a preceding match) meant that our hero, Harry Chambers, had to be given his opportunity. It was nine months since Harry had signed, but never had he played in the first team. 'A 'journeyman' joiner, at present unemployed, with a month-old baby and a sick wife, the chance of £2 for an appearance, or even £10 in the unlikely event of a victory, was as heaven-sent.

' "Didn't I say all things come to those who waited— long enough?" cried his wife, tearful with joy. "It's nine months since you signed that League form and now your chance has come." '

The match took place. The section that deserves anthologising comprised the last quarter of an hour. We come in just after play has been held up for what seemed a minor injury.

'. . . the back misses his kick. Inside-right shoots wildly, strikes the cross-bar, and the ball bounds back; but Harry, with a mist before his eyes, is there, and steers it, amid frantic cheering, into the net. The whistle blows. "Time's up", and the eager spectators crowd upon the field to carry their hero shoulder-high to the dressing-room.

'But, instead, they gather in a vast circle. Something is wrong. Aye, Harry has swooned, and soon the news goes round that Harry Chambers has been playing for fifteen minutes with a broken collarbone, and he is ten times the hero he was before.'[8]

During Harry's convalescence the Ramblers played in the semi-final. A collection on the ground realised £50 for Harry, a reward for one who knew his station in life.

The voice of the master was heard by the man from all angles. So we may find even a great footballer of the old school—William Isaiah Basset, the famous outside-right of West Bromwich Albion—advising the aspirant players of *c*. 1906:

'There used to be', he wrote, 'a lot of wild doings in the old days, and they make very interesting reminiscences . . . [but] there is every encouragement given today for the formation of character. There is a daily increasing tendency for clubs to look askance at men who have not a clean record. Clubs have begun to learn—nay, they have learned! —that it does not take many black sheep to lead the whole flock astray. So long as I am connected with football I shall never sanction the admission into a team of any man who has not a clean record. It is all very well to be a fine footballer; but the man who can play good football and is occasionally unfit to do so, is of doubtful value to a side.

'I have even gone to the length of seriously advising players to pay some regard to their personal appearance. This may appear to some as a rather small matter, but personally I regard it as a somewhat important one.

'I do not like to see footballers getting £4 per week—or even £3, if you like—slouching about in mufflers and dispensing with collars. It brings the game into contempt with the very class we want to draw to our matches.

'There is no reason why footballers should not always look neat and trim; they will be doing good to the pas-

8. *Twenty-five Football Stories.*

time generally if they are reasonably careful as to their personal appearance.'[9]

Cleanliness thus is shown as conjoined with godliness as assurance of professional security; and all underwritten with plenty of skipping, country walks, cold baths, hot baths, douches, vigorous rubbings down, and optional exercise with Indian clubs, punch-balls, and even golf clubs.

The player had one relationship with his direct employers—the management of his club, but another with his indirect patrons—the crowd. With the one the relationship was, and has tended to remain, feudal. The other—a series of variations on a love-hate relationship—is more diverse. The interplay of these relationships led the thoughtful professional to reconsider his situation, in terms of security and remuneration, on a comparative basis. If he was a craftsman, then his rights should be those of other workers.

To safeguard these rights a Union of Professional Footballers was founded at a meeting held in the Spread Eagle Hotel, Manchester, on January 12, 1898. After a decade of ineffectual effort—the authorities proving as obstructive as could be—the Union was recognised, but only after strong backing by the Federation of Trades Unions, with which the League had at first refused to sanction affiliation.[10]

The subject of footballers' wages has been a perpetual issue for contention. In a capitalist system there should, of course, be no complaint if footballers play the game according to the established rules. There is always trouble when they do.

'Sir: I should like to hear your readers' opinion of the wage-limit question in football, at present so prominent.

9. 'The Day's Work: How the Professional Footballer is trained', *The Book of Football*, p. 113.
10. The pioneers of Unionism within football were the players of Manchester United. See Percy M. Young, *Manchester United*, London, 1960, pp. 67–8.

I may say I am in favour of it. I think in the interest of the game generally it has proved itself to be good and wise legislation and has secured for all players a good and substantial salary all the year round, work or play. Some clubs have given benefits which have materially increased the limit, and as such a salary should pay for the best exponent, why increase it? A labourer is worthy of his hire, but the profits as shown a few weeks ago in the cup-ties would warrant a £20 limit. The whole thing becomes absurd. Have our clubs become too rich.[11] Look at the transfer fees. I well remember £350 being an exorbitant price, but take the Middlesbrough-Sunderland transfer, £1,000. Is this to become a common experience, or where will it end?

'I venture to suggest the turn has come of the public who bring the grist to the mill. Why not covered accommodation for spectators, dry ground to stand on, and a reduced admission if possible. The profits will stand it. Many a wreath has been purchased by standing on wet ground on Saturday afternoons. If there is going to be unlimited wage [*sic*] and unlimited transfer fees, the business will become a complete farce. There is nothing to prevent a rich club becoming possessors of an international eleven. How will clubs perform when say, A has £8 per week and B £4 per week? A could not secure his £8 without his colleague. Would the play degenerate? I think so. Players have played much better together since the limit. I should say to them, "Be satisfied. You are lucky men. Let your supporters have something." '[12]

Much of this makes familiar reading in the light of more recent events and we now know the answers to some of the

11. The list of accounts on p. 213 of League clubs for the season in question (1904–5) reveals a widening gap between rich and poor and the writing on the wall is clear enough. The figures in parentheses give final League positions. Missing accounts from this list are those of Manchester City (3), Sunderland (5), Stoke (12), and Notts Co. (18).
12. Letter signed A. H. M., *Birmingham Mail*, March 16, 1905.

pertinent questions raised. We do not know, however, if they are the right answers.

If the player is minimally guaranteed by a wage structure he neither is nor was protected against often ill-informed criticism. Criticism is often sparked off by amelioration of players' conditions.

'Sir: Observing the continual absence of players from the football field through injuries and sickness I can not help thinking that our present day professional player is not so hardy as the players of a decade or more ago, who worked hard through the week and played hard on Saturday. Our professional of today, although surrounded by F.A. rules that do not permit of rough play, is continually out of harness through injuries, sickness and colds. He appears to be a more fragile athlete than the "old school", who thought nothing of playing through a season without laying up, and dearly loved a good shoulder charge. I think there is too much pampering of the men at present to produce hardy footballers.'[13]

There is a moral undertone audible in this. But English Puritanism, shaded off into class-consciousness, is at its most characteristic when seen growing direct from its bourgeois roots. Thus the Victorian and Edwardian employer found that in a conflict of interest his own profits in some mysterious way represented what was best in the national interest. One such employer (writing anonymously) took up a point raised in the *Birmingham Mail* by another employer (also anonymously) and then moved off into the field of education. In this connection it should be observed that an increased interest in schoolboy football had taken place since the institution of the Elementary Schools Football Association in 1904 (English Schools F.A., 1905).

' "An Employer" has certainly exposed a very great evil of the present day. Working men are too anxious to leave their work for the sake of seeing their favourite team play

13. Letter signed 'Old Player', *Birmingham Mail*, October 9, 1907.

Name of Club	Net Gate			Season Tickets			Wages and Transfers			Training, Travelling and Hotel Expenses			Net Profit or Loss		
	£	s	d	£	s	d	£	s	d	£	s	d	£	s	d
Aston Villa (4)	14,329	14	2	621	0	6	5,940	5	5	2,499	19	1	1,876	18	3 (p.)
Small Heath (7)	7,209	3	1	559	8	0	4,438	3	6	820	7	6	949	9	6 (p.)
Wolverhampton Wanderers (14)	5,450	15	4	380	2	0	3,617	17	1	844	6	5	119	6	8 (p.)
Newcastle United (1)	17,065	0	5	715	10	6	5,118	9	2	*3,265	14	6	5,487	17	4 (p.)
Middlesbrough (15)	8,177	14	2	525	10	6	7,730	2	7	1,209	5	8	1,035	2	5 (l.)
Woolwich Arsenal (10)	8,600	14	3	1,000	10	6	5,802	10	0	1,003	19	6	1,674	2	5 (l.)
Everton (2)	14,053	14	4	333	17	9	3,748	9	7	1,780	15	7	5,108	17	7 (p.)
Sheffield United (6)	8,074	13	1	362	9	6	4,039	12	2	570	4	11	†1,473	19	9 (p.)
Sheffield Wednesday (9)	8,983	5	6	203	3	6	4,733	9	0	748	17	3	1,433	8	8 (l.)
Blackburn Rovers (13)	5,743	2	0	380	4	0	5,174	5	0	964	11	9	1,542	13	10 (l.)
Bury (17)	5,181	13	9	330	18	0	4,848	17	6	945	19	1	1,049	18	0 (l.)
Preston North End (8)	6,957	13	11	131	15	0	4,345	17	0	895	9	10	917	5	0 (p.)
Derby County (11)	4,410	17	10	745	1	3	3,998	1	3	930	3	7	1,467	4	7 (l.)
Nottingham Forest (16)	5,504	0	0	750	0	0	4,645	0	0	455	0	0	545	0	0 (l.)

* Indicates police, gatekeepers, advertising, etc.   † Gross profit.

football. Sport is very good in its way, but it must always hold a subordinate position. The end and aim of life is not sport, but to fill one's station in life in the most capable manner. When it takes first place it is usurping its position. It is well known to all that in factory, school, and office the common every day talk is sport, and the real business of life is neglected. Employers, I fear, have only too good reason to complain when they see thousands of working men hurrying off to a football match on a Monday afternoon, heedless of the effect their neglected duty may have on their employer's trade. And I would remind such men that their masters' trade is the British trade which we are all so anxious to encourage and increase. The worship of sport commences at school. Our school competitions in football and other sports have now become a severe tax on the strength of any boy, and particularly on the poorly-clad and ill-fed. It is forbidden by the Board of Education to prepare a few boys for a particular examination, to the detriment of the remainder, the same regulation should apply to sport. In many cases a team from a poor district has to compete with a school in a better neighbourhood, where the boys are better fed, and much evil must result. A sound elementary education has become a thing of the past in many schools. Exhibitions, both in school work and sport, are the order of the day, to the great majority of the scholars in a school. Our best schools today are not those which produce a brilliant few, whether in school work or sport, but where all the scholars are considered, and where sport holds a subordinate position.'[14]

The letter comes to a strong finish, with 'Another Employer', favouring the principle of comprehensive education, showing himself well ahead of his time.

14. *Birmingham Mail*, September 8, 1908.

13

Realism

Partly because of its long history and traditions, partly because of its virtue in supplying an aesthetic satisfaction to a people frequently denied other opportunity, and partly because of its intrinsic nature and its personalities, British football (of whatever kind) has always appeared to possess a kind of wayward charm. This has been reflected in many ways: most of all in its literature. The literature of football has been undervalued, largely because until later years it has, unlike the literature of cricket, been considered ineligible for the department of *belles lettres*.

There are two classes of football literature: the fantastic, and the realistic. In the first are to be found much of the day-by-day reporting of the past—and some of the present, inflated anecdotes, hero-size biographies of players, as well as a considerable body of poetry; in the second lie the factual and statistical magazines, annuals, and so on, as well as a certain amount of cool journalism. Apart from the statement of individual facts and irrefutable figures, however, there is little in the way of objectivity. In one way or another we are all involved, all are interested parties.

The early years of the present century brought the dichotomy symbolised by the literature of the game into the open. Was a condition of Arcadian simplicity to remain? Or was the game to be brought into conformity with modern ideas? Attempts to resolve these questions represent the history in modern times.

Apart from the idealisation of celebrated players in coloured prose it is to poetry that we should look for an appreciation of the romantic impulses that inspired our grandfathers to brave the elements at least fortnightly in order to lift their otherwise earth-bound spirits. Conditions for spectators—and also for players—were often appalling[1] and it was only a determination not to see things as they were (a national malady?) that enabled those involved not only not to complain of discomfort but even to persuade themselves that they were enjoying themselves.

The fantasy of football is well illustrated by the songs (perhaps a hundred) that were issued in the field of popular music during the late Victorian and Edwardian eras. Some were virtuous pieces intended to spread the moral purposefulness of the public school game.[2] Some—a large number—stemmed from folk-song, and in these the incipient sense of rebellion that is never far distant from the thoughts of player and spectator is sublimated. In 'The Football Match' (words by J. Curran, music by E. Jonghman) an imaginary match between 'Swifts' and 'Macalvenney Wallopers' is described. In the second verse the 'Swifts' scored a goal:

'At this result there was a bit of wrangling,
The Wallopers swore the Swifts deserv'd a mangling,
They claim'd "Off-side" and the Referee, big Stevenson,
Disallowed the goal just to make the game an even one.

1. Thus when Manchester United played against Portsmouth in the first round of the F.A. Cup on January 26, 1907, the *Manchester Guardian* described how 'All the time the struggle was waging the thirty Clayton chimneys smoked and gave forth their pungent odours, and the boilers behind goal poured mists of steam over the ground. To visitors from the South coast Clayton in midweek must have seemed a strange scene indeed for sports on the field.'

2. e.g. 'Football Song' by Julius David, appears effectively to have caught the enthusiasm for football displayed by his colleagues at Uppingham (see p. 119). Joseph Barnby, Precentor of Eton, a virtuous composer of church music, also savoured the moral qualities of the game in a 'Football Song'.

The Swifts gave way and then to work they flew
    again,
They captur'd the ball and swore they'd put it
    through again,
One of them jump'd on the Wallopers custodian,
And he lost more teeth than there are keys in a
    melodion.'

If this belongs to the province of music-hall then the
Chorus from L. E. Mongiardino's 'Football' (stirringly set
to music in the key of B flat) derives from Verdian Grand
Opera:

> 'Never on the football field
> To the foreman shall we yield
> Never shall we cravens be
> Cravens ne'er win victory.'

An anonymous contributor to the Nottingham *Football
Post*[3] made effective use of parody to present his critical
theories, taking as his model W. S. Gilbert:

The 'Wab' Ballads

WANTED

(An Advertisement)

Wanted, by Forest, at once: first of all,
A sound line of halves—like the halves we recall.
Wanted, some man of superlative rank;
Wanted, a Forman, in fact (to be 'frank').
Also required a vanguard who can
Not be dependant [*sic*] on just an odd man:
Wanted, a right flank both 'heady' and deft—
Wanted, a right wing as good as the left:

3. October 10, 1903.

Also required less play of the kind
Which leaves us a goal—by our giving—behind!
Wanted, more wins to chalk up on our card—
For terms and requirements—write Maypole-yard.

The immediate inspiration for this verse came from the fact
that Frank Forman,[4] one of the greatest of Forest players,
had been dropped. The team thereupon appeared to be on
the verge of disintegration. On the day that the above was
published, however, Forman was restored to the team and
to his captaincy, and Sunderland were easily defeated by
3—0.

It will be recognised that the poetry of football served a
quasi-liturgical purpose. It existed not only for itself but as
an aid to illustration, as a guide-line to magical experiences. During times of dislocation the need to reassure that all
will be well again, that all will be as it was once thought
to be, is acute. So we read the nostalgias of the period of
the First World War. :

'When the sun is hot and the sky is blue,
When golden September smiles fair on you,
And the team gathers up, old hands and new—
Sing hey! Sing ho! for football.

When the fog rolls in and the sky is grey,
When the gloom steals down ere the close of day,
And you're only warm when the ball's your way—
sing hey! Sing ho! for football.

4. Forman came to Forest from Derby County as a wing-half. He
succeeded to the centre-half position and to the captaincy on the retirement of John McPherson. An attacking player, Forman was outstanding in his era and was capped for England nine times. In 1898 Nottingham Forest won the Cup for the first time, Forman then being captain.

When a cup-tie comes and the play is keen,
When there's just a hint of wigs on the green,
But right to the finish the game is clean—
Sing hey! Sing ho! for football.

The rough-and-tumble, the dash and the skill,
The single aim, and the curbing of will,
Make men who can face good fortune and ill—
Sing hey! Sing ho! for football.'[5]

One could, it is clear, compile a 'Hymns Ancient and Modern' for use at football matches. The incentive to liturgise the game is still present, and the community singing of the 1960s is but another aspect of the hidden forces illustrated above. At the beginning of the century the exposition and interpretation of these forces was left to the individual—as Saturday-night issues of local newspapers all over the country show. Now, however, conditions for better of worse, stir collective creativity—such as it is: hence the parodied hymns, psalms, and other spiritual songs, that are to be heard from behind the goals on most modern British football grounds. The spirit of the present age stands on its head. So, at every football match, what was sacred is profane, what was reverenced is irreverenced, by those who in uncertainty look for some consolation from unknown gods. It is one of the paradoxes of today that there are those (excluding policemen and reporters) who go to football matches not only to watch the players but also (some of) the spectators. It may be that some players have become to a large extent spectators; it is certain that many spectators have become, if not players, at least performers.

It is, in fact, the spectator who has made the modern game of football. His power, however, has been slow to develop, as witness the deplorable conditions that are still

5. *British Sports and Sportsmen*, 'The Sportsman', London, 1917, p. 316.

to be encountered on the majority of British football grounds.

The former relationship between professional player and spectator was fairly clear. Both were members of the one class, with little opportunity to escape it. Across this century, however, the barriers between classes have been more and more eroded, so that by now the relationship that once existed between player and spectator no longer stands. If anything, it might appear to some that many professional footballers so far from being under- are, perhaps, over-rewarded. The fight for recognition has been a long one, and marked by a number of belligerent episodes.

The odds at the beginning were all on one side. When the professional footballers formed the Players' Union they were met with an instinctive determination on the part of their employers and legislators to oppose their efforts on principle.

In 1908 Manchester United, led by their great captain Charlie Roberts, played a match against Newcastle United in order to raise funds for a provident fund for the Union. They did this despite the disapproval of both League and F.A. During the next year the Players' Union sought affiliation with the Federation of Trades Unions. In this they had the support of the Federation, and when the F.A in conjunction with the League suspended the Chairman and Secretary of the Players' Union, and ordered all members to resign, there was prospect of a political conflict. The players were backed by Arthur Henderson, who attempted to have the matter taken to arbitration. But the Football Association refused to agree to this. The players therefore determined on strike action (precisely what the football authorities sought to prevent by their attempt to isolate footballers from workers as a whole).

Two days before the opening of the new season in September, the League clubs had signed on sufficient amateurs to allow them to undertake their immediate fix-

tures. On August 31, however, a compromise was reached.
The Players' Union was accorded recognition, and it was
accepted that where it seemed expedient cases could in
future be taken into court under the terms of the Work-
men's Compensation Act of 1896. The suspensions were
removed and arrears of pay were allowed. When Manchester United took the field against Bradford City on
September 1 they were warmly welcomed by their supporters as apostles of freedom. The particular issue, of course,
was limited, but in those days of struggle for a higher standard of social justice it could be seen as a general one.

It was, however, but a half-way stage to freedom. The
F.A. (alone among the national Associations) had, as has
been seen, stipulated a maximum wage limit. In 1910–11
the Football League took over the maximum-wage principle
while the F.A. included a minimum-wage clause. The
League at the same time introduced talent- and place-
money. After the First World War, in 1922–3, the maximum wage approved by the League was £8 a week, with £6
in the close season. The regulation of wages in this manner
—related to the financial standing and resources of the
average club and to a sentimental concern for keeping
weaker clubs in being—was an early attempt by a private
body to organise a prices and incomes policy. Its imple-
mentation was to lead to many difficulties in the future.

These developments took place against a complex background. As interest in competitive football had intensified
so too had the involvement of bookmakers and newspaper
proprietors, who saw the profits that could accrue from
football 'competitions'.[6] The temptation to 'fix' matches by
bribing indigent or improvident players, or those who

6. In 1909 *The Racing and Football Outlook* instituted a weekly prize
of five guineas for the correct forecast of six away winners. National
papers were quick to follow this example. In 1928 a judge of the King's
Bench ruled that such 'competitions' were illegal, by which time the
'pools' which had operated locally were ready to take their place in the
national framework of recreation.

might have been thought to have a grievance, was strong. It was not always resisted. So it was that in 1912–13 the Management Committee of the Football League, aware of attempts to involve players, came out strongly against all forms of betting on football, describing it as 'a detriment and menace to the game'.[7] Legal actions concerning the acceptance of bribes were not unknown during the early part of the century, and continued at least until 1964–5 when the most notorious of all, perhaps, took place.[8]

It is probably true that all ages are ages of unrest and the security that is sometimes considered to belong to past eras is no more than the result of wishful thinking. But the twentieth century has been more turbulent than most, and has appeared so because of superior means of communication. When footballers found themselves drawn into the politico-industrial maelstrom they were at least unconsciously affected by general as well as particular conditions. Up to the outbreak of war in 1914 the tempo of industrial strife quickened, and disputes, especially in the coal and transport industries, that took place between 1911 and 1915 had their effect on footballers who came from those com-

7. C. E. Sutcliffe, J. A. Brierley, and F. Howarth, *The Story of the Football League, 1888–1938*, Preston, 1938, pp. 18–20. On April 24, 1915, a firm of bookmakers inserted a notice in the newspapers (supposed generally to relate to a match between Liverpool and Manchester United) stating their belief that 'a certain First League match . . . was "squared" . . . and that several of the players of both teams invested substantial sums on having the correct score of this match with our firm and others'. The firm withheld all payments; the clubs involved by implication, and the League, held inquiries; and eight players were permanently suspended. In 1918 a libel action by Enoch James West against the *Daily Dispatch* and *the Athletic News* arising out of this case, was dismissed by Mr. Justice Ridley. See 'West *v.* Football Association (Ltd.) and Hulton & Co. (Ltd.)', *The Times*, February 12 14, 15, 1918, for the dismissal of the appeal by Lords Justices Pickford, Warrington, and Scrutton.

8. 'At Nottingham Assizes, trials for conspiracy before Mr. Justice Lawton and a jury resulted in prison sentences for professional players, including two current internationals, followed by their inevitable disqualification by The Football Association from their subsequent participation in the game at any level'. *F.A. Year Book*, 1965–6, p. 14

munities and had frequently worked in those industries.

The growing tensions within professional football were regarded with concern by the amateurs and the division between professional and amateur widened. It is easy, with hindsight, to blame the amateurs for failing to understand the scale of the problem. But for the most part they were, if over-simplifying issues, acting with the best of intentions when they determined to take steps to preserve what they thought to be the pristine purity of football.

In March 1905 the Council of the F.A. proposed to the Surrey, Middlesex, and London Associations that they should take over the responsibility for professional clubs in their areas, which should, therefore, be admitted to membership of the Associations. Already irked by the lessening influence of their side of the game, and convinced that the F.A. had lost interest, a considerable number of influential amateurs resisted the order and in 1906 established a break-away body: the Amateur Football Association (later Alliance).

The F.A. acted as a government against a rebellious colony. In 1907 other national Associations were persuaded to support lawful authority and to refuse recognition to the secessionists (thus the traditional Queen's Park *v.* Corinthians fixture was prevented).[9] The power of the F.A. was such that even continental bodies came into line—a particularly hard blow in view of the success achieved by the best amateur teams in the mission field.[10] The issues involved in

9. 'In terms of the international agreement between the English, Scottish, Irish and Welsh Associations, each Association was bound to recognise the prohibitions and suspensions of clubs and individuals by other National Associations. . . . So the New Year Game [Queen's Park *v.* Corinthians] was in jeopardy. The Queen's Park approached the Scottish Football Association on the subject, but that body had no alternative but to uphold the authority of the English Association, as it would expect, in a similar case, its own decisions to meet with the support of all kindred associations'. Robinson, op. cit., pp. 239–40.

10. The separation between amateur and professional was further marked during this period by the institution of Amateur International

any dispute are seldom clear-cut, and while the F.A. may seem to have acted severely in this instance, the matter of ultimate authority was involved. On this the F.A. was sensitive, and any affront to its authority was taken as blasphemy.

In 1903 when the idea of an International Federation of Football Associations (to become known as F.I.F.A. in 1904) was first mooted the English Association had stood aloof, but stating a willingness to confer 'on all matters upon which joint action was desirable'. A year later, however, after a conference called by the F.A. at the Crystal Palace a form of recognition of a European Federation was approved in these terms:

'That it is desirable that the National Associations of the countries of Europe should associate in an International Union for the promotion and control of the game of Association football, each Association reserving its own jurisdiction within its own area, but co-operating with the other Associations.

'No Association shall be eligible for Membership until it satisfies the Union that it is the only National Association.

'The Union may arrange an International competition to which the entrance by Members shall be optional.'

As at a later date with the Common Market, the English remained apart, and as dignified as possible, until it became apparent that nothing was gained by so doing. The dissident amateurs of 1907 were an embarrassment, since they brought to the forefront the reciprocities implied in any international commitments.

In fact not all the amateur clubs joined the A.F.A. and during the obligatory absence of Corinthians from Hampden their place was successfully taken on two occasions by

matches: against Ireland and France, as from 1906; The Netherlands, 1907; Wales, Belgium, Germany, and Sweden, 1908; Switzerland, 1909; and Denmark, 1910.

In 1908 England won the Olympic Games tournament at Shepherd's Bush, and again in 1912 at Stockholm.

Northern Nomads, a team which then enjoyed a brief period of renown. At the end of 1913 the F.A. and the A.F.A. agreed a truce and came to an agreement, which was further ratified—and the relationship between the two bodies more fully defined—by the F.A. Council on April 13, 1934.[11]

The secession of certain clubs into the A.F.A. was a symptom of a general discontent within the organisation of football. There were others. So far as League football was concerned there was also an abiding sense of injustice in the under-representation of southern clubs in the competition. By 1905 the two Divisions of the League comprised forty clubs, which number was increased to forty-four on the resumption of football after the First World War. But the majority of clubs in the South were still confined to the Southern League—a combination that lacked the acute competitiveness and prestige of the national league. Of the southern clubs that had gained admission to the English League[12] the most successful in the first decade of the century was Bristol City. In 1906 the City was promoted to Division I, in which it took second place in 1907. In 1909 the Cup Final was between Bristol City and Manchester United. The latter won by a single goal, scored by 'Sandy' Turnbull, who five years later volunteered for war service and soon afterwards was killed in action. Although Bristol tried hard enough they were beaten by superior skill, more particularly by the disconcerting artistry of Meredith. The 'sturdy toilers', who supported the United 'even if they wish above all things to see their own side win, [have] a real understanding of the *nuances* of scientific football.'[13]

Scientific football was hardly the rule in those more in-

11. See Walter E. Greenland, *The History of the Amateur Football Alliance*, London, 1966.
12. Arsenal, 1893; Luton Town, 1897–1900; Bristol City, 1901; Chelsea, Clapton Orient, 1905; Fulham, 1907; Tottenham Hotspur, 1908.
13. *The Times*, April 24, 1909.

H

tuitive days, but it was more so in the North than in the South, hence the continued monopoly of the F.A. Cup that lasted until the second success of Tottenham in 1921.

Before the First World War recognition of the function of the spectator, and of the fact that his interest must be sought and sustained, came tardily. True, prospective profiteers were ready to exploit the spectator as and when it was possible, especially in the field of gambling. Pie-makers, pudding-manufacturers, and brewers, also increased their takings, and other peripheral industries benefitted. But the conditions for watching football conformed to a familiar pattern. Association football was a working-class game, patronised only by the superior classes when Members of Parliament condescended to their constituents, or when ministers of the Government were concerned about impending Election prospects. The Cup Final was exceptional, and as a national ritual came under the protection of the nobility until their vanishing mystique demanded their replacement by the Monarch. King George V attended the Cup Final in 1914 between Burnley (1) and Liverpool (0). In view of the domestic and international political climate it is clear that the King's advisers sought thus to signify a national unity.

Attempts were, of course, made both to publicise the game and to enhance its attractions. Some of these attempts, however, were premature. In October 29, 1907, one James E. Bland, having watched the recently touring New Zealand Rugby football team, wrote a letter to the *Manchester Guardian* in which he advocated that soccer players should be distinguished as were the New Zealanders, by numbers on their jerseys. This drew a sarcastic reply from one 'H.K.', who retorted that footballers might just as well have their 'names emblazoned on the front of their costumes'.[14] The matter of numbering waited for some twenty-five years

14. In 1909 the Football League decreed that goalkeepers should wear distinctive colours.

until Tottenham Hotspur, supported by certain other clubs, unsuccessfully brought it up again in 1933. Six years later numbering became compulsory.

This brings us to the true revolutionaries of the era: the two clubs who were determined to pull the English game out of the nineteenth century. With Hampden Park and Ibrox, Scotland had taken the lead in supplying more or less adequate amenities and comfortable viewing places on their spacious terraces. The English Cup Final, however, was still kept at Crystal Palace, where although the annual gate was gratifyingly large the actual number who saw the game was lamentably small. For many the only sight of what was going on came when a player kicked the ball into the air. The largest attendance at a pre-war Cup Final was in 1913, for the meeting of Aston Villa (1) and Sunderland (0). There were 120,081 spectators present.

In 1896 where there is now the Stamford Bridge head-quarters of Chelsea F.C. was the ground of the London Athletic Club. H. A. Mears, the imaginative and enterprising son of a local contractor, envisaged the transformation of the site into a grand new arena, on which the Cup Final and other important football matches could be played. Mears, helped by his brother J.T., started to put his intention into practice but was immediately frustrated by the reluctance of the freeholder of the site to die. However, after this unhappy event had taken place and after the late summer meeting of the Athletic Club in 1904 the site—together with an adjacent market garden—became the property of Mears. Temporarily put in doubt about his investment by an offer from the Great Western Railway Company, Mears consulted a knowledgeable and experienced friend, Frederick Parker, as to whether he should re-sell at a profit or play his first hunch. Parker, fortunately, was sanguine about the prospects of the use of the acquisition for football. Mears, therefore, refused the offer from the Railway Company and at once travelled by a rival concern to inspect the great Scottish stadiums. Inspired by what he saw at Hampden, Ibrox, and Celtic Parks, he put the work of reclamation and transformation immediately in hand. Within a year the new ground, capable of seating 5,000 spectators, and (at a push) accommodating a further 95,000 standing clients, was thrown open for inspection. 'Chelsea,' said one eupeptic reporter, 'will stagger humanity.' So blessed, the Chelsea Football Club—the titles London F.C., Stamford Bridge F.C., and Kensington F.C. having been considered and rejected—came into the world.

The team in fact was something of an afterthought. Mears thought first of the unique properties of his ground. Afterwards it occurred to him that to use it to best advantage he should construct a football club. Under the chairmanship of Claude Kirby a manager was appointed. The successful candidate was John Tait Robertson, a Scottish international who had won twenty-two caps, now in his last season with Rangers, for whom he played at wing-half. Robertson, a shrewd player according to the classical Scottish pattern, had a wealth of experience, even of English football. He had had spells with Southampton and Everton.

Not unnaturally Robertson signed on a number of Scottish colleagues and the character thus imparted has remained with the club. Having a ground and a team was one thing; to find a league in which the club would be accepted was another. The Chelsea directorate put out feelers to the Southern League and the Football League. After a deal of lobbying and other behind-the-scenes activity Chelsea were elected to Division II of the Football League. At the end of the season 1905–6 they were in third place. A year later they were runners-up. In the two seasons a reputation for dashing play was established; in the first ninety goals were scored, in the second eighty. Thus the club brought back a cavalier spirit, the effect of which has by no means been diminished by later vagaries on the field of play. At best Chelsea were a side worth watching;

at worst they were good for a laugh. Such was the force of the skilful public relations operation that has brought the club into being.

The second major exercise in improving the player-spectator relationship was the brave enterprise of Manchester United in building a new and splendid ground at Old Trafford. On January 22, 1910, United played their last match on the mud-flats at Clayton, making a valedictory gesture to the spirits of the past by beating Tottenham Hotspur 5—0. Shortly afterwards, on a tempestuous day, the stands collapsed. On February 19 the club moved to the new ground that had been in the planning stage for two or three years. Publicity again had been skilfully fed out, and when the stadium was ready for view the Pathé Film Company came to record it for posterity.

So far as the players were concerned Old Trafford offered hitherto unheard-of facilities: billiard-room, recreation-room, massage-rooms, gymnasium, plunge-bath, and so on. For the spectators there was more than a touch of class about the place. There was capacity for 80,000, of whom at least a sixth could be under cover. The grandstand was the last word in Edwardian luxury—with attendants to point patrons to their tip-up seats, and to the new tea-room. Prices, let it be noted, were 6*d.* for admission to the ground, 1*s.*, 1*s.* 6*d.* and 2*s.* to the covered stand, while one could obtain a reserved seat in the centre of the stand for 5*s.*

In this way J. H. Davies, the Chairman of Manchester United and the biggest investor in the company, sought to change the image of the game, and to make his club an attractive centre of social activity for the more prosperous, and refined, citizens of Manchester. This was during the first noteworthy period in the history of the United. They won the League in 1908 and again in 1911. As has been noted already, they were Cup-winners in 1910. In 1911 the Cup Final at Crystal Palace, between Bradford City and Newcastle, ended in a goal-less draw. The replay—won by a single goal by Bradford—took place at Old Trafford.[15]

There were few to be found who did not proclaim the infinite superiority of the Manchester to the traditional London enclosure. The turn of the Stamford Bridge as a venue for the Final was yet to come, though it staged the England–Scotland match of 1913. After the 1914–18 war three finals were played at Stamford Bridge, in 1920, 1921, and 1922.

The outbreak of war in 1914 brought to an end a footballing era. On November 3, 1913, the Football Association celebrated its Jubilee with a sumptuous banquet that comprised fifteen courses. That, too, marked the end of an era. During this period the progress made on the broad front was astonishing. What had been a private recreation, or a folk custom, had become a world-wide pastime. In that the British pioneered this universal extension it was the great age of British football. This was acknowledged by the presence at the F.A. Jubilee Banquet of representatives of Associations from many European countries, but also from Argentina (where Southampton—also the first professional team to play in Hungary, in 1901—toured in 1904), Australia, and Jamaica. After the war things were never to be the same again. That this was so was due to the commanding position held by the professional game. While the position of the individual professional player, socially and economically, was often uneasy, it was his expertise that determined the pattern of the spectacle. Not only this, but because of the heroic qualities into which he was endowed by the young (and not always the young) his example moulded the *mores* of the game.

15. In 1911 a new trophy was designed to replace the existing F.A. Cup, the pattern of which had been pirated. But the F.A. in producing a replacement were able to mark Lord Kinnaird's twenty-one years as President of the F.A. by presenting him with the Cup made after the loss of the prototype in 1896 (see p. 192). Appropriately enough the third cup was made in Bradford by the firm of Fattorini. In 1914, on the outbreak of war, this firm helped to stimulate recruitment by retailing 'patristic badges' each enshrining the picture of a prominent footballer, and edged with red, white and blue.

When the F.A. came into being, and for some time afterwards, the amateur was the arbiter of style and method. In the decade before the outbreak of war the professional came fully into his own. On the field at least he was more or less a free agent. The control of the manager had not yet extended so far as to comprehend the detailed direction of tactics and strategy. Since the transfer system had not yet reached wholly scandalous proportions (though there was a well-known scheme of under-cover incentives in operation as well) there was a reasonable equality of competence, at least in the First Division. Neither Cup nor League was dominated by a small group of clubs. Between 1905 and 1914 only Aston Villa won the Cup twice—in 1905 and 1913, while the best League record was that of Newcastle United, champions in 1905, 1907, and 1909. It was a period in which the unfashionable could attain unexpected glory. So, in 1910, Barnsley reached the final of the Cup, to be beaten in the replay by Newcastle. Two years later Barnsley —still in the Second Division (but only just, for re-election had been necessary at the end of the previous season)— came into the final again.

A resolute progress had entailed no fewer than twelve games, of which six had ended without score. That year Barnsley met Birmingham (twice), Leicester Fosse, Bolton Wanderers, Bradford City (four times), Swindon, and, in the final, West Bromwich Albion. This was played in two instalments. The first meeting, in London, was goal-less. At Old Trafford the only goal by Barnsley's inside-right S. Tufnell.[16] And this was when only two minutes of extra time remained. Since the finals of 1910, 1911, and 1912 had

16. The ball used in this final was presented to Prebendary Tiverton Preedy, who, as a curate of St. Peter's Church, Barnsley, had founded the town football club in 1887. Preedy's name is still given in the Barnsley match programme. After his death in 1928 the ball was bequeathed to Barnsley F.C.

See letter from Rev. Clifford Warren, *Daily Telegraph*, September 15, 1966.

all required replays it was decided by the F.A. that thereafter extra time should be played, if necessary, after the expiry of the statutory ninety minutes of the first meeting. Since that time replays have, in fact, not been required, and extra time only on five occasions.

If in England there was a chance for a number of clubs to shine in the major competitions, in Scotland it was otherwise. Rangers and Celtic dominated the scene. In the first fifteen seasons of the twentieth century Celtic won the Scottish Cup seven times. They held the League Championship consistently from 1906 to 1910, and from 1914 to 1917. In the intervening years Rangers were champions. In international matches with England during the same period Scotland won five and lost four. In connection with this record it should be noted that at that time the football drain from Scotland was severe—so severe that in 1907 the Scottish team included only two members currently active in Scotland. The rest were Anglo-Scots.

If the Scottish style was established anywhere with particular distinction in England it was in the north-east, where Newcastle, Sunderland, and Middlesbrough were convenient of access for Scottish players. Thus it was that the masters of the more delicate Scottish manner were the pre-war Newcastle United. Winners of the F.A. Cup in 1910, the United also appeared unsuccessfully in the finals of 1905, 1906, 1908, and 1911.

At that time there were two contrasting styles, both being based on man-to-man marking, on an attacking centre-half, and on triangular motifs worked out between wing-halves and outside- and inside-forwards. Newcastle, with such practitioners as Colin Veitch, Peter McWilliam, and Bill McCracken in their ranks, played their game with delicacy and distinction. So too did Sunderland (Cup Finalists in 1913), with the famous right-wing trio of Mordue, Buchan, and Cuggy. The contrasting style, skilfully managed by the Villa and effectively by Barnsley in their Cup frays, made

more use of the long pass. In the final issue both Newcastle
and Sunderland failed too often at the last hurdle for their
method to be accepted in its entirety. More pragmatic plans
have prevailed, and what is known on the Continent as the
'English style' has emerged: a blend of quickness and corporate skill, supported by physical determination. Some of
this, of course, was there in the beginning.

14

The Age of the Manager

Football was kept going during the First, as during the Second, World War by regional competitions, and teams by the dedication of directors and the readiness of players—when and if they were in England—to play temporarily for the most convenient club. Many players ended their careers before the outbreak of war. Some who had been stars in the making returned to find themselves in positions of seniority. Every team needed to be rebuilt to meet the challenge of a soccer-hungry community. All of this tended to turn the game in on itself again, to rekindle the old parochialism. In so far as the international scene was concerned, the frontiers, once so reluctantly opened, were closed again. The F.A. withdrew from F.I.F.A., wishing not to have dealings with former enemy countries. In 1924 the F.A. took up membership once more, only to resign yet again in 1928 over the issue of 'broken time' payment for continental amateurs.

In the briefly euphoric state of the country after the cessation of hostilities, however, crowds flocked to football grounds to reassert the primacy of traditional values. Later on they went in order to assuage the anxieties that came with a contracting economy and with the long and disastrous period of unemployment. For a great number of British people football between the wars represented a way of escape. For young players of talent, handicapped otherwise by social background or inadequate education, football opened the door to a relative prosperity that was otherwise unattainable.

League football recommenced in the season 1919–20 with twenty-two clubs in each Division, at the end of which the champions (for the first time) were West Bromwich Albion, who also defeated the Second Division champions, Tottenham Hotspur, for the F.A. Charity Shield.[1] A compact side, devoid of stars, the Albion went through the first post-war season with only eighteen players appearing in the first team. The secret of success in League football depends on a good start. Albion scored 36 goals in the first 11 matches and, having established an unassailable lead, and with 9 points between them and the runners-up—Burnley. Those were the days when pride was taken in local talent and the success of the Albion depended a great deal on Fred Morris, of Tipton, who at inside-left scored more than a third of his team's total.

The Midlands took the other major trophy that year, for the Cup-winners once more were Aston Villa. At that time the Villa supporters and management accepted such honours as if by right. The classic days of the eighties and nineties were never out of mind: nor, to be truthful, are they even at the present time. But a fine history can be a snare and a delusion. Winning the Cup in 1920 was in a way unfortunate, for it bred a state of complacency that fed on itself until in 1936 the team dropped into the Second Division.

The writing was on the wall at the beginning of the 1919–20 season, for after playing ten and winning only one game the Villa were at the foot of the Division. The situation was restored by the transfer of Frank Barson from Barnsley. Barson had enormous vitality, and no sense of fear. He was ruthless and indefatigable—a man for emergencies. He was said to be rough, but held no ill-will against an opponent

1. Instituted in 1908, and won in that year by Manchester United, Football League Champions. Their opponents were Queen's Park Rangers, Champions of the Southern League. Later the match was between amateurs and professionals, but since 1930 the League Champions and the Cup-winners.

who returned his charge. He survived a broken nose four times, and two spells in hospital with back injuries. Behind the outward show of a man of action (which the crowds loved) there was, however, a shrewd footballing brain. Barson put the Villa back on even keel, and after two seasons was transferred to Manchester United and put in charge of another rescue operation.

If Barson was not cast in the true Villa mould, Billy Walker, who joined the club in the same season, certainly was. Walker's skill at centre-forward complemented Barson's mid-field dominance and he it was who was the effective agent in winning the Cup in 1920. Walker spent his playing career at Villa Park, played for England sixteen times, and then went on to manage two famous clubs: Sheffield Wednesday and Nottingham Forest, both of which won the Cup under his management.

Management now becomes the operative word. Villa's opponents in the 1920 final were Huddersfield Town, then just arrived in the First from the Second Division. In the final Huddersfield were unlucky to lose. For the first time in history the match was extended to extra time, and it was after seven minutes of this period that the ball cannoned off Kirton to Wilson, the Huddersfield centre-half, or off Wilson to Kirton, and thence into the net.

Hitherto Huddersfield had been an insignificant factor in English football. For some time, however, they were now to dominate the scene, and in no uncertain manner.

The record of the next few years becomes virtually the story of one man. That was Herbert Chapman, a native of Kiveton Park, Yorkshire. An averagely industrious player, though with no claim to great distinction, Chapman took over the management of Northampton Town—a Southern League club of modest attainment—some seven years before the war for no better reason than that a Tottenham colleague, Walter Bull, thinking better of his own acceptance of the post, recommended it to Chapman. After some success in revitalising the fortunes of Northampton Chapman moved to his native county, to Leeds.

In Yorkshire there was acute competition between soccer and Rugby League for the support of the public. Chapman met the challenge and at least managed to keep Leeds City (as it was then) together as a going concern in the Second Division. During the war years, however, the club suffered from its directors, who, by making illegal payments to players and then refusing to produce their books, landed themselves in disgrace and the club in oblivion. In 1919 Leeds City was expelled from the League and its place taken by Port Vale. Meanwhile at Huddersfield the condition of the club was perilous, and a proposal to remove the whole concern to Leeds was seriously entertained. Instead, some of the playing assets of Leeds were absorbed, and Chapman—suspended at Leeds, although personally uninvolved in the indiscretions of his employers—was taken on as manager. He remained with Huddersfield until 1925.

After thrusting into prominence in 1920 Huddersfield Town kept within sight of the leading teams of the First Division for a couple of years before reaching third place in 1923. They won the Championship in the following season, in the one after that, and the one after that. Following this hat-trick of success—a feat without precedent—the team finished the next two seasons in second place: a remarkable achievement for a club situated in what was not the most congenial climate for soccer. Huddersfield had some fine players, S. J. Wadsworth and E. Barkas—classical and poised defenders; the half-backs Tom Wilson and William Watson (father of the cricketer, and football international of recent times), who missed respectively only two and three matches in three championship seasons; and Clem Stephenson, inside-left, the constructive force of the forward line.

Chapman had the talent not only to assess the individual merits of a player but also to anticipate the relationship between that player and others. The Huddersfield team had a clever and interlinking right wing in Kelly and Alex Jackson, and an orthodox outside-left in W. H. Smith. Chapman, an authoritarian, made his team into a machine, each part functioning in relation to the whole. He was, of course, fortunate in achieving early success. Skill is one thing: luck is another. Outstanding achievement depends on the union of skill and luck. A football manager devoid of one or other of these qualities can no longer survive.

While Chapman was beginning to prove this as axiomatic, other developments were taking place. For a long time the Southern League clubs had been dissatisfied with the restrictions imposed on them by geography. In 1919 discussions were initiated to determine if a merger with the Football League could be effected. In this form the proposal failed, but in 1920 a new Third Division of the League was started, which embraced twenty-two clubs of the Southern League. These ranked as associate members of the parent body. A year later a northern section of the Third Division was formed to satisfy the aspirations of those northern teams who felt their claims to be as strong as those of the newly enrolled southerners. At first the northern section contained twenty clubs, but in 1922 this number was increased to twenty-two. At this stage then there was a grand total of eighty-eight clubs in the Football League. Unfortunately a number of the Third Division clubs never got over the dignity of belonging, however obscurely, to the Football, instead of to some regional, League. Many, starved of funds, have been dying a slow death ever since they were admitted to the League, and, by congesting fixture-lists, have tended to hinder the progress of the professional game as a whole.

More important than the multiplication of League clubs, however, was the alteration in the Laws of the game that was introduced in 1925.

For obvious reasons (for the view of the game is different for referees and linesmen than for spectators) the administering of any offside law is liable to produce contention. Behind the law as it was until 1925 there was a separate history of Scottish objection by the agreement reached in 1882. Between 1882 and 1925 a man was off-side if he was in the opponents' half of the field in front of the ball, and there were fewer than three players between him and the goal. After the war it had become standard practice for a defending back to linger up-field so that he could easily disrupt any plan of attack by slipping forward in order to throw an attacker off-side. This resulted in frequent stoppages and a reduction in the number of goals scored. The game began—neither for the first nor the last time—to suffer a defacement of image. At an International Board meeting held in Paris on June 12, 1925, the Scottish F.A. proposed that the number of defenders required to be between the opposing side and the goalkeeper should be reduced to two.

The immediate effect was considerable. We may contrast the figures, for example, of Aston Villa before and after the change. In the season ended in 1924 Villa were sixth in the First Division, having won 18 matches, scored 52 goals and having had 37 goals scored against them. Two years later the final position was the same, but with two fewer victories. There were, 86 goals for, and 76 against. It is worthy of comment that on the day of which the new law was first introduced the Villa took advantage of the new licence to score goals by beating Burnley 10—0. In 1925 Huddersfield won the championship having scored 69 goals against 28 (58 points). A year later, still Champions, they scored 92 goals against 60 (57 points).

The problem for the club manager, then, was to devise an effective anti-goal-scoring device. There emerged the 'stopper' centre-half. About who was the first of this race there is liable to be dispute but the originator of the fully defensive role of the centre-half would seem to have been Robert Gillespie, of Queen's Park. Gillespie, a large man and captain of the club, simply made it his duty to blot out the centre-forward. Other clubs followed suit. For the time being the day of the fluent, attacking centre-half was past. The next strategic task centred on the discovery of centre-forwards capable of destroying the plan. It was Herbert Chapman who built a team to conform to the pattern prescribed. That team was Arsenal.

While interest in football was thus quickened by the upgrading of clubs, and by the introduction of a radically changed style, the dedication of a new stadium to the Cup Final was in the long run to prove the most significant factor of all. The first three finals after the war (like the last prewar match against Scotland played in London, in 1913) took place at Stamford Bridge. But this was as far as Mears's dream of Stamford Bridge becoming a national centre came to fulfilment. Wembley Park, to the north of London, had been in the news for some time. It had been intended at first to build a tower there, to rival the Eiffel Tower in Paris. This grandiose scheme was dropped, but one even more grandiose took its place. The site was selected for a British Empire Exhibition, to be housed in palaces of various exotic kinds and to be held in 1924. The Exhibition, like the Empire whose obsequies it began to prelude, came and went. But the Stadium, for the use to which Sir Charles Clegg, President of the F.A., had negotiated a twenty-one-year contract in 1921, has remained. On April 28, 1923, the first Cup Final took place at Wembley, between First Division Bolton—who had dismissed Huddersfield Town, the Cup-holders, in the third round—and West Ham United, about to be promoted from the Second Division.

Wembley Stadium, stated the official programme, was 'incontestably the finest sports ground in the world . . .' It was 'the largest in the world, the most comfortable, the best equipped, holds more than 125,000 people, and will accommodate 1,000 athletes. In area it equals the Biblical City, Jericho. The circuit of its walls is half a mile in length. . . .'

The advertisement of the vast capacity of the Stadium

had disastrous consequences. While it may very well have been able then to contain 125,000 spectators in relative comfort, it could not cope with the estimated 200,000 people who decided to put the ground to the test. There was chaos. It was a miracle that no calamity occurred. It was a miracle that the game, seen by King George V, started, and another miracle that it continued to the end.

In any case Bolton, for whom the master-players were Ted Vizard, a Welsh international outside-left of long standing, David Jack and Joe Smith, clever and dangerous inside-forwards, won the match by 2—0. In 1926 Bolton won the Cup again, and yet again in 1929. The secret of these three successes was experience. R. H. Pym, the goalkeeper, played in three finals, as did R. Howarth, H. Nuttall, J. Seddon, W. Butler. A. Finney, W. Jennings, David Jack, the Smiths, and Vizard, each played in two finals. Among the Bolton players of that time the star was David Jack. On him the story now begins. But to discover how we must retrace our steps.

The early League record of Arsenal was relatively inglorious, and there were few who were prepared to take the club seriously. One who was, however, was (Sir) Henry Norris, a wealthy estate agent, sometime Mayor of Fulham and M.P. for Fulham East: a man who saw in the renascence of a football club the possibility of his own eventual apotheosis. Norris in another age and place would have been a determined and extravagant patron of the arts. In Britain in modern times that prospect was not one likely to touch the mind of a self-made magnate.

From 1910 onwards, Norris, then Chairman of Fulham F.C., made the salvation of Arsenal his mission. First he tried to amalgamate Arsenal with Fulham, but the League disapproved of the proposal. A year or two later he determined to move Arsenal from Plumstead to an attractive site at Highbury. After negotiating satisfactory terms with the Ecclesiastical Commissioners—from whom the site was acquired—Norris prepared to do battle on two fronts. The residents of Highbury took exception to the threatened interference with their amenities, and made strong representations against the likely intrusion of the 'undesirable elements of professional football'. Tottenham Hotspur and Clapton Orient, while accepting each other's presence, were agreed that a third professional club in north London would prove disadvantageous to all parties. In fact Norris rode over all obstacles (though leaving behind a residue of strain between Spurs and Arsenal that was for some time reflected on the field of play) and on September 6, 1913, Arsenal played their first match at Highbury, beating Leicester Fosse by 2—1.

Arsenal remained a Second Division side until the war, Norris reflecting that the chances of being repaid anything of his investment of about £125,000 were dim. After the war Norris, whose determination was the rock on which the modern Arsenal was built, appointed a new manager—Leslie Knighton, who had previously administered the affairs of Huddersfield Town and Manchester City. His instructions were to make a First Division team, but not to exceed £1,000 in respect of any transfer. As a result of inflation and a sellers' market so far as footballers were concerned the transfer fee of a reasonably good player was in the region of £3,000. Knighton, therefore, started under a disadvantage. However, he enjoyed one major stroke of luck. When the League was re-started the First Division was, as has been seen, extended. To make up the required complement of twenty-two it was necessary to elect two clubs from the Second Division. One of these clubs was expected to be, and was, Chelsea. In respect of the other vacancy it was generally anticipated that it would be filled by Tottenham. If not Tottenham, then either Wolves, or Birmingham. What none had fully realised was the extent of Norris's machinations behind the scenes. As a consequence of secret bargaining the application of Arsenal was unequivocably backed by John McKenna, of Liverpool, President of the League. Thus it was that, unloved and unwanted, Arsenal slid into the First Division.

Handicapped by Norris's *ipse dixit* on the subject of transfer fees,[2] Knighton augmented his tenuous playing resources from the amateur ranks—his notable captures being the ex-Queen's Park wing-forward Dr. J. Patterson, who was to play for the Football League against the Scottish League in 1921—and Alex Mackie from the Falls Road district of Belfast. For an Irishman living below the line of subsistence and under the shadow of Civil War it seemed that the streets of Highbury were paved with gold. Such was the lure of a certain £5 a week. Knighton also searched for talent amid the slagheaps of Glamorgan. His course of action was not only limited by Norris's zeal for economy but also by reason of the fact that the Chairman disapproved of small players. Intrigued by the impudent success of 'Midget' Moffatt, of Workington, Knighton signed him—and his own warrant of execution. Norris, irked at lack of progress[3] and intolerant of insubordination, advertised for a new manager.

So it was that Herbert Chapman, looking for fresh fields to conquer came to Highbury. The one man able to take the measure of Norris, Chapman, unafraid of responsibility, acted according to his own judgement, confident that time would justify his actions. Recognising the unreality of the limitation on transfer fees in the light of the past years of failure he straight away plunged into the market. The man he wanted was Charles Buchan, once an Arsenal reserve and for years the mainspring of Sunderland's era of suc-

2. At the Annual General Meeting of the Football League in 1922 Norris unsuccessfully proposed a general limit of £1,650 on transfer fees.

3. As preparation for the first round of the F.A. Cup in 1925 the Arsenal players, unwilling subjects for biochemical experiment, were dosed with 'pep-pills'. See Bernard Joy, *Forward Arsenal*, London, 1952, pp. 32–3.

cess. It was as long ago as 1910 that Buchan went to Sunderland, where he was to score 200 goals and to become the English captain. In his middle thirties Buchan had lost none of his craft and his experience was invaluable. Arsenal overtly[4] paid £2,000 for his services, with an understanding that for every goal scored during the first season a further £100 would accrue. During that first season with Arsenal Buchan scored nineteen goals. Other importations were Bill Harper, the Hibernian and Scottish goalkeeper, and Joe Hulme, of Blackburn Rovers, the finest outside-right of his generation in England. In 1925 Arsenal had finished three places from the bottom of the First Division. A year later they were runners-up.

Within two years Arsenal had paid out £25,000 in transfer fees. Faithful to principle, the club still sought the limitation of such fees, unsuccessfully bringing the matter up both in 1926 and 1931. But when reproached by Chelsea for joining in the mad rush the official programme riposte was: 'If insanity is to continue in this matter, then we will be insane with the rest.'

Chapman arrived at Highbury in time to assess the effect of the new offside law. On his reading of the new situation the phenomenal period of prosperity that was to follow depended. Chapman not only had to invest in new players, he had to select players to meet a particular contingency. The first general of the football field to plan campaigns from his office, he furnished a system whereby a generally profitable balance between goals won and goals lost could be achieved. That, in the long run, is the acid test, and the yardstick by which the manager expects to measure his futurity.

Forwards were chosen who could out-manœuvre held-back defences and who were sufficiently direct and confident

4. But see p. 246. At the High Court case of February 5–6, 1929, the case of Buchan's transfer was particularly mentioned, since Norris offered other inducements to Buchan to leave Sunderland.

themselves to score. The secret of the attacks at first mounted by Hulme, Charlie Jones (Welsh international outside-left), and Jack Lambert (centre-forward from Doncaster) was simplicity and economy. As few moves as possible was the distinctive mark of Arsenal, in contrast with the more intricate planning of, say, Tottenham. In defence the key was a resolute, watchful, centre-half, flanked by solid full-backs detailed to neutralise opposing wing-forwards, and supported by wing-halves on the look-out for marauding inside-forwards. The gap between attack and defence was filled by inside-forwards, kept back to act as link men. The first centre-half of the new dispensation was Herbie Roberts, of Oswestry, who came to Arsenal in 1926. The first of the great Arsenal full-backs was Eddie Hapgood, whose composure saved many matches for England between 1934 and 1939.

Chapman had the genius to understand that while he as manager had to take overall responsibility for the grand design he also had to delegate duties to a specialist staff of technicians. He knew the game as a whole, from boardroom to arena, and recognised that the pattern of functions in the field needed its analogy behind the scenes. He appointed Tom Whittaker as trainer in succession to George Hardy, and in so doing revolutionised the whole approach to physical fitness.

'Whittaker brought all the resources of modern science to treating the player. Sun rays, heating apparatus, and electrical equipment of all all kinds were installed at Highbury, and his ideas were as advanced as his tools. He went further. When a specialist said, "He'll be playing in three or four weeks" Whittaker aimed to halve the time.'[5]

Training routines were also revised and made both more intelligible and more intelligent—with exercises devised to correct particular weaknesses or to enhance particular qualities. Whittaker treated each player as an individual and

5. Bernard Joy, op. cit., p. 48.

in so doing became not only a highly valued technical adviser but also a frequent father-confessor. The value of this quality in the dressing-room—where were inexperienced young men often straight from the coal-fields—is obvious. Whittaker sustained his charges by an unusual psychological insight into their problems, realising that personal difficulties more often than not were the cause of professional uncertainty and decline in form. His influence spread. He accompanied F.A. teams on tour, and advised and treated athletes of many kinds. It may be said that the improvement of the physique of the nation as a whole, and the care taken to maintain it through all forms of physical recreation, is to a great extent the result of Whittaker's work between the wars. In certain other countries at that time young men were being made fit by government decree.

Arsenal had become highly professional in every detail. This, however, did not endear them to other clubs, where most directors liked to amble along in the way to which they had become accustomed. The board-room, peopled by the elderly, was (and in some cases has remained) a symbol of parochial worthiness and a centre for the exchange of reactionary opinions on many topics. Any breach in the conventions was unwelcome; despite occasional and sporadic expressions of belief in the necessity for keeping up with the times.

Norris, the progressive, came unstuck in the end, whereat some were not displeased. Arraigned by the F.A. in 1927 for non-compliance with the rules, he and a fellow director were suspended, the club censured, and the facts of the case published. Norris took action for libel, and the ensuing case in the King's Bench Division, before the Lord Chief Justice (Lord Hewart) and a special jury, is a classic of its kind.

Although represented by Sir Patrick Hastings, K.C., and Mr. R. Fortune (Mr. Holman Gregory, K.C., Mr. Norman Birkett, K.C., and Mr. Paley Scott appearing for the F.A.) Norris lost his case, the verdict being that the occasion was privileged and that there was no evidence of malice. During the hearing Norris's activities, however well intentioned, were made to appear at least as foolishly irregular. What he had done in fact underlined the fragile state of morality of the transfer system. Outside of the transfer fees involved he had offered further inducements to players to come to Arsenal. He had, for instance, compensated some for loss of income derived from sports businesses in the town in which they lived. (It was the known continuation of such practice that in due course proved to be a decisive factor in removing the maximum wage and increasing the player's share of any transfer fee, but this was more than thirty years later.) Not only this, but Norris had irregularised the books of Arsenal. He had, it is clear, acted, as he thought, for the benefit of the club—which owed its existence to his benefactions. But he had broken the law.[6] Norris's career and his downfall illustrate the classic principles of tragedy as enunciated by Aristotle. He died on July 30, 1934, an exile from football.

The successor to Norris as Chairman of Arsenal was Sir Samuel Hill-Wood, who wisely became a constitutional ruler, leaving all matters of club policy to Chapman.

The key to successful team-building in modern times is to find the right man for the right place. In 1928 Charles Buchan retired from playing and began a new, and successful, career as a sports-writer. His decision meant that Chapman had to find a successor. There was only one player who measured up to his requirements: the graceful and mesmeric David Jack, of Bolton. Themselves in process of rebuilding, Bolton, with no intention of parting with Jack, coolly asked a fee of £13,000—twice the existing record fee paid by Sunderland for Bob Kelly. After prolonged discussion Chapman beat the figure down to £11,500, below which the Bolton directors would not go. So, to a general

6. For reports of the case, see *Manchester Guardian*, February 6–7, 1929.

raising of eyebrows, Jack became an Arsenal player. A year later Alex James of Preston, and one of the stars of the so-called 'Wembley Wizards' Scottish team that defeated England by 5—1 in 1928, joined the club. The fee in his case was £9,000. At this juncture a split between clubs may be seen to appear. On the one hand are those with ample, on the other those with modest resources. The extravagance of the transfer market rapidly began to lead to a vicious spiral, with the rich becoming richer and the less rich progressively poorer. Where now are the glories of Bolton and Preston— and of many other clubs that once were household names?

And what was achieved? In 1927 Arsenal played in their first Cup Final—to be defeated by a single goal by Cardiff City, who thus became the first club to remove the F.A. Cup from English possession. The losing of this match was a personal disaster for the young Arsenal goalkeeper—Dan Lewis—himself a Welshman. Lewis made the one mistake that is not allowed to a goalkeeper. He let slip an innocuous ball and then knelt transfixed to watch the ball roll into the net. Three years later Arsenal reached the final again, their rivals, and the favourites, being Huddersfield Town. Huddersfield, inspired by Alex Jackson, had seven internationals in their team. The team as a whole still bore testimony to the fine management of Chapman during his tenure of office.

Chapman's intimate knowlege of the opposition enabled him to plan measures and counter-measures. The main requirement was to contain the mercurial Jackson, who was liable to use the whole field as his domain and not merely the statutory strip traditionally allowed to an outside-right. Young Hapgood was deputed never to lose sight of Jackson. Jackson was thus effectively controlled, and with defensive anxiety removed (save for the frequent and daring excursions of the Arsenal goalkeeper, Preedy), the forwards were able to get into their stride and strike with confidence. The forward line of Hulme, Jack, Lambert, James, Bastin—recruited from Exeter in 1929—was perhaps the best ever to represent Arsenal. James and Lambert scored the two goals that brought the Cup to Highbury for the first time.

Arsenal were at Wembley again in 1932, losing to Newcastle United (1—2) through a highly disputed goal, and in 1936, when they narrowly defeated Sheffield United by 1—0. Collaterally the League Championship was won in 1931,[7] 1933, 1934, and 1935. Arsenal were champions again in 1938.

Chapman died in 1934, and was succeeded by George Allison, one of the first radio commentators on football,[8] who in turn was succeeded by Whittaker in 1947. The fame of Arsenal resounded in unlikely places. So John Drinkwater wrote account of a suppositious first-round Cup replay against Aston Villa, at Villa Park. Drinkwater gave Arsenal credit for adventurous play. A goal up at half-time all looked well. But Villa took charge when 'the second half began, and it was soon clear that Arsenal were going to be hard put to it to hold on to their lead. To do them justice, they did not fall into the error of concentrating on defence. Their forwards made raiding movements at the smallest opportunity', but the Villa equalised. In extra time the tension mounted. Minutes from the end Arsenal were awarded a penalty. And the Villa goalkeeper saved it! 'The game,' added Drinkwater, 'in spite of its severity, had been played with a fairness that was a credit to professional football.'[9] A fantasy, maybe, but perhaps not too far from the truth. Drinkwater, no doubt, had in mind the rivalry of Villa and Arsenal in the early 1930s, and the third-round

7. With a record number of 66 points. Arsenal lost only 4 out of 42 League matches.
8. The B.B.C. began to transmit commentaries on the game in 1927. This innovation was resisted by some clubs, as, at a later date, incursions by television were opposed.
9. John Drinkwater, *Robinson of England*, London, 1937, Chapter 9, pp. 205–16.

tie of the season 1930–31, when, in fact, Villa lost the replay at home by 1—3.

Mindful, perhaps, of the social consternation created when the club first invaded Highbury the Arsenal directors pursued a single aim during those climactic years: to provide entertainment for all. It was necessary, then, to persuade the doubtful that professional soccer was no longer the prerogative of one class; that it was worth watching for its own sake. To achive this meant more than merely providing a good team. It meant utilising all the means available to establish a satisfactory public relationship. Knowing the mystical regard in which the nobility was held by the English, Chapman hoisted Lord Lonsdale on to his board of directors. Recognising the effectiveness of subliminal advertising he persuaded the transport authorities to re-name the adjacent underground station 'Arsenal'. In 1932 a new stand was opened by the then Prince of Wales and in the same year floodlighting was installed. Chapman also erected a forty-five-minute clock. Of this the F.A. disapproved, as of his experimenting with a white ball, and his numbering of players—first tried by him in 1928. When the F.A. encouraged a scheme for coaching public-schoolboys, however, Chapman was entirely in favour and put Highbury facilities at the disposal of the F.A. for this purpose.

The meteoric rise of Arsenal was not predictable. The later diminution of the club's reputation was. In the first place a conjunction of men and circumstances was fortuitous. In the second the precedents established challenged complacency, and by stimulating envy encouraged a revision of attitudes elsewhere.

During the twenties and thirties there were, of course, other teams of excellence than Arsenal, but none with the same collective zeal and determination, and the apparently limitless backing. It was on the whole an era of workmanlike football. With occasional glimpses of individual talent of a high order. The status of the player, however much he was (during the period of his competence) idolised on the terraces, remained much as it had been. His playing days over, he sank back into obscurity, content to own a small retail business, to take over the management of a public house, or, more reluctantly, to return to industry. A good deal of profit was being made out of football. The last person to benefit from it was the individual footballer.[10]

Clubs which made history during that time, apart from Arsenal, still belonged to the North and the Midlands. Sheffield Wednesday, promoted from the Second Division in 1926, reassembling their forces round the steadiness of Ernest Blenkinsop, the inventiveness of Jimmy Seed, and the wing-thrust of Mark Hooper and Ellis Rimmer, won the Championship of the League in 1929 and 1930. Their achievement was enhanced in the eyes of John McKenna, the League President, by reason of the fact that, staunchly patriotic, the Wednesday relied on English footballers. In 1931 West Bromwich Albion, led by W. G. Richardson at centre-forward, not only gained promotion to the First Division but, by defeating local rivals Birmingham, also won the Cup. Four years later the Albion, spirit compensating for any lack of individual brilliance, were back at Wembley. This time they lost, by 2—4, to Sheffield Wednesday, who thus marked their all-round standing.

In 1928 Manchester City returned to the First Division and after stabilising their position proceeded to storm the Challenge Cup citadel. Semi-finalists in 1932 (losing to Arsenal by 0—1), they reached the last stage in the following year. They lost to Everton (0—3), but according to a tradition they succeeded in the following year by defeating Portsmouth in the closing minutes of a memorable match. Frank Swift,[11] a novice goalkeeper, fainted at the end of the

10. If a competent footballer was earning upwards of £8 a week, however, it should be remembered that at that time the average skilled workman earned 60s. to 65s. a week.

11. Who later became a football writer and died in the Munich air disaster in 1958.

1934 Final. The City side of those years, with Busby, Cowan, and Bray the prominent forwards, was attractive to watch; quick, elegant, and fallible. It seemed that then the quality of play was of more significance than the results achieved. Everton, too, were a stylish team, centred on the greatest, most daring, and most successful of all centre-forwards of the inter-war years—Dixie Dean, who broke every goal-scoring record that existed.[12] The alleged value of a period in the Second Division (thrown as a crumb of comfort to the relegated with unfailing regularity) certainly seems borne out by the evidence of those years. Everton left the Second Division as Champions in 1931. The next year they dominated and won the First Division title. And in 1933 they won the Cup. Despite the rampages of the voracious Dean, Everton were a calm, methodical team, serenely guided from the rear by a classical defensive formation in which Sagar, the goalkeeper, Cook and Cresswell, full-backs, and Britton, at right-half, were, as near as makes no odds, peerless.

At the end of 1923 Wolverhampton Wanderers were in deep disgrace, relegated to Division III (Northern Section). The insult to the pride of an old and famous club was a traumatic experience only equalled by that suffered more recently when, after a sequence of mighty years, First Division status was lost (but quickly regained). The directors built a new stand, new lavatories, and invested in a new centre-forward, Tom Phillipson—a north-easterner currently playing with Swindon. Faith, perseverance, and Philipson's accuracy took Wolves out of Division III after only one season. At the end of 1932 the Championship of

12. Dean joined Everton from Tranmere Rovers (Birkenhead) in 1925, remaining with the Club until 1938, when he was transferred to Notts County. In 1927 he scored 60 goals in 39 League matches, and 22 in other games (cup-tie and representative). In all his League matches he scored 379 goals, the previous best total having been Bloomer's 352. It should be pointed out that the most impressive goal-scoring record in Britain is that of J. McGrory, of Glasgow Celtic, who retired in 1936, having amassed a grand total of 410 goals in league football.

Division II was attained. In 1938 Wolves were runners-up in Division I, and in the season following—according to majority opinion—all set for a Cup and League double. In the event Wolves, beaten by Portsmouth in the final, had to remain content with second place in both competitions. But it was a marvellous transformation of fortune—the prelude to the greatest era in the club's history—and Wolves on the outbreak of the Second World War were the golden boys of English soccer. Not only in Britain but also in foreign parts those deficient in general knowledge no longer needed to ask where Wolverhampton was. Nor did they need to ask who Major Buckley was.

In 1927 Wolves directors, acting in defence of their own interests after a dismal season, sacked their manager, appointing in his place Frank Buckley, who had managed the Norwich and Blackpool clubs. Prior to that he had served in the regular army, played at centre-half for Aston Villa, Birmingham, Derby County, and once (1914, against Ireland) for England. There was no reason to suppose that Buckley would do more than keep Wolves afloat. But he rose to the challenge in a remarkable manner. Resilient in manner, imperious by temperament, and never lacking for words, Buckley determined to make the best of the situation as he found it. Wisely, he refrained from asking for the moon. Chapman had all the money in the world at Highbury. Buckley virtually none. The assets of the club lay in an indelible loyalty. The new manager recognised that this asset must be turned to the best purpose. His first job was not to buy but to make players. Having made them, he was often to be found suffering from an *embarras de richesse*. Thus he was able to sell players at a considerable profit. The club became among the wealthiest in Britain.

Like the Jesuits Buckley believed in the virtues of early instruction. He sought out likely-looking boys in the neighbourhood of Wolverhampton and taught them the essentials of the game. His 'youth policy', forced on him by circumstance, became the envy of other managers and in due course football nurseries attached to senior clubs became the rule. Among the players whom Buckley brought into prominence were Stanley Cullis and Billy Wright, Jimmy Mullen and Bryn Jones. In 1938 the latter became an exhibit on the open stalls of the transfer market. Allison, of Arsenal, distraught for lack of a class inside-forward, bid £10,000. Enquiries from Tottenham Hotspur stirred the Wolves directors to put up the price to £12,000. Before the last gasps of astonishment at such audacity had died away, Allison was back with a revised offer of £14,000. The bidding closed and Jones went to Arsenal, with the record fee hanging round his neck like an albatross.

Ruthless in his defence of his club's interests, Buckley was avuncular in his relationship with his players. His directors, appreciating a 'card' when they met one, did not disapprove his theatricality. Buckley made news. He introduced new training routines. He was an early advocate of involvement with European football. He watered the pitch to prevent, so he said, injury to his players, but, according to his opponents, to place them at an advantage. He experimented with intravenous injections of, according to sceptics, 'monkey-gland' for his players. He investigated the possibilities of psycho-analysis. It was all rather febrile, but it was exciting. In that his team collected no major honour, however, Buckley was in one sense a failure. It was left to his protégé and (after an interregnum) successor, Stanley Cullis, to complete his work. Buckley died in 1964 at the age of 82. Modern management is based largely on the pioneer work of Chapman and Buckley, the two dominant influences of the first half of the twentieth century.

During those inter-war years British football certainly developed. But it developed in isolation. And it inculcated isolationism. Content to believe that by divine ordinance British football was the best in the world the British people watched it increasingly, and in so doing helped themselves to ignore the tumult of Europe. Although it was a shock for the first time to lose an international match abroad— against Spain in 1929—the growing strength of European and world football was largely an irrelevance. In 1930 Uruguay won the first World Cup in Argentina : But the fact that Brentford won all their home matches in the League was considered more newsworthy. Italy's success in the next World Cup in 1938 was overshadowed by the Jubilee of the F.A. (where Stanley Rous had succeeded Sir Frederick Wall as Secretary in 1934).

And then came the Second World War.

15

Brave New World

As seen in retrospect British football of that part of the twentieth century that has already dissolved falls into three compartments, the division between them being clearly marked by two world wars. Before the first war football, still earthy in character, was fitfully struggling to escape from the paternalist conventions of the Victorian era. In the twenty-year period laying between the wars the game was marked by a certain suspension of disbelief. Competitive football, urged on by ambitious managements and conducted by a growing number of talented players who could carry their professionalism with more ease than their predecessors, grew in theatrical interest. Over and above the arithmetic of results there was a conviction that spectacular football was its own justification.

One may argue that the thesis is reasonable. The 'escape' provided by the spectacle is temporary, and thereafter morale rides higher than before. Internationally, the relief of tension afforded by a game and the promise of amity contained in it are valuable. Such arguments have a grain of truth, but their total acceptance betrays a singular ingenuousness.

More and more in modern times the symbol of sport has become a political factor. Between wars the resurgence of extreme nationalism in various European countries led to the sportsman becoming a combatant in the contest of ideologies. In 1934 the Italians turned an international match against England, at Highbury, into a 'punch-up'. A battered and bruised home side, with seven Arsenal players included, surprised not only at their treatment but also the cause of it, survived the day and won the match 3—2. Four years later an English team submitted to instructions from a supine Embassy and with raised arms hailed Hitler in a prestigious new stadium in Berlin. The 'world game' was in a sorry state. In the gathering gloom of the late 1930s the label 'prestige' was firmly affixed to football. It has remained.

The new look of the game since the Second World War has been affected by consideration of prestige on all levels, so that in modern Britain, for better or worse, an arm of government is stretched over the game and an Under-Secretary of the Department of Education and Science watches over its interests.

However, the British place their faith in evolution rather than in revolution, and many of the radical changes in football have come about almost imperceptibly. The spectator, if not the player, generally prefers to keep his eye on the ball.

Conservatism and regard for tradition preserve a sense of apostolic succession. There is—and this is is the point from which this book started—the ideal of football. There may be many falls from grace but throughout the game there runs the image of the perfect footballer. A few footballers have become legends in their own lifetime: none more so than Stanley Matthews.

The Matthews era ran from 1932, when he first played for the senior club of his native town—Stoke City—until 1966 when, having in a football sense outlived the illustrious Meredith, he bowed out of the game, also with Stoke City. Matthews entered the game as modestly as he left it, but more obscurely. An unfashionable club, with no high successes engraved on its register, Stoke City was accustomed to cutting its coat according to its cloth. In an age of depression and unemployment its existence depended on the development of local resources. The manager of that time

J

was the Scotsman Bob McGrory—who spent in all some thirty years with Stoke, and deserves his place in the saga.

The boy Matthews was one of the relatively few natural geniuses of football. His sense of ball-control was superb, for he was one of those for whom a football was an extension of a bodily member. To dispossess Matthews was a task normally too considerable for any opponent. That this was so was not only due to ball-control but also to a sinuosity of movement, an uncanny judgement in altering tempo, and an endless, teasing patience.

The development of Matthews was aided by the corporate spirit of the Stoke club, and by the contemporaneous emergence of other fine players. In 1937 Stoke had three English internationals in the forward-line: Matthews, on the right wing, Johnson, on the left, and Freddie Steele, at centre-forward. Johnson was efficiently orthodox. Steele, whose career was destroyed by injury, was one of the most incisive and direct leaders of his generation. Matthews, intuitive and unorthodox, fed his artistry, which was supported by the charming embellishments of such fine players as Frank Soo and George Antonio, to his understanding colleagues. Matthews, in the end, made Stoke, but he was made by Stoke. Across the years he played for England, but not with the unfailing regularity that his genius should have commanded. Football selectors in Britain typify their race by having a general mistrust of genius. In subsequent years Matthews's sometime rival and sometime colleague (for he was also played at centre-forward) was the graceful Tom Finney of Preston. The English selectors were in a quandary when inevitably faced with the names of these two players.

In 1938 Matthews spoke of wanting a transfer from Stoke. The citizens rose in a body and hung out banners with the device: 'Matthews must not go'. Nor did he, until 1947, when with a home and business interests in Blackpool he joined the Blackpool club. By the ordinary laws of the game Matthews by this time was a veteran. Yet his skill shining out even more brightly and with no signs of diminishing, the best was to come.

In 1948 Blackpool met Manchester United in the Cup Final and were beaten 4—2. Three years later Blackpool were again unsuccessful, being beaten by Newcastle United, by two goals from Jackie Milburn. This, incidentally, was the last period in which Newcastle United lived up to their meticulous traditions, and their inspiration for the finals of 1951, 1952 (Newcastle 1, Arsenal 0), and 1955 (Newcastle 3, Manchester City 1) was the couthness of Milburn, a versatile forward endowed with some degree of infallibility. The greatness of that Newcastle team lived on, vicariously, until the European Cup Final of 1967: Simpson, Newcastle's Scottish goalkeeper of 1952 and 1955 was the Celtic goalkeeper of the last year!

Fading memories of another club of honourable and honest traditions were revived at Wembley in 1953, when Bolton once again reached the Final. In this team there was still a good deal of fire in the belly. Lofthouse, a player who combined vigour, determination, and generosity, and who had won a historic match for England, in Vienna, in 1952, was the Bolton centre-forward. The scorer of six goals between the English and the Irish Leagues in the autumn of 1952, and at the end of that season crowned as the 'Footballer of the Year', Lofthouse was confidently predicted as the likely determinant of the Cup Final of 1953. In the end that Cup Final was handed down to posterity as 'Matthews's Final'.

It might have been otherwise. Lofthouse scored for Bolton within the opening minutes of the game. Half an hour later, a Bolton half-back having been injured and sent on to the wing, Blackpool equalised through Mortensen, a player not improperly described in his heyday as dynamic. But Bolton scored again before half-time, and yet again soon after the interval. To all intents Blackpool were defeated, but refused to believe that they were beaten. Mortensen, controlling a ball that had eluded a Bolton defender on its way from Matthews, scored again. Within two minutes of full-time—Matthews now commanding the field like a Caesar—Mortensen scored again from a free-kick. There remained the time added for injuries. Matthews to Perry, outside-left, and the winning goal.

The mystique of Matthews continued. The man himself, shy, reserved, dedicated, silent amid rising torrents of volubility, went on. Long past the normal term of super-annuation for even the most durable footballers he was per-suaded back to a dishevelled, relegated, Stoke City. In 1963, with renewed spirits, the club returned to the First Division. Before his final retirement Matthews became the first pro-fessional footballer to be awarded a knighthood, in 1965.

This unique and continuous career was laid out against a rapidly changing background, and to some extent the fantasy of the one career for a time at least veiled the magnitude of the changes.

After the end of the Second World War in contrast to the conditions obtaining in 1919 there was a general and earnest impulse to reconstitute the social order. That many of the hopes of those days ended either only in partial fulfil-ment, or, finally, in disillusion, does not detract from the sincerity of the impulse. The rank and file footballer was alive to the fact that the conditions of his employment left him with a considerable handicap in the race towards equality. He was, more than most, the servant of his masters, and controlled by a contract that was both unfair and out-of-date. On the other hand the concept of the in-evitable superiority of British football—which had suffered some blows in the inter-war years—was being destroyed by the facts of the post-war international situation. Britain, now no longer even *secundus inter pares* and gravely im-poverished, had to fight for her place in the world.

In 1938, to mark the seventy-fifth anniversary of the F.A., England beat the Rest of Europe in a commemorative match at Highbury that was the prelude to a banquet 'at which it was even more apparent in what high esteem the F.A. was held throughout the football nations and how far the fun of football itself had spread'.[1] Nine years later a side representing Great Britain beat the Rest of Europe in a match marking the return of the British Association to membership of the F.I.F.A.[2] In 1948 the 26th F.I.F.A. Congress was held in London—a gesture signifying a new relationship for British football. The relationship, however, was one that needed getting used to.

Soon after the end of the war the first Russian team to visit Britain, Moscow Dynamo, gave several exhibitions of the Soviet will to succeed: at Stamford Bridge, Ninian Park, White Hart Lane, and Ibrox. Unhampered by niceties of genteel behaviour the Russians drew with Chelsea—before the largest crowd ever to occupy Stamford Bridge—and Rangers; beat Cardiff by 10—1, and, in farcical and foggy conditions, Arsenal by 4—3. The quality of ruthlessness that characterised both training and playing methods caused a certain concern, just as the fluidity of movement, and the retreating defensive plan, of the team aroused incredulity. If football could be taken as seriously as this, then some revision of approach would be needed.

In the spring of 1947 England lost face by losing to a country reckoned among the weaker football-playing nations, Switzerland, in Zürich, while Scotland suffered a similar fate in Brussels. Balance was somewhat restored by victories by the English over Portugal, and by Scotland over Luxembourg. But the defeats needed some explaining.

1. *Association Football*, ed. A. H. Fabian, 4 vols., London, 1960. I., p. 31.
2. The growth of the influence of this body is shown by the expansion of its membership. In 1904 there were 6 affiliated Associations; in 1914, 24; in 1923, 31; in 1938, 51; in 1950, 73; in 1954, 84. From the public point of view F.I.F.A., the headquarters of which are in Zürich, arouses interest as the body responsible for the organisation of the 'Jules Rimet' trophy—the 'World Cup'. In 1961 Stanley Rous, previously Secretary of the Football Association, was elect ed President of F.I.F.A

At this juncture the F.A.—hampered as always by the conflicting claims of international duty and league requirements—appointed a team manager to supervise the national team. This was Walter Winterbottom, at one time a wing-half-back with Manchester United. The task facing Winterbottom was formidable, not least of all because of the English inability to adjust their inclinations to the demands of the new nationalism. The English director, player, spectator, at that time thought in terms of club rather than of country. In Scotland, Wales, and Ireland, for obvious reasons loyalty to a national team (often assembled with difficulty in view of the claims on many key players by their English clubs) was more strongly developed. Thus, while England was never deficient in players of high quality there was insufficient opportunity to unify their actions and thoughts.

In international matches the home countries did well enough during the first few post-war seasons. Though the defeat of England by Sweden, in Stockholm, and a dismal tour by Wales in Portugal, Belgium and Switzerland, in 1949, shook complacency, in the following year England entered in the World Cup for the first time. The contest in 1950 took place in Brazil, which fact gave many their first opportunity to realise the full potential of soccer fanaticism.

England were placed in Group 2, with Spain, the U.S.A. and Chile. The English party, which included Williams, Ramsey, Aston, Wright, Dickinson, Finney, Mannion, Bentley, Mortensen, Mullen, and Matthews—a galaxy of talent in every department—was expected at least to reach the final. In the event the excursion culminated in anti-climax. England lost to the U.S.A., and also to Spain. After all excuses were made—obstructive tactics by opponents, inferior refereeing, climate, and so on—the fact remained that the team had not been geared to this kind of occasion. The English (and they won some credit for this) treated the game as a game: an out-of-date attitude, however commendable. One comfort remained: the final between Brazil and Uruguay, and won by the latter, was refereed by an Englishman, George Reader, to the satisfaction of both finalists and public alike. As with British policemen, so with British referees, it is understood to be correct for a courteous foreigner to say that they are wonderful.

So far as Europe was concerned the outstanding soccer country of the early post-war period was Austria, then occupied by both Russian and Western soldiery. Football, as will be seen in other cases, tends often to reach a climax in times of distress. It is, then, of bardic significance: an expression, in symbolic terms, of the will of the people. The Austrians, backed with half a century of tradition, combining Teutonic and Italian influences in their football as in their music, introduced a new finesse to the game, playing with a deceptive delicacy of touch. In the season of 1950–1 they defeated Scotland twice. In the following year they drew with England at Wembley in a match memorable for the mastery of the great centre-half Ocwick, and the tenacity of Ramsey and Lofthouse for the home side. The return match, in Vienna, was that in which Lofthouse, by scoring a spectacular goal to win the match, earned his place in the footballer's Pantheon. So, too, did the half-back line of Wright, Froggatt, and Dickinson.

The turning-point in the history of modern British soccer was November 25, 1953. On this day, at Wembley, England met Hungary.[3] For the first time in history England was made to look a second-rate soccer power. Hungary—their team including Kocsis, Hidegkuti, and Puskas as the spearhead of attack—combined the individual skills characteristic of the best continental tradition with the enterprise and initiative hitherto thought of to characterise the British style. Hungary, scoring within sixty seconds, completely outplayed the English, leaving them slow-footed and insecure

3. *England:* Merrick; Ramsey, Eckersley; Wright, Johnston, Dickinson; Matthews, Taylor, Mortensen, Sewell, Robb.

at almost every turn. The half-time score was 4—2 to Hungary. The final score (Ramsey having converted a penalty and Hidegkuti having completed a hat-trick) was 6—3. Of the English team of that day only three remained (Merrick, in goal, Wright and Dickinson) to face Scotland at Hampden Park. The Scots, also in a state of transition, were unable to compete with an English side determined to restore at least a little of their pride, and lost by 2—4. But English confidence evaporated in the spring. The match against Yugoslavia at Belgrade was lost by a single goal, and the form of the forwards was lamentable. On May 23, 1954, the team went to Budapest. The Hungarians improved on their Wembley scoring feat and massacred the English to the extent of 7—1. Those matches are talked of to this day in Budapest.

There is one consideration lying outside the immediate field to be taken into account. The Hungarian nation at this point in history was once again rediscovering its identity. Nationalism is one thing; this kind of nationalism is another. After centuries of catastrophe and under a burden of recent doubts and difficulties the post-war Hungarians in seeking a new sense of cohesion invested their faith in those activities which indigenous skills could be given fullest scope. Throughout history the Hungarians had distinguished themselves, by courage, by a talent for graceful and co-ordinated movement (so men spoke of the 'dancing Magyars'), by quickness of intellectual perception, and by imagination. An artistic nation, they imbued football with a sense of artistry, but did not cancel either its virility or its chivalry. Thus we may begin to see the international pattern of modern football in its psychological context.

It took further disappointments in the World Cup Series of 1954 and 1958 to get the British really to readjust their sights, although, as will be seen, individual clubs were moving rather faster in what may be called the right direction than the national authorities. In 1954 both Scottish and

English teams presented themselves as World Cup candidates in Switzerland. The former, outclassed in every department, failed to score a single goal in their group—while conceding eight. The latter reached the quarter-finals, to lose to Uruguay by 4—2. Crumbs of comfort were found in the sportsmanship of the British representatives and (again) in the admirable control of a number of difficult games by British referees. The final, between West Germany and Hungary, was refereed by W. Ling, whose experience of supervising international matches of the top grade went back to the Olympic Games of 1948.

Until the Munich disaster of February, 1958 (see p. 269), the English had been rated as favourites for the World Cup, to be played that year in Sweden. For the first time all four British Associations were represented, and as it happened each team was linked either directly or indirectly with Manchester. Winterbottom was a former United player, while Doherty, team manager of the Northern Irish side, had played for City. Jimmy Murphy, in charge of the fragile Welsh hopes, was assistant to Matt Busby at Old Trafford. Busby himself prior to Munich, had been team manager of the Scottish team.

The champions that year were Brazil: a classic, virtually flawless combination, with a virtuoso in every position. England, for three matches using the famous Wolves half-back trio of Clamp, Wright and Slater in its entirety, only failed to make the quarter-finals after a play-off to determine the leadership of their group with the Soviet Union, who won by 1—0. Northern Ireland, inspired by Danny Blanchflower, and not lacking in the finer skills of the game, did reach the quarter-finals, but found Brazil and France too experienced opponents. Wales, with the brothers Charles, Ivor Allchurch, and Cliff Jones, as the mainstays of the side, also needed a play-off—to determine the second place in their group. This they forfeited by losing to Hungary. Of the British entrants the Scots, drawing one match and losing two, were the least successful. Wales, Ireland, and Scotland are at a great disadvantage in international football, being reliant to a great extent on the munificence of the English clubs to which many of their best players migrate.

During his term of office as manager of the England team Winterbottom effected a quiet revolution. Recognising that in England, in spite of foreign effervescense on the international plane, there is a broader base for football than anywhere in the world he worked on the assumption that the foundations should be secured. Thus he extended the whole system of F.A. coaching—the results of which may be best exemplified in the overall raising of standards on the schoolboy level, and in the universities. In this connection should be mentioned the fact that in recent years changing attitudes to the nature of football, and to the social system in general, have made it possible for young men who have learned football at grammar school and university to embrace it as a profession. On the top level Winterbottom not only assembled England players for more thorough and co-ordinated training (there now being national training establishments at Lilleshall in Shropshire, and at the Crystal Palace) but also indicated to them that, as the Austrians, the Hungarians, and the Brazilians had shown the game was not only a physical but also an intellectual exercise. Winterbottom made systematised football, as exploited by the Brazilians, credible to the British. Indeed, for some years the supposed merits of 4–2–4, 4–3–3, have caused a good deal of innocent bemusement.

A further point of involvement in world (or, at least, European) football came during this period through the slender soccer brain-drain that was caused less by interest in the game than by the lure of the rewards available to the talented few abroad, in contrast to the more modest earnings then customary in Britain. John Charles, exceptional in his talent for acclimatisation, was the star of Juventus, Turin, for a number of seasons. Greaves, Hitchens, and Denis Law also expatriated themselves to Italy with varying degrees of success.

The 1962 World Cup series, held in Chile, and remembered less for the quality of football than for the fracas between Chile and Italy which was of such ferocity that even the most bloodthirsty among the spectators called for an incompetent referee to put a halt to the proceedings. The English team, still showing little change of approach to the game, reached the quarter-finals, but were comprehensively beaten by the Brazilians. In 1962 Brazil still played eight of the victorious 1958 side and had the illustrious Pele been fit there would have been nine. The duty of a football manager is to achieve success. Winterbottom though the architect of future success had, in his own right, achieved too little. In 1963 he was replaced by Alf Ramsey, a Tottenham and much-capped England player of the 1950s. It was for him to fashion the shape of things to come.

It was in 1955 that the French newspaper *L'Equipe* convened a meeting of prominent European clubs in Paris. This was in order to discuss a project to inaugurate a continental championship, based on a home-and-away knock-out competition between the various national league title-holders. British delegates at the meeting were Chelsea (English champions for the first time in their Jubilee year of 1955) and Hibernian, representing the Scottish League. The new competition was approved, and was inaugurated in the season 1955–6. In keeping with the cautionary principles that underlay English football Chelsea were advised by the League to withdraw from the European Cup[4] on the grounds that it would interfere with their domestic programme. Since, however, Sir George Graham, Secretary of the Scottish F.A., was on the international committee of management for the European Cup no hindrance was placed in the way of Hibernian, who not only reached the semi-

4. Properly, European Champion Clubs' Cup.

final at the first time of asking but, it is believed, made a profit of £25,000 on the enterprise. The Cup was won for the first time by Real Madrid, who went on to win it for each of the four succeeding seasons.

During the second year of the competition Manchester United made their bow on the redesigned European stage. Here some recapitulation is necessary. At the end of the war this club, like every other, needed to reconstruct its playing resources. It was also necessary to rebuild the ground and its complex of buildings, which had suffered considerable war damage. In 1945 there was, it happened, a vacancy for a team manager. Hearing of this Matt Busby sent in an application. This, together with his known experience of the game and his palpable shrewdness, impressed the Chairman of the club—H. P. Hardman, himself a former amateur player of distinction, and an international—and Busby was appointed, at first with a contract for five years. By 1948 Busby had constructed the most stimulating team known in England during the first half of the century and had also formulated a clear, decisive, progressive policy for his club. Success could only be assured by planning in depth— through the reserves to the junior and youth teams. For three years running, in 1947–8–9, United were second in the League. In 1951 they were also runners-up. Inevitably, perhaps, the Championship was won in the following year. Further Championship honours followed in 1956 and 1957; which meant qualification for Europe. Meanwhile, in 1948 the United were Cup-winners. In 1957 and 1958 they were losing finalists.

When Manchester United presumed to enter the European Cup in 1956 the Football League, as in the case of Chelsea, advised against the undertaking. But Busby, confident in the strength of his playing staff, and having calculated for just such a contingency, observed to the League that, while appreciating the point of view put to him, he could guarantee that League commitments would not suffer. Nor, as the results prove, did they. The United, young, keen, adaptable, reached the semi-final of the European Cup, losing to Real Madrid. By their performance up to that point the Manchester team had made its impact on the European scene. This, it was agreed, was English football at its best.

Thus when in the next season Busby's players looked set to offer a real challenge to Madrid excitement was general—abroad as well as at home. The United disposed of the Czech team Dukla, of Prague, in the first round proper, and in the quarter-final were drawn against Red Star, Belgrade. Such was the strength of the United that Busby (whose Youth team had won the F.A. Youth Cup five times in five seasons) could afford to omit five seasoned internationals. At Old Trafford the United beat Red Star by 2—1. On February 5, 1958, the return match took place in Belgrade. After half an hour the United were three goals ahead, but had to fight desperately to save the match, which ended in a draw, 3—3. The United, however, were once again through to the semi-final, where they would meet Milan.

And then on the way home, on February 6, tragedy struck. The aeroplane carrying the team, its officials, a number of journalists, as well as other passengers, crashed on the snow-and ice-bound airfield at Munich. Seven players, three other members of the staff, eight journalists, and three other passengers were killed outright. Nine players and their manager were injured, some severely. Two weeks after the accident Duncan Edwards, then, perhaps, the most talented player in England, died. The shock of this disaster brought the world together in sympathy and respect, and messages of condolence came from monarchs and heads of governments, from the Pope, and from thousands of other notable persons and institutions.

On February 17 a memorial service was held in St. Martin's-in-the-Fields, London, and the Bishop of Chester gave a moving address. In the course of this address the

Bishop beautifully indicated the present-day responsibilities of the footballer, and also the way in which Manchester United had fulfilled their responsibilities:

'. . . Those well fitted to express an opinion have spoken of the quite outstanding quality which Manchester United has displayed, and, during the last ten years under the genius of Matt Busby, young men have not only been trained to a high standard of technical efficiency but they have also been inspired with a loyalty to the club and to the game which has been a pattern for the best that men can achieve. This character has brought the team to the highest places of the game in the country. It has made the name of Manchester United a household word. It has also given the team an opportunity of travelling to many foreign countries and there, in addition to playing good football, they have proved themselves fine ambassadors on the football ground and off it.

'When we remember that during the season a million people each week in this country watch professional football, we can appreciate the responsibility which is laid upon these young players. They are admired, idolised, glamourised, imitated. They set a standard which, unseen, perhaps, certainly leaves its mark on the moral standards of our society. They have a responsibility not only to play efficiently but to play well, and it is because Manchester United have acquitted themselves so splendidly in the wider as well as the ultimate discharge of their duty that the team has become a by-word for those who play a good game wherever football is played.'[5]

5. cf. '. . . in 21 seasons since the Second World War Manchester United have finished first or second in the First Division on 11 occasions and for good measure, they have made four appearances in the F.A. Challenge Cup Final, two of them successfully.
'Over the years United have figured prominently in the European and international scene. Individually and collectively they have been no less triumphant as ambassadors for the game overseas than they have in this country. Season after season making history all the time.
. . . 'And so United, Champions again this year, have made history

For the time being Jimmy Murphy now controlled the United team, which with former reserves and one or two new signings beat Milan in the first leg of the semi-final of the European Cup (losing on aggregate, however, by 3—4), and reached the final of the F.A. Cup. At Wembley, in an emotionally charged atmosphere, the United lost to Bolton Wanderers—still directed by Lofthouse, who scored the only two goals of the match.

By this time the magnitude of the challenge of the European clubs was clear. The outstanding performers in the Spanish, Portuguese, and Italian teams, who dominated the final with a monstrous regularity, were drawn from various countries. The directors of Real Madrid, Benfica, Milano, were prepared to invest sums of money almost beyond belief in the purchase of great footballers. In Britain there was, and to some extent remains, a prejudice against this parody of capitalistic philosophy. The foundation of a good British side was the education of youngsters to the standard required for First Division competence. Good club sides won the national leagues, but in the major European competition did not get beyond a certain point.

Wolverhampton Wanderers[6] (pioneers of post-war fixtures with foreign teams and remembered for stirring contests particularly against Honved of Budapest, and Spartak and Dynamo of Moscow), Burnley, Rangers, Ipswich Town,

---

as it was foretold, and they will contine so to do. Not necessarily because they have so much prolific talent, not necessarily because they are so self-assured, not necessarily because in Matt Busby they have probably the kindliest and shrewdest manager in the business, today. There is a dedication throughout the club that cannot be denied, a dedication that above all else makes it "tick" so smoothly . . .'.

Eric Todd, 'The History Makers', in *The Guardian*, May 13, 1967.

6. In their most successful period in the fifties and early sixties the Wolves were captained by W. Wright (also captain of England, and the first player to play in 100 internationals—reaching this peak of achievement in 1959) and managed by S. Cullis. After thirty years, as player and official of the club, Cullis was removed from his post in the autumn of 1964. The team were doing badly, and at the season's end were relegated.

Dundee, Tottenham Hotspur, Hearts, Celtic, Liverpool, all went so far but no further. It seemed that the best British teams were for ever cut in the mould of gallant losers. The reason for the efficiency bar becoming effective at latest at the semi-final lay not only in the strategic blue-prints, well studied beforehand, by which they worked. The science of football becomes a reality. The British by nature are un-addicted to science, preferring to work by the light of nature.

It is, perhaps, significant that prior to 1966–67—the *annus mirabilis* of British soccer—the outstanding British successes in respect of European competitions were in the European Cup-Winners' Cup, instituted in 1960. Cup-winners are a different breed from League winners and the secondary competition (as it is regarded) attracts a different participation. Some clubs make their way into the competition somewhat impertinently. In 1963, for instance, Bangor City—modestly housed in the Cheshire League and represented either by those not good enough or too old for a senior League—took part in the European Cup-Winners' Cup. They were so entitled since they had won the Welsh Cup. What is more, before burying their unexpected crock of gold in Snowdonia, they forced their first-round oppon-ents, Naples, to the indignity of a play-off. This, however, was the year in which a British side did win a trophy, for the visitors in the final of the Cup-Winners' Cup were Totten-ham Hotspur. A sensitive, cultured side, League champions and Cup-winners in 1961 and Cup-winners also in the following year, the Spurs beat Atletico Madrid by 5—1: the notable men of that Spurs team were Danny Blanch-flower, John White, Jimmy Greaves, and Cliff Jones (from Ireland, Scotland, England, and Wales respectively), players of great talent, but also imbued with a sense of *joie de vivre*. Two years later another English side, playing at Wembley, won the same trophy. This was West Ham United. Their rivals were T.S.V. Munich The significance of this match in particular was that West Ham, managed

by Ron Greenwood, played in a more calculated manner
than had hitherto been seen from an English team free-
flowing movements, part prepared but part extemporised,
bewildered the German side (who displayed more of what
might heretofore have been described as the 'English style'),
and West Ham were able to finish their movements con-
clusively. This victory had further consequences in that a
strong West Ham influence was thereafter brought to bear
on the English national side.

In 1963 the Football Association celebrated its centenary.
The manner in which this event was celebrated marked the
changed condition of the game. The home international
championship, won by a renascent Scotland, took place as
usual—but with diminished splendour. Of more significance
were the celebratory visit to Wembley of Brazil (the match
ending in a 1—1 draw and hardly living up to its billing),
the spring tour of the English side (which, for the first time,
played at Leipzig against Eastern Germany), and the
attractive eight-nation amateur international tournament
that took place in the north-east, with the final (won by
Scotland against Western Germany) at Sunderland. Also in
honour of the festival year the European Cup Final, between
Milan and Benfica, was staged at Wembley. This was not,
however, the first occasion on which this final was staged in
Britain. That between Real Madrid and Frankfurt-Ein-
tracht took place at Hampden Park, where the gate receipts
of £55,000 constituted a British and European record. Real
Madrid beat the German team by 7—3, the latter having
eliminated Rangers in the semi-final by 6—1 in Frankfurt,
and 6—3 in Glasgow.

Thus the second hundred years of organised football
began on a new note. Domestic professional football is seen
to exist almost entirely as a testing ground for a more
universal game.

In the transitional period—of the late fifties and early
sixties—the character of football changed. Experimentation

in the 4–3–3 *and* 4–2–4 formation abounded. A general run of substitutes was permitted, after an experimental period in League football in 1965–6. In the fight to reach the top a tendency to replace keenness with malevolence of rivalry emerged, both on the field and, more frequently, on the surrounding terraces. Football—despite the reservations of clubs and League over some years established as a regular television entertainment—received more publicity than ever before. Its patrons were thereby drawn from a wider section of the community, and its financial structure became more involved.

But, paradoxically, the numbers watching football matches declined. In 1948–9 the aggregate attendances came to 41,271,414; in 1966–7 the comparative figure was 28,902,596. This falling-off is due to a variety of causes— more counter attractions, more opportunity to travel, more participation in sport,[7] and a preference for sitting at home and watching the televised game, among them. But it is also due to a new selectivity. The old-style spectator supported his team through thick and thin. A few of this type survive, but the connoiseur will only watch attractive football while the materialist will patronise only a winning side. The sentimentalist deplores the sad plight of once famous British (more particularly English) clubs. Notts County (with a hundred years of history), Bolton Wanderers (eminences of forty years ago), Aston Villa (until recently described as 'aristocrats of the game'), and many more, languish far away from the pastures of Europe. Once again facts speak. In 1948 the average gate at Villa Park was 41,436, but in 1967 it was only 16,757.

The key figure is, of course, the player himself, who now enjoys an enhanced status. The top player enjoys his fame earlier than used to be the case. This is due to two reasons. First, the obvious quickening of the pace of the game.

7. There are 2,500 amateur football clubs (some of high standing) in England under the jurisdiction of the F.A.

Second, the general adulation of youth by youth. The theatricality of football has, as has been shown, been a constant factor in the history of the game. In the long course of its story one picks out some figures who behaved as tragedians—judging by his portrait Alf Common, of Middlesbrough, belonged to this class—or as comedians—here the claims of the irrepressible Charlie Tully, of Celtic, rank high. In the lower leagues there was not one club in the past that did not have its music-hall turn. The great majority, however, were good, constant, repertory men. To-day the emphasis is on extreme youth; the most talented among the prodigies model themselves to fit into the so-called 'pop world'. Off the field (but not always on) the idol of the teenagers is, by style, dress, and coiffure, often a dandy. He also enjoys emoluments once unheard of, and withal a degree of independence unknown to his predecessors. The football player has seen the game become a top entertainment. He has seen no reason why he should not be rewarded according to his drawing power as entertainer. The logic of his case is irresistible—the more so since the P.F.A., with commendable generosity, has supported the principle of just rewards for high skill as well as remembering the claims of the average.

Dissatisfaction with archaic procedures, stringent conditions of employment, and scales of pay incommensurate with talent, was expressed soon after the Second World War. In 1952 the findings of a Committee of Investigation appointed by the Ministry of Labour, after a deadlock in negotiations between the Football League and the Players' Union,[8] were published. The Committee suggested that maximum wages[9] (more recently settled by the National Arbitration Tribunal of 1947) could reasonably be raised, that match bonuses and talent-money payments should be

8. Now known as the Professional Footballers' Association.
9. Then standing at £20 (£17 in the close season) a week for a full-time player aged twenty and over.

made obligatory, that in disciplinary matters players should be able to have legal or Union representation. But the Union's main submission, for the removal of the maximum wage limit and of restrictions on the freedom of players to move at their own request, were turned down. A cogent passage in the report reads:

'Although the existing provisions concerning maximum wags and transfers were "unusual", the Committee did not think that the alternatives suggested by the Union would make for the continued success of the League, or would prove to the ultimate advantage of the professional player. Richer clubs would undoubtedly be at an advantage in the competition for players, and, unless clubs had a right to retain any players, they might be faced with the task of trying to build an entirely new team after each playing season. Star players would tend to be concentrated with a few rich clubs, and thus the general standard of League football would decline. In many cases this would lead to a fall in gate receipts and in a worsening in the conditions of professionals of average ability.'[10]

It took the Professional Footballers' Association nearly nine years to reach their main objective, the abolition of the maximum-wage system and of the former type of contract between club and player. At the end of 1960 negotiations between the League and the P.F.A. (predictably) broke down—and the Association threatened strike action. As on a former occasion the strike did not take place, being called off, after a meeting engineered by the Ministry of Labour, two days before the first League matches to have been affected took place. The maximum wage was abolished, and new contractual agreements were formulated. Thus we arrive at the point where a few professional footballers may earn more than £100 a week and on transfer deals that, reaching to the skies, now top £200,000 receive 5 per cent of

10. See 'The White Paper on Professional Players', *F.A. Year Book*, 1952–3, pp. 20–2.

the agreed figure.[11] In the negotiations that have taken place since the Second World War the P.F.A. have been led by able men—particularly J. Guthrie, J. Hill and D. Dougan. Hill demonstrated his versatility by renovating the fortunes of Coventry City, of which he became manager, and taking them, in a sky-blue vapour of publicity, to Divison I.

The result of this, as foreseen in 1953, has been to tend to concentrate the best talent in a few wealthy clubs, and to make life much more difficult for the small clubs. Although this situation is not entirely new (the Arsenal led the way in buying up rare skills a generation ago, while power in Scotland has always reposed in a few hands) it brings a new set of factors into the English game. Thus, the law of diminishing returns makes the prospect of clubs that have fallen on evil times look particularly gloomy. While the demands not only for quality football but also comfortable amenities for spectators make it seem likely that in the not too distant future some towns with two first-class (by courtesy, at least) teams, will have to make do with one. The fight for the survival of the club of average repute is really on. There are many whose hopes are centred on a minnow's follow-through in the F.A. Cup, on one or two profitable encounters in the Football League Cup, or on the providential arrival of a soon-to-be-sold boy prodigy; but whose finances are precariously guaranteed by bingo sessions, private football pools, and the social activities of the Supporters' Club. About the Third and Fourth Divisions, the Scottish Second Division, and the Irish League, there is a certain pathetic charm. But—as the passing of the once famous Accrington Stanley showed, in 1962—pathos and charm, in the temper of the present age, are expendable.

11. This does not obtain if the player himself seeks a transfer. A report, generally critical of the controlling organisations and the financial structure of the game, prepared by Political and Economic Planning (P.E.P.), was issued under the title of *English Professional Football*, in August, 1966.

16

Tribal Ending

During its last phase—that is, since the foundation of the
F.A.—British football has increasingly reflected the detailed
pattern of social, political, and economic forces at work
within the body politic. On the grand scale there may be
observed in its development the rise and fall of an imperial
philosophy, a sense of superior virtue in respect of the
world at large, an hostility to newer ideals promulgated
from abroad, a retreat to isolationism, and a final attempt to
readjust to new circumstances. After the Second World War
the overriding national problem has been to accommodate
internal ideas to external standards. Underlying the problem
there has been a traumatic experience—more often felt subconsciously than consciously, and born of the realisation
that Britain does not stand where she did.

By 1966 the nation as a whole awaited a miracle. And
there was a miracle: the English football team won the
World Cup. Less than a year later Scotland, represented by
Celtic, won the European Cup. So there was dual opportunity to recollect the virtues of the past and to rehearse
the certainty of further triumph in the future. At no time has
football signified more to the British people.

It may also be observed that the events of 1966 and 1967
were watched by the world at large (the estimated television
audience being 400,000,000), and that the achievements won
a new kind of respect. If, unfortunately, swords have not
been turned into ploughshares it is clear that the symbolic
warfare of the football field has caused the sublimation at
least of some hostilities. In a sense the ritual of modern football—the universal pageant—represents for the many what

the stylised *Calcio* of the Florentines did for the few. There
is a point at which a game is no longer a game, but
a general statement of human practices, principles, and
ideas. By referring to the first chapter it will be recognised
that the wheel has come full circle.

The fate of nations often seems to depend on individuals.
So it was, at this point in time, with English football.

'. . . England bulged with great footballers and yet the
World Cup of 1966 was decided by a young inside-forward
who, only one month before, was given scarcely an inside
chance of playing in the series. Geoff Hurst may have
proved that in football this is the age of the common man,
just so long as he can do something as uncommon as scoring three goals in a World Cup Final.'[1]

But in the new context the individual is not self-sufficient.
The fact that the right person was in the right place at the
right time was not in this case fortuitous. The three goals
that Hurst scored against West Germany were the culmination of intricate, and many-sided, organisation. That
Hurst was the player of quality that he was derived from
the excellences of his own club, West Ham, and its able and
engaging manager, Ron Greenwood. That he was finally
chosen for the climactic occasion by the decision of the England team-manager, Ramsey. Behind Ramsey was the
expertise and phlegmatic efficiency of the F.A., of which
the capacity for superb organisation by a few highly competent hands is unrivalled. And there was the Government.

In general the age of private patronage is past (in football the antique principles linger on, as is shown in England
by the resurrection of Coventry City through the subsidies of
a local worthy) and governments are required to supply the
want. In the year before the World Cup was to be staged in
England the British Government made a grant of £500,000
to the F.A. (of which 20 per cent was to be repaid). 'The
F.I.F.A. Committee', observed Sir Stanley Rous, 'will be

1. *World Cup '66*, ed. Hugh McIlvanney, London, 1966.

very pleased. When the World Cup was given to England I do not think that anybody thought the government would be so interested and generous. I feel that much of this has been due to Mr. Howell (Minister with Special Responsibility for Sport)'.[2] The F.A. itself laid out £150,000.

Such funds were primarily invested in the renovation and modernisation of grounds on which the matches in the series were to be played. It is, perhaps, characteristic that whereas in countries where the World Cup had previously been played new, often magnificent stadiums had been specially designed and built, in England the traditions were served. Historic grounds—of Aston Villa, Everton, Manchester United, Middlesbrough, Sheffield Wednesday, Sunderland, and at Wembley—were given extensive face-lifts.

The onus of ultimate justification lay with Ramsey. His mission was to develop not so much a winning team, but a team with the will to win. That he was capable of conceiving and executing long-term strategy was demonstrated when in the 1961–2 season he made Ipswich Town—the most unlikely candidates of all time for high honour—League champions.

Ramsey had many assets. He spoke and acted with authority, but without ostentation. A quiet determination akin to, but different from, ruthlessness, enabled him to control the occasional volatility and other temperamental quirks of the players under his command. Thus he was able to plan for contingencies in the confidence that those who were to execute his strategies could do so with a sanguine understanding. Himself a full-back, Ramsey recognised that the crux of modern international football was inviolable defence. Prevention being better than cure he adopted,

2. The report of the Public Accounts Committee issued a year after the winning of the World Cup was critical of the investment: 'A loan was made to the Football Association towards the cost of staging the World Cup without any provision for giving security or for action by the lender in case of default'. Which shows now hard it is to please all the people all the time.

but varied, the fashionable current theories of the Brazilian-type 4–3–3 formation. Having played in the disastrous match of 1953 against Hungary he carried with him the memory of that day, and a conviction that the match could at least have been saved. 'Four of those goals,' he once said, 'came from outside our penalty area. We should never have lost.'[3]

At the same time the ideal purpose of an invincible defence is to act as a spring-board for attack. Defence is not, though it may sometimes appear to be so, an end in itself. In the days of specialised function the forwards were the engineers of attack; but deep in the British tradition was the admired convention of the aggressive defender—particularly the attacking half-back. A review of the conditions then obtaining led Ramsey, in the days of team-building, towards a new form of stylistic flexibility. In short, the player (except, of course, the goalkeeper) required a new kind of versatility, to be able to adapt himself to circumstance and occasion. In the end, after trying more than fifty players, Ramsey arrived at a team which understood the basic principles on which he worked. The 'personalities' of the World Cup team were, of course, built up in deference to public demand: but the individuals were not cast in the heroic mould of former days. Each was equal to other, even though individual flair had its frequent opportunity. It is arguable that the eleven that won the Cup represented the ultimate in team organisation, as also in team spirit. This, perhaps, is what George Raynor meant when he said: 'There's no substitute for skill, but the manager's job is usually to find one. Ramsey obviously found one.'[4]

3. *The Times*, August 1, 1966.
4. Quoted by Stephen Fay, in 'Rebirth of English Football', *The Observer*, July 31, 1966. George Raynor, once a Bury player, and later manager of Coventry City, was highly successful as coach and manager in Sweden. He was responsible for the Olympic Games success in Sweden in 1948 and for that country's successful showing in the World Cup of 1950, when the Swedish team, unexpectedly, finished third.

On July 11, 1966, England opened the World Cup tournament at Wembley with a match against Uruguay. The team was: Banks (Leicester); Cohen (Fulham), Wilson (Everton); Stiles (Manchester U.), J. Charlton (Leeds), Moore (West Ham); Ball (Blackpool), Greaves (Tottenham), R. Charlton (Manchester U.), Hunt (Liverpool), Connelly (Manchester U.).

In a competition in which the names of Pele and Eusebio were on every lip the English team looked fairly anonymous. With the possible exception of Greaves and R. Charlton there was not an acknowledged world-beater on the list. But there was experience, unimpaired by sagging vitality, and resolution. For all its failings the English League is the best of all training grounds for the inculcation of the latter virtue, and this was never better demonstrated than in the quality of such players as Banks, Cohen, Wilson, Stiles, and J. Charlton. There was also a zest for adventure, particularly exemplified by R. Charlton and Ball. The creativity of the last-named, often marred elsewhere by a demonstrative irritability, came to florescence during this series of matches.

The Uruguayans, vastly experienced in all the arts of defensive strategy, blotted out the potential of the English team. By concentration of forces, physical, robustness, and (the *bête noire* to the English crowd) body-checking, English scoring attempts were few and far between. But so too were those of Uruguay. A goal-less draw was unsatisfactory as a curtain-raiser, but as the first skirmish in a comparison was not without its value.

The opening match attracted 75,000 spectators. The next, on July 16, against Mexico, was attended by 85,000. Paine (Southampton) replaced Ball, and Peters (West Ham) came in for Connelly. The Mexicans played the fashionable neutralising game, and it was not until thirty-five minutes had passed that the English players were able to bring their techniques to coherence. Deliberation and occupation of open spaces saw a fluent sequence of movements between R. Charlton, Hunt, and Stiles, which led to a centre to Peters and a head-flick to Hunt, who put the ball into the net. Only to be ruled off-side. But the action destroyed Mexican confidence. Within two minutes R. Charlton, having taken the ball in mid-field and retained possession, made a characteristically individual burst to score. From this point English pressure became remorseless, and the concern caused to the Mexicans by J. Charlton's habit of coming forward for corner-kicks was considerable. Towards the end of the match Greaves shot. The shot was only parried, by the goalkeeper Calderon, and Hunt had no difficulty in bringing the final score to 2—0.

Against France, on July 20 (attendance 92,500), Hunt scored two goals.[5] Of these, one, scored while a French player was out of action following an unpenalised foul by Stiles, was disputed. This was an unsatisfactory match, spoiled by insecure refereeing and by the wayward and sometimes perplexing eccentricities of Stiles. But England led their group with 5 points—followed by Uruguay (4), Mexico (2), and France (1).

On July 23 England played against Argentine in the quarter-final (attendance 88,000).[6] What should have been an exhibition of the higher skills turned out to be an occasion of anarchy. Coming into the match fresh from a bruising encounter with West Germany, the Argentinians were dismayed to discover that a German referee was in control of the game (that is to say, he should have been, but in the event was not, in control). They were not pleased that the commissar appointed by F.I.F.A. to overlord the game was an Irishman. From the outset the English team moved with brisk confidence, and, launching frequent attacks, drove the Argentinians back to their storm stations. Since legal methods were insufficient to effect a change of balance the

5. Callaghan (Liverpool) replaced Paine.
6. Forward line: Ball, Hurst, R. Charlton, Hunt, Peters.

Argentinians resorted to illegality. Each English attacker was then brought to a halt by a deliberate foul.

The Argentine captain, Rattin, was ordered off. He refused to go. For some time operations were suspended while the visitors laid siege to the referee, and while officials and police came to the relief of beleaguered authority, and spectators adjusted their appreciation to a new game. Eventually the match was re-started, and when it seemed that the reduced opposition, now playing with more of style and resolution, might hold out, Hurst scored a winning goal. Subsequently the Argentinians, having gone home in dudgeon and disgrace, were called on for guarantees of good behaviour in the future, and Ramsey was called to order for comments (through a televised interview) that were construed as marked by a justifiable indignation but somewhat lacking in discretion.

For the semi-final, England, lacking an injured but otherwise below-his-best Greaves, were unchanged. Their opponents were Portugal—Pereira; Festa, Figueiredo: Lucas, Hilario, Graca; Coluna, Augusto, Eusebio, Torres, Simoes. The match was played on July 26, before 90,000 spectators.

The issue resolved on the contests between the impeccable fluent English defence and the inventive and beautiful Portuguese attack on the one hand, and between the (by highest standards) moderate English attack and the fallible Portuguese defence on the other. The key man was Eusebio, the greatest individual footballer of the decade. The English problem was the containment of his genius. This was solved by a policy of isolation. Stiles and Moore, by standing off in order to nullify the results of his calculations and gestures by more of less remote control, succeeded admirably in frustrating both his designs and his colleagues. (So in former times was the menace of Matthews best met.) For half an hour the English probed for weaknesses. The game unfolded ballet-wise, there being no foul for a full half-hour.

Soon after the half-hour a traditional English ploy was introduced: the long pass. Wilson sent the ball ahead of Hunt who shot. Pereira, confused by the quickness and simplicity of the action, was able only to let the ball rebound to R. Charlton, who promptly scored. A dominant figure in the English march to victory, he was finding opportunity to display the richness and the hidden subtleties of his talents. And as he did so Alan Ball was commanding more and more attention by the intensity of his energy: he became, one might say, a Ball of fire.

It was now that the English showed their versatility and adaptability. The rigours of Ramsey's direction had not obliterated either individual or collective initiative. If the first goal sprang from the depths of the traditional English game, the second was the apt consequence of modern science. The precision of J. Charlton, Ball, Moore, Cohen and Hurst led the Portuguese defence into distraction, so that the thrust of R. Charlton was momentarily overlooked. Thus he scored his second goal of the match. At this point the Portuguese awoke to the seriousness of the situation and with a penalty (given against J. Charlton for a handling offence) Eusebio began to close the gap. In the final issue it was only a peerless, story-book save by Banks that ensured the English victory.

The final was between England and West Germany, the teams being: *England*: Banks; Cohen, Wilson; J. Charlton, Moore, Stiles; R. Charlton, Ball, Hunt, Hurst, Peters. *West Germany*: Tilkowski; Höttges, Schulz; Weber, Schnellinger, Haller; Beckenbauer, Seeler, Held, Overath, Emmerich.

The nature of German fooball is akin to that of English: keen, fast, uncomplicated, and physically hard. The final, therefore, presented few difficulties in respect of style. Throughout the series the individual players of both teams had both hardened and matured, and by July 30 respect both for the teams and for certain players as individuals was high. On the German side the outstanding player was reckoned to be Schnellinger, while each forward was potentially dangerous.

The English side were first to come to terms with the occasion, and played in relaxed manner. A feature of the team was the ease with which interchanges of position were effected, but without loss of defensive certitude. In the early stages of the match R. Charlton was nomadic, and as he wandered he diffused confidence in one direction but alarm in another. And yet, as sometimes happens, confidence led to carelessness. It was as simple as this: Wilson, with time enough to clear properly, tamely headed the ball to Haller— thus completing the intention of Held who had attempted to centre. And Haller scored. Two minutes later Moore was fouled. Taking the free-kick, he floated the ball directly to his colleague Hurst, who headed a flawless equalising goal.

Moore, the English captain, placed himself in the gallery of great English half-backs by his imperturbability, technical assurance, and tactical control during the series, but particularly in the final. As the game went on he tightened his grip on its pulse so that the English players were able to combat transient misfortune.

In the second half the game belonged largely to the effervescent Ball. With a quarter of an hour to go he took a corner-kick. The ball was diverted to an unmarked Peters, who put England in the lead. As has been said, the nation hoped for a miracle. Here, within moments of its occurrence, the England spectators (rather irrelevantly) threw up the chorus of 'Rule, Britannia'. But in the last minute of normal time—the game having ebbed and flowed continually—the Germans equalised. A free-kick, after an infringement by J. Charlton, went to Weber (possibly the ball was helped on its way by Schnellinger's hand), who put the ball past Banks.

After ten minutes of extra time Hurst scored a fine goal: that is, if the ball, which hit the underside of the cross-bar, had passed over the line. After consultation with a Russian linesman the Swiss referee decreed that it had. (Doubts about the correctness of his decision are still entertained in some German circles.) But the last gesture of a pulsating match—that made up with drama for what it lacked in elegance—put the issue beyond all question. Moore worked the ball clear out of his own area and sent it to Hurst, waiting a few yards inside the German half. Instead of playing out time Hurst, gathering momentum, swept down on the German goal, and with a last thrust of defiance sent a vicious shot beyond the grasp of the opposing goalkeeper. England had won the World Cup, and a new era had begun. Or had it?

The Brazilians faded from view in 1966. With the remnants of former achievement draped round shoulders too old to wear them the old masters departed gracefully and sadly. The memory remains of Pele, injured against Portugal at Liverpool, taking his leave. The Italians went home in disgrace, defeated by North Korea at Middlesbrough before a crowd of Tees-siders dedicated to the cause of the Asiatics to a man. Through Albert and Bene and a fine victory over Brazil at Goodison Park the Hungarian team added to its reserves of credit in Britain. Russia supplied a father figure in the shape of Yashin, the great and chivalrous veteran goalkeeper.

The critics began their preparations for the next competition, in Mexico, and already speculated which of the English team would survive the hazards of four years.

At this juncture a new helmsman was required at the Football Association. During the preparations for the World Cup Mr. J. H. Mears, son of one of the Chelsea founding brothers and himself Chairman of Chelsea as well as of the F.A. and the League Management Committee, died suddenly. His successor was announced in January, 1967, as Dr. Andrew Stephen, Chairman of Sheffield Wednesday. In addition to presiding over the F.A. Council Dr. Stephens retains membership of the League Management Committee. In this way a community of interest between the two main bodies may be preserved. It is to be remarked that Dr. Stephen is a Scotsman.

The World Cup made a profit of approximately £1,000,000 as a result of the 1966 competition. Of this the F.A. received perhaps £400,000, which left a profit of about half of that sum. The clubs which staged the matches received about £235,000, over and above any grants for improvements previously obtained. The cost of the English team, in fees, was £27,960, divided among twenty-two players. Covered in its entirety by television the World Cup not only aroused world-wide interest and enthusiasm but also won many converts to the game. Not least of all in the U.S.A., where subsequent attempts to popularise the game have threatened a new brain-drain, as well as optimistic offers to buy up several English club sides.

By reason of the dependence of their best players on the English market neither Wales nor Northern Ireland (nor Eire) are to be contemplated in the world class. With Scotland, despite consistent plundering of her resources, it is otherwise. There are two or three great clubs in Scotland with as much potential as any clubs in Europe. In respect of the 1966 World Cup, mismanagement and ill-fortune conspired to eliminate Scotland in the qualifying matches. There was little organised preparation and a change of direction, bringing Jock Stein into management of the team in place of Ian McColl, who was too late to enable the disparate talents of the best available players to be harmonised. At the end of the qualifying competition Scotland needed to draw against Italy in Naples (on December 7, 1965) in order to earn a play-off.[7] English League commitments meant travelling without Law (Manchester U.), Baxter (Sunderland), and Stevenson (Liverpool); while Henderson—a

7. Previous matches: Scotland 3, Finland 0; Poland 1, Scotland 1; Finland 1, Scotland 2; Scotland 1, Poland 2; Scotland 1, Italy 0. That the Poles defeated Scotland at Hampden Park was the surprise of that series; but also a demonstration of the virtues of organised competition over uncoordinated brilliance.

Rangers player eyed enviously by Real Madrid—was unfit. Scotland lost to Italy by 0—3.

It was left to Celtic to restore the traditions of the North
British, and this they did in no uncertain fashion.

Towards the end of the 1964–65 season Celtic, with a
decade of frustration and the memory of four failures in
the Scottish Cup Final behind them, appointed a new
manager. This was Jock Stein, than whom no man knew
more about the Celtic tradition on the one hand and the
revitilisation of jaded hopes on the other.

Stein once played Second Division football with Albion
Rovers. From there he went into the wilderness of non-
league football, joining the South Welsh club, Llanelly. In
dejection, in 1952, he was on the point of resigning from his
contract when a message came from Scotland, calling him to
Parkhead. Celtic had lately earned disgrace for losing a
Scottish Cup replay (in the first round, against Third
Lanark) for the first time in fifty years.

This was the period in which the club had first undertaken American tours—arriving back with a goalkeeper
(Kennaway) from Fall River Club from one, and a
Jamaican forward (Giles Heron), of Detroit, from another.
Even then the missionary spirit was strong at Parkhead,
and Celtic recognised the attractions of a world game. Stein
arrived to take his place at centre-half. The triumvirate of
Evans, Stein, and McPhail represented one of the most accomplished of all British half-back lines, and was the power
behind the success of 1953 and 1954.

In 1953 the English and Scottish Associations and League
jointly promoted a 'Coronation Cup', to be played for by
what might have been subconsciously considered as a basis
for a 'British League'—the idea of which is never far out of
sight. The competing clubs were Arsenal, Manchester
United, Tottenham Hotspur, Newcastle United, Rangers,
Hibernian (League champions), Aberdeen (Scottish Cup-
winners), and Celtic. At this point, having tried nine centre-

K

forwards during the season, Celtic obtained Mochan, from Middlesbrough, on transfer. Scoring two goals, and making a third, Mochan was largely responsible for the victory of Celtic over Queen's Park in the final of the Glasgow Charity Cup. Thus encouraged, the team defied all prognostication by beating Arsenal in the first round of the Coronation Cup, and Manchester United in the semi-final. Since Hibernian had beaten Newcastle in the other semi-final it was an all-Scottish final. On May 30, 1953, 117,000 spectators assembled at Hampden to see a sparkling display of high-quality football. Celtic won a hard-fought match 2—0. In the following season, in which Mochan, now playing at outside-left, scored 26 goals, Celtic won the League title, by beating Aberdeen by 2—1, also the Cup. Behind this lay the other double achievements of 1907, 1909, and 1914.

After 1954, as happens, a successful combination broke up, and the succeeding years were relatively dismal. In the meantime Stein had taken up management with Dunfermline Athletic, and then with Hibernian. On April 22, 1961, Dunfermline, managed by Stein for the past twelve months or so, unexpectedly drew with Celtic in the Cup Final. Four days later, having been given no chance of survival, they upset every calculation by defeating Celtic 2—0, and thus winning the Cup for the first time in their history. There followed three years of dominance of Rangers (Celtic reaching the Final again in 1963 to lose in a replay), but in 1965 Celtic were again Cup-winners. Now managed by Stein they turned the tables on Dunfermline. Just as Stein had formerly taught Dunfermline to make the most of their relatively limited potential, so now he showed Celtic how to win victory out of adversity. In the 1965 final the team was twice behind, but, undaunted, they faced the game so well that by the middle of the second half there was no doubt about who was going to win. In an interview—quoted in a Berlin newspaper—Stein on a later occasion said that his footballers must be made to believe 'that they are the best footballers in the world'.[8] By 1965 the Celtic players were beginning to feel that they were on the way: at least they had now caught up with Rangers' record of eighteen Scottish Cup victories.

In the next year Celtic developed into a team that combined the old tradition of elegance with a new-found power. So far as the manager was concerned it was a matter of psychological insight on the one hand, and acute perception of technical capacity on the other. Stein re-made reputations, because he was able to urge ordinary talents towards extraordinary effort. The goalkeeper, Simpson, formerly with Newcastle and Hibernian, was brought to Celtic at the age of thirty-five, at the point when he was about to retire. His experience and confidence were important factors in the successful dénouement of Stein's scheming. Auld had once left Celtic for a discouraging spell with Birmingham City. Stein brought him back, moved him from outside- to inside-left, and re-created a career. Similarly Stein renewed the confidence of his other forwards, as well as of McNeill, a centre-half apparently destined for honourable oblivion, until the whole team moved as one precise mechanism. A summer tour of the United States gave Celtic opportunity to revise method, to place the emphasis on attack, by speeding up the play of the backs. A feature of the play of Celtic in the past two seasons has been the overlapping of forwards by backs; and the spectacle of graceful aggression practised by the Scots has begun to have repercussions in Europe. For Celtic proved the fallacies underlying the most recently fashionable continental-style defensive procedures.

In 1966–67 Celtic won their way to the final of the European Cup by defeating Zürich (2—0, 3—0), Nantes (3—1, 3—1), Vojvodina Novi Sad, Yugoslavia (2—0, 0—1), and

8. 'Das schottische Jahr', in *Neues Deutschland*, June 19, 1967.

Dukla Prague (3—1, 0—0).[9] At the same time they were winning the Scottish League Cup, the Scottish League Championship, the Scottish Cup, and the Glasgow Charity Cup.

The final of the European Cup was played in Lisbon, on May 25, 1967. Celtic was represented by: Simpson; Craig, Gemmell; Murdoch, McNeill, Clark; Johnstone, Wallace, Chalmers, Auld, Lennox. Their opponents, Internazionale Milan, deprived of their commander-in-chief, Suarez, and their Brazilian winger, Jair, through injury, lined up as follows: Sarti; Picchi, Burgnich, Guarneri, Facchetti; Bedin, Corso; Bicieli, Mazzola, Cappellini, Domenghini.

After seven minutes of the final Milan scored from a penalty. This came after a foul by Craig on Cappellini. The scorer was Mazzola. And that, decided the Milanese, was that. From now on they would make sure of their winning. Thus the cast-iron defence stations were manned. Celtic, infuriated, put into operation all their aggressive energy, and mounted attack after attack on the Milan goal. What disturbed the Italians—saved on a number of occasions by the goal-posts and bar, and by Sarti, the goalkeeper—was the presumption of Gemmell in thrusting swiftly, deeply, and frequently into their lines. It was Gemmell, aided by his fellow-back, Craig, who scored the equaliser. The second half was all Celtic, and it was no surprise when, five minutes before full-time, Gemmell fed Murdoch whose low shot was diverted past Sarti by Chalmers.

Inter Milan, through their manager, Helenio Herrera, sought to exculpate themselves. They had endured a hard season, and had played, in the 'Sunday-Wednesday-Sunday rhythm', no fewer than sixty matches. Stein observed that Celtic, during the same period, had played sixty-two matches. Milan's decline was complete. They went home to lose a vital League match to Lazio, Roma, and surrendered the League title to Juventus, Turin; and the semi-final of the Italian Cup to a second-class side from Padua. Because

9. Result of home tie given first in each case.

A.C. Milan were the eventual Cup-winners Inter just managed to qualify for admission to the 'Fairs Cup'—Europe's consolation for those who also ran.

The Celtic players returned home to be greeted by a quarter of a million jubilant Scotsmen who lined the route from airport to city, and by 50,000 or so loyalists packed into Celtic Park. When West Germany reached the World Cup Final Germany was reunited for two hours as Germans both in West and East prayed for national victory. The victory of Celtic also brought a temporary resolution to Scottish strife, as Protestants, burying ancient prejudice for the time being, joined in celebration. The General Assembly of the Church of Scotland made one of the greatest ecumenical gestures of all time, by placing on record its delight at the success of Celtic.

We were back at the beginning. Football, in Britain, is the game of the people. In respect of the European Cup it was written:

'The scenes at the end were almost tribal. Thousands of Celtic supporters invaded the pitch waving their banners and uttering wild whoops of joy. Hundreds knelt to kiss the ground and, having cut slices from the turf of Wembley last month (when Scotland defeated England), these Scotsmen now did the same to the Cumberland soil of the stately National Stadium here.'[10]

10. Geoffrey Green, in *The Times*, May 26, 1967.

17

New Roles

A backward glance at Chapters 3 and 4 may persuade the reader to the conclusion that it was really during the seventeenth century that organised football assumed a socio-political, if not a politico-philosophic role. The consequences of the fusion of football and other more general interests within the period of the Renaissance were considerable: how considerable is for each student of the facts, as hitherto presented, to determine for himself. The part of modern times which we currently occupy is similar to that earlier period in many ways. Old principles and dogmas are under assault from advocates of new orthodoxies, or heterodoxies; western man again loiters between extremes of optimism and pessimism. In the particular, this condition is not unfamiliar to the dedicated football fan. But now he finds that between hopes and fears there is frequent intervention by the element of doubt. Will the Rangers supporter, or the Arsenal supporter, wake up one morning to find that there is no longer Rangers, or that Arsenal has been thrown into an outer darkness?

Such gloomy hypotheses no longer seem quite unwarrantable. In 1972 Rangers supporters—or some of them —nearly killed the thing they purported to love in a new Peninsular war. After the Scottish team had beaten Moscow Dynamo in the Final of the European Cup Winners' Cup, at Barcelona, some of those who had accompanied the team rampaged to such effect that the Rangers Club was for a time suspended from European competitions. The occasion and the events deriving from it at the very least demonstrated how the psychological stresses of individuals and groups (supporters of the Glasgow clubs are conditioned by external syndromes of great malignancy) seek expression on the terraces of, and the territory adjoining, footbal arenas.

As to the matter of the impermanence of great institutions (and Arsenal may claim a place among these) one may only point to the decline and fall of institutions in general. In the narrower sphere of football the names of numerous once eminent clubs are to be found in the lower reaches of competition, while some are not to be found at all.

The rat race, whose only end is the survival of the fittest, is no longer confined to the British Isles. It is continental, and ultimately global, in scale. The Championship of the Football Leagues and the winning of the F.A. Cups of the four home countries are no longer ends in themselves, but staging-posts on the way to larger challenges. The diminution of significance of these competitions at present may seem more apparent than real. But the fate of the home international championship is both apparent and real. Contests that once set nerves atingle are now confined within an end-of-season appendix, and serve only to test candidates for the next World Cup—or the one after that.

The success of England in the World Cup of 1966, in the football sense, marked the end of Empire. It was at that time expected that England should and would win as in public duty bound, and as of right. England, after all, was the original provider and law-giver of football, and defeat in the end-game at Wembley was not to be thought of. Four years later, in Mexico, the English team was eliminated in the quarter-final by West Germany, which in the department of football is like East Germany in the province of athletics—the parvenu. There were, of course, excuses for a moderate showing in Mexico—the absence through illness of Banks, one of the best of goalkeepers—but not too many recriminations. It is still fair to say that

English sportsmen are good losers—which in a chauvinistic age is no back-handed compliment. The idea that the English team was not the best in the world nonetheless has taken some time to sink in. In fact, it will probably be several generations before it has finally been assimilated. Long experience of football, however, has given English crowds a capacity for appreciating the talents of world class players, whatever their origins.

The fact that horizons have so recently been widened has had immeasurable consequences. These relate to the place of the player in the game, his new social standing, and his professional dignity; to the organisation and administration of clubs; to the function of the manager; to the politics of football, both in the narrow and the broad sense; to the parasite industries which have more and more come to make demands on the game; and to the fan, whose favours so many covet and whose well-being too few consider.

For almost ninety years professionalism in football afforded for the talented few a means of emancipation from the worst of the disadvantages of an inegalitarian society. The struggle for freedom within the profession, however, has been hard and is surely a continuing one. The manner in which the game has been controlled has readily induced paternalistic concepts that to many may seem to be proper provided that they apply to others. Even now the most skilled of professional footballers accept—or, at least, do not openly question—prohibitions that in any other calling would lead to immediate withholding of labour. The player may be, and often is, instructed as to how he should dress, where he should live, what he should eat, and (implicitly) how he should think. In matters of discipline the odds are certainly stacked against him, and methods of imparting a disciplinary sense may seem to the objective observer to be more than a little primitive. There is no doubt that premises which have hitherto been accepted will come increasingly under critical scrutiny as the professional footballer's own organisation becomes more aware of its own dignity and potential effectiveness vis à vis the other bodies concerned with the government and control of the game. Within the last few years the P.F.A. has spoken with authority on a number of issues, and its standing has been enhanced by wise and sometimes eloquent leadership.

As the result of a growing consciousness of professional propriety and determined action two significant restrictions have been relaxed and this relaxation has helped to adjust the balance between player and employer, to the manifest advantage of the former. There is no longer a 'maximum wage', and in consequence of the judgement in the Eastham case in 1963 a club may no longer lay claim to the services of an unwilling player. In both instances, astute and patient advocacy by the P.F.A. proved the value of this body. Arising from all this is the fact that the talented player is now free to conclude a contract with a club on much more favourable terms than was previously the case, and to attain a standard of living commensurate with the apparent value set on his high skills (so long as these shall last) by the community at large.

In a notable judgment in the High Court in October 1972 Mr. Justice Bristow determined that in an appeal case in respect of the sending-off of Ernie Machin, of Coventry City, in 1970 a disciplinary committee of the F.A. had acted without a due regard for 'natural justice'. The conclusion to be drawn from this judicial decision is that footballers on trial before a committee convened by one of the organising authorities shall in future be entitled to the normal rights of any citizen judicially called to account. The conduct of this case had covered two years in the course of which the P.F.A. had already won a right of appeal for players and legal representation at appeal hearings. In establishing the rights at law of its members the P.F.A. has made it plain that there is no question of claiming 'victory' over any parent body, and that in pressing claims due regard has been paid to the Chester Report of 1968.

The good player is now assured of his place in the community; in economic terms he is now well within the middle class, whereas formerly—and not so long ago—he was denied this cachet. The incentives now provided are palpably broadening the base of recruitment. Players with greater educational experience are being persuaded to devote some years at least to a career in football. In the long run the game can only benefit, since there will be a larger pool of men of all-round competence available for management and administration at various levels. Although this may have a ring of novelty, it may be remembered that the famous amateur sportsmen of the past were (to put it delicately) so comfortably supported in their amateur status that they could, and did, acquire professional habits. That Britain is incapable of maintaining a challenge in football in the modern Olympic Games, is, of course, the results of an elasticity in terminology that British football administrators do not tolerate.

A high degree of professionalism, in whatever field, inevitably intensifies competition in that the ultimate rewards for success are greater. The opportunities for a player to move into affluence are related to the success of his club, and the success of a club patently depends on the selection, management, and training of players, and on their maintenance of both fitness and loyalty. Experienced players—the foundation of any team—are expensive to engage; among the supply of players of genius active at any time the cost of any one is prohibitive for all but a handful of clubs; and—since on the whole success tends to beget success—there is an ever increasing tendency towards concentration of talent.

In world football this tendency has long been apparent, for in most countries the level of club football outside a restricted circle is relatively low, and in many cases the chief concern is with the 'national' side. How much this is not the case in England is shown by the obstacles often put in the way of the manager of the national team by clubs pursuing their own ends. If it were not for the uncomfortable fact that the Scottish (as also the Irish and Welsh) F.A. depends on the whims of English clubs for the maintenance of a fully competent national side the position in Scotland would closely resemble that in most European countries. For the fame of Scotland as a footballing nation has largely been based on the premise that Celtic and Rangers should flourish at the expense of practically every other League side. In England the number of clubs thought up for the inauguration of the Football League in 1888 looks about right for an estimate of how many teams of high excellence the English game can afford. And, even then, twelve may be an over-estimate. It is fortunate, however, that from time to time computer mathematics do not apply, and that an unfavoured outsider arises to mock the pretensions of powerful and/or rich clubs, and to fracture complacency. In 1962 Ipswich Town won the League Championship. Ten years later Derby County—after many years in the wilderness— took the same prize. In the intervening period the Championship had gone four times to Merseyside (Liverpool and Everton twice each), three times to Manchester (United twice, City once), once to Leeds and once to Arsenal. In the same period in eight of the Cup Finals contested there were representatives from this same select group. Success in these competitions are passports to entry into the major European contests—the 'Champion Clubs' Cup' and the 'Cup-Winners' Cup'.

Celtic won the former trophy in 1967, and were runners-up in 1970, and Manchester United in 1968; Manchester City won the latter in 1970, and Chelsea a year later, while Rangers were unsuccessful finalists in 1967. The U.E.F.A. (formerly Fairs') Cup collects the next merit among the European teams and in this competition English clubs have done especially well. This is effective evidence of the depth of the British club tradition and gives support to the often held contention that the English league competition is the most testing of all such competitions. A tendency to write down the U.E.F.A. Cup as a kind of economy-class affair is certainly unwarranted, in view of the fact that in the Cup-Winners' Cup in particular there are entrants from domestic competitions drawing on limited resources. In Britain, for instance, the winners of the Welsh Cup (if other than Cardiff City), and of the Irish F.A. Cup, are likely to find virtue accorded for valour rather than skill, and only a brief excursion in the lusher pastures.

The more prestigious competitions have brought fresh experiences all round, but also some disillusionment. Matches between top clubs are fabulous in prospect, but in reality too often rigid in monotony. The principle of no surrender away in the expectation of capitalising on local fervour at home has too often diminished football as a spectacle. It was succinctly put by one writer that 'defensive play requires no genius, and, indeed mediocrity can match greatness if mediocrity is confined to the negative'.[1] The victory of Manchester United in the European Cup in 1968 was based on the creativity of fluent attack. The progress of Wolverhampton Wanderers to the U.E.F.A. Final in 1972 was similarly based. Such clubs provide the allure of football and the arenas for the display of untrammelled genius.

The English League Cup competition was instituted after the manner of the Scottish League Cup, but for a different purpose. The Scottish competition helps to fill out a programme which otherwise would be too sparse for the fans and which would be inadequate to support even a modest degree of professionalism. The English League Cup came into being for the benefit of the lesser clubs, and for a time it was boycotted by the more eminent. But since success now provides one certificate of entry to the U.E.F.A. Cup competition it has assumed a greater significance, even

1. *F. A. Year Book*, 1966-7, p. 23

though the winners of the trophy still tend to come from out of the pool of dark horses than from that of certain favourites. The more famous teams appear to prefer to keep their sights trained on the traditional blue ribands. In accordance with modern egalitarian trends which would see everyone offered at least the opportunity of competing for some sort of certification of qualified superiority there are new competitions. Of these, one of the most encouraging is the F.A. Challenge Trophy, for teams outside the Football League. This stimulates grass roots growth and brings out local patriotisms when—in a wider sense—these are of increasing importance. Within football it is the hardworking committees of clubs in the lesser and provincial leagues, and of county associations, who have done much for the game in the past and who have much to offer in the future. The F.A. Challenge Trophy gives them encouragement to continue in their good works. In 1970 the winners were Macclesfield Town—where football has been played in its modern form for a hundred years (see p. 143). In 1971 the unsuccessful finalists of the previous year won the cup— Telford United. Telford, unlike Macclesfield, is a new town, and a football team is one means of providing a community spirit. The fertility of this whole area in respect of football talent is emphasised by the fact that the next winners of the F.A. Trophy were Stafford Rangers.

This competition has now replaced the F.A. Amateur Cup, which itself was established as a supplementary contest, because at long last the technical term 'amateur' has been abolished. The final degradation of the term, of course, has been in its application to the winners of the Olympic Games. It is, however, still to be remarked that the ultimate strength of British football does lie in purely recreational football. There are 25,000 amateur clubs affiliated to the F.A., and it is from these clubs, and from the schools from which they draw membership, that basic skills and knowledge, as well as enthusiasm, derive. In this connection it is significant to note that Association football is increasingly cultivated in schools and universities in the United States, partly because of an appreciation of the intrinsic qualities of the game, partly because of student dislike of the exclusivism of American football. Patient missionary work on the part of certain eloquent and dedicated expatriates, among whom the best known is the former Welsh International Phil Woosnam, is beginning to show a generation of zealous converts.

Throughout its long history football has mirrored social patterns and ideas. In an era of growing materialism and commercial development the signs of new values (if that is the correct word) and intentions are to be seen. So it is that 'sponsorship' (another term much devalued by contemporary usage) has come to football. Not altogether willing players of certain teams play for a 'Watney' Cup before the beginning of the season proper, and for a 'Texaco' Cup in the interstices of an already overloaded programme. Such innovations, however, have begun to appear counterproductive, and instead of selling more football are having the effect of reducing overall attendances. Spectators are not less, but more discriminating, it would seem.

The end of a materialistic philosophy is 'success' and the adoption of such a philosophy imposes on all parties involved in pursuing the chimera of success. The greatest strain is on managers, and also on an handful of top class players.

The casualty rate among managers remains high. But, escape clauses in contacts being what they are, this is less important than the fact that the modern manager is hardly left alone by the various agencies of news dissemination for a single day. The spillage of words—of which a number are inevitably less than discreet—is neither helpful to amicable relations in general nor to the nervous condition of the manager himself. Driven by his employees, the manager in turn often tends to identify efficiency with 'drive', so that one must once again wonder at the patience displayed by many players under the compulsive harassment of ambitious overseers.

Of the managers of the 1970s the greatest impact, perhaps, has been made by Brian Clough of Derby County, whose professional success is matched by a strong determination to be his own man and to speak his own mind. Mr. Clough's comments sometimes offend, and invariably provoke, but they stem from a concern not only for the football community but for society as a whole. In this respect he has given additional distinction to his calling.

The incentives provided by participation in European competitions—which do not, alas, generally include opportunities properly to meet people of different countries and cultures—have progressively pushed up the emoluments of the best players, the fees asked for transfers, and the stresses of life at the top. In one way or another the star player (there are relatively few of these at any time) earns the stipend of a Cabinet Minister. (In either case peak earning capacity may be short-lived, and the position is at all times insecure.) It is now no longer sensible to refer to records in the transfer market since a new one is established almost daily. In commercial terms, however, it may be crudely put that in 1973 a player of First Division standard, and on the way up, is labelled £200,000 plus.

In spite of the fact that in this way money appears to be more eloquent than once it was, it may truthfully be said that in contrast with many countries football in Britain remains commendably free of corruption.

Society looks for scapegoats. Because the footballer is in the public eye more than most he is often the butt for censure. This is no new phenomenon, but that is small comfort to those who are traduced. Insofar as behaviour on the football field is concerned it is, it may be objectively proposed, doubtful whether any other collective human activity involving physical expression is conducted with more honesty and less malice. The apportionment of responsibility for crowd violence to football players—modern life being what it is—is singularly ungenerous. To one's certain knowledge such apportionment is usually made by those who have no first-hand knowledge of football at all. Violence is only endemic to football terraces, and to the streets near football grounds, because it is endemic in modern urban society. It is true that sometimes on the field tempers get out of hand— but this is in no way condoned by the general community of footballers. What appears to be particularly unjust is that in some other games violence is condoned. So on the same page of an account of Rugby football matches in one issue of *The Guardian* one could read of one match, that 'at the beginning it was all very intense, with tempers occasionally flaring as players were chopped down savagely in full stride', and of another, how 'there was a flurry of punches in a fierce maul on the touch-line during which the *** prop forward was laid out. He was carried off on a stretcher and taken to the *** Hospital . . .' It is doubtful whether this would be tolerated within professional football, and certainly not by officials or spectators. There is some substance in the claim that 'the game has created a more universally accepted and effective international law than any other sphere of international society . . .'[2]

The ramifications of football were, and are, many and various, so that the history of British football in large part is also the history of the British people. The same is true of any institution, or corporate activity, of long tradition. But in its own way football arouses awareness of the individual and of the responsibility of the individual. Great footballers to some extent are isolated by their excellence. In an extreme case this is borne out by the turbulent career of George Best—perhaps the most naturally gifted British player of his generation. Best, with a Celtic flair but the victim also of a Byzantine complexity, is on one side of the

2. ibid., 1967-8, p. 15

Romantic tradition. Within this same tradition are also to be found Best's fellow-countryman, Derek Dougan, whose ultimate triumph as a footballer lies in an exquisite refinement of style, and Dennis Law, the quintessential Scot. On the other hand there is the effective and business-like English manner exemplified by the phlegmatic Bobby Moore and Arsenal's Bob Wilson, conspicuous both for tidiness in keeping goal and also in dialogue—or monologue. Reputations come and reputations go. Once or twice a generation throws up a candidate for immortality. One such, whose credentials are impeccable, and whose qualities are a distillation of the British way of football and as a lodestar to the whole world of football, is Bobby Charlton. Perhaps it is only Charlton who could compel the attendance of 60,000 spectators at his testimonial match—Manchester United *v* Celtic—on a September night in 1972. Testimonial match is a misnomer. This was a kind of liturgy, celebrating football itself through a tribute to one of its most classical and chivalrous exponents.

From here we bounce back across the organisation of more than a hundred years to the tribal football admired and —in the proper sense of the word—sponsored by Walter Scott; from thence a further hundred years to the recorded games of Wales and Ireland; and beyond those days to the footballing rituals of English Renaissance and medieval life. It is one, unified, pattern, reflecting the way life is lived, and, maybe, the way in which it ought to be lived. Football in Britain is not only a game to be played, or watched : it is to be lived with.

Time-chart

6th century B.C. Report of Greek ball-game by Antiphanes.

1st–5th century A.D. Roman–Celtic–British ball-games.

217 A.D. Defeat of Roman military team by British (mythical).

1175. The popular *ludus pilae* as described by William Fitz-stephen.

13th century. St. Hugh of Lincoln (1246?–1255) noted for ball-control (legend).

1303. English footballer attacked and mortally wounded by Irish students in Oxford.

1314, 1389, 1401. Royal disapproval of football in England.

1321. Head of John de Boddeworth used as football in Cheshire.

1423. Scottish king proscribes football.

1425. Prior of Bicester inaugurates professionalism by paying 4*d.* to footballers.

after 1471. Miraculous preservation of the life of William Bartram, a footballer from Newark.

16th century. Wide enthusiasm for football, despite frequent legislation against it.

1561. Richard Mulcaster, schoolmaster, suggests improvements in the game and advocates appointment of trainer/referee.

1581. Cambridge University team runs into trouble in neighbouring village.

1583. Philip Stubbs condemns football, as also do other Puritans.

1585. Scottish minister arraigned by Synod of Lothian for playing football.

1600. John Chamberlain invites Dudley Carleton to watch football.

1613. Wiltshire vicar arranges football match for a royal visit.

1620. Football favoured at St. John's and Trinity Colleges, Cambridge.

1656. Italian football (*Calcio*) described in Henry Carey's translation of *I Ragguagli di Parnasso*.

1698. French visitor commends the quality of London football.

1700. Scottish minister acts against Sunday football.

1719. Cumberland vicar promotes Sunday football.

1720. Anna Beynon, Welsh football fan, describes a local Derby.

1720. Matthew Concanen's poetic account of Irish football, in which we learn of transferred players.

c. 1755. Football played in Bolton.

1772. A well-established game in Hertfordshire.

1793. Famous football match between Sheffield and Norton.

1801. English football at low ebb according to Joseph Strutt.

1814–15. Organised football at Harrow School.

1821. Ballad in praise of football sung by John Fawcett.

1823. William Webb Ellis repeatedly breaks rules at Rugby School, and subsequently much praised for so doing.

1827. Rough play at Eton College brings game into disrepute.

1845. Office of referee instituted at Eton College.

1846. Rules defined at Rugby School.

1847. Attempt to suppress folk-football in Derby.

1848. Rules drawn up at Cambridge.

1855. Oxford *v.* Cambridge match; more rules at Cambridge.

1857. Sheffield Football Club founded.

1859. Forest Club founded by J. F. Alcock and other Old Harrovians.

1860. Prohibition of folk-football in Ashbourne: appeal by natives to Queen's Bench dismissed.

1861–2. Charity matches in Sheffield and neighbourhood.

1862. Rules for the 'Simplest Game' issued by J. C. Thring at Uppingham. Rules for Old Etonian *v.* Old Harrovian match at Cambridge.

1863. Cambridge Rules inspire formation of Football Association in London (October 26). Promulgation of Association Rules.

1863–70. Proliferation of football clubs, and regional variants of basic rules.

1867. Foundation of Queen's Park Club, Glasgow.

1870. England *v*. Scotland.

1871. Establishment of F.A. Challenge Cup: formation of Rugby Football Union in protest against humanitarian principles adopted by F.A.

1876. Bad language at Scottish football match deplored.

1878. Football under electric light at Sheffield.

1880. Riots at folk-football match at Dorking, Surrey.

1885. International Football Association Board, comprising Associations of England, Scotland, Ireland, and Wales. Professionalism legalised in England.

1888. Foundation of Football League.

1889. Foundation of Scottish League.

1890. Foundation of Irish League.

1891. Introduction of goal-nets.

1892. Second Division of Football League.

1893. Institution of F.A. Amateur Cup: professionalism accepted in Scotland.

1895. F.A. Cup Final transferred from the Oval to Crystal Palace.

1898. Promotion and relegation in League football.

1901. Tottenham Hotspur break the hegemony of the North by winning the F.A. Cup after a replay.

1902. April 15: collapse of stand at Ibrox Park, Glasgow, during Scotland *v*. England match; 25 dead, more than 500 injured.

1904. Foundation of F.I.F.A.

1905. New stadium at Stamford Bridge, and foundation of Chelsea F.C.

1907. Amateur clubs break away from F.A. and from A.F.A.

1908. England win Olympic Games football tournament.

1909. Opposition to Players' Union attempt to affiliate with Federation of Trades Unions, and threatened strike. English team in Austria and Hungary.

1912. England win Olympic Games tournament in Stockholm.

1913. Arsenal F.C., under patronage of property magnate, move to new Stadium at Highbury despite protests from class-conscious residents.

1914. King George V present at last Cup Final held at Crystal Palace.

1918. Case of West *v.* F.A. and Hulton & Co. Ltd.

1923. First Cup Final at Wembley Stadium, and chaotic scenes. Hereafter Wembley regarded as national shrine for football.

1925. Playing style revolutionised by change in off-side law proposed by Scotland. Mastery of method by Arsenal F.C., under management of H. Chapman.

1927. Cardiff City win F.A. Cup, which thus temporarily leaves England. F. Buckley appointed manager at Wolverhampton.

1928. Irregularities at Arsenal F.C. lead to suspension of directors and High Court action.

1932. S. Matthews makes his debut at Stoke.

1933. Players numbered in Cup Final.

1939. System of numbering applied to League football. Rangers *v.* Celtic match attracts 118,567 to Ibrox Park.

1945. Moscow Dynamo visit England, Scotland and Wales.

1946–7. British football begins affiliation with European; England appoint a team manager; Wage structure altered as result of National Arbitration Tribunal.

1950. England fail in World Cup, in Brazil.

1953–4. England twice severely defeated by Hungary: shock to morale.

1954. Scotland and England fail in World Cup: further shocks to morale.

1956. European Championship Clubs' Cup and frosty attitude of Football League. Hibernian enter the competition.

1957. Manchester United, managed by M. Busby, reach semi-final of European Cup.

1958. February 6, accident to aircraft at Munich and deaths of Manchester United players. World-wide sympathy. Manchester United nevertheless still play in semi-final of European Cup and reach final of F.A. Cup.
Brazil win World Cup. British National team languish in disgrace.

1960. Institution of European Cup-Winners' Cup.

1961. Tottenham Hotspur win League and Cup. English players, seeking new deal, again threaten strike action. Sir Stanley Rous elected President of F.I.F.A. June 30: ending of maximum wage restrictions.

1962. Brazil win World Cup in Chile.

1963. F.A. celebrates its Centenary.

1965. Knighthood for S. Matthews. West Ham F.C. win European Cup-Winners' Cup.

1966. World Cup competition takes place in England and won by host country.

1966. National euphoria. A. Ramsay, team-manager, knighted.

1967. Glasgow Celtic, managed by J. Stein, win European Cup and practically everything else.

1968. Manchester United win European Cup. Publication of Chester Report as a result of an enquiry into football ordered by the British Government.

1970. Brazil win the World Cup in Mexico.

1971. Chelsea win European Cup-Winners' Cup.

1972. Rangers win European Cup-Winners' Cup. October 20: Bristow judgment in the High Court in the case of E. Machin.

Index